Social Work
and the
Black
Experience

Social Work and the Black Experience

ELMER P. MARTIN
JOANNE MITCHELL MARTIN

NASW PRESS

NATIONAL ASSOCIATION OF SOCIAL WORKERS
Washington, DC
Jay J. Cayner, ACSW, LSW, *President*
Robert H. Cohen, JD, ACSW, *Executive*

Linda Beebe, *Executive Editor*
Nancy A. Winchester, *Editorial Services Director*
Maben Publications, Inc., *Project Manager*
Wolf Publications, Inc., *Copy Editor*
Annette Hansen, *Proofreader*
Susan J. Harris, *Proofreader*
Oneida Indexing Services, *Indexer*

Library of Congress Cataloging-in-Publication Data

Martin, Elmer P.
    Social work and the Black experience / Elmer P. Martin and Joanne
Mitchell Martin.
        p.   cm.
    Includes bibliographical references and index.
    ISBN 0-87101-257-X
    1. Social work with Afro-Americans.   2. Afro-Americans—Attitudes.
    3. Afro-Americans—Psychology.   4. Afro-Americans—Social
    conditions.   I. Martin, Joanne Mitchell.   II. Title.
    HV3181.M37 1995   95-38881
    362.84'96073—dc20   CIP

Printed in the United States of America

To our friends
Elizabeth Peavy and Milton Morris

To our teachers
Oliver C. Cox
Gordon Morgan
James Bryant
Frances Holiday
Edythe J. Thurston
Juanita Armstrong
Thomas A. Blue
Maybelle Evans

And to our fathers
Elmer P. Martin, Sr., and Jeremiah Mitchell, Sr.

Contents

Acknowledgments

This book was done in the African tradition, which calls for communal or collective endeavors over individual effort conducting hard, good work alone. Although we are the authors and the ones responsible for this book's shortcomings, we were not alone in producing this seminal and challenging work. We first owe thanks to our social work students at Morgan State University who, since 1976, have been helping to shape our thoughts and who, since the early 1980s, have been engaged in "social experimentation," shaping and refining the theory and practice of black experience–based social work. Our students are too many to mention each by name, but they know who they are and they know that we are eternally grateful. We also express gratitude to the following librarians at Morgan State University's Soper Library: Vivian Njeri Fisher, Edith Murungi, Diane Daley, Eva Colbert, Jean Wheeler, and Juliette Mitchell. They went above and beyond their duties to find the material we needed to put this book together. We particularly made extensive use of Morgan's Davis Room, which houses its special collection on African American scholarship. Along these lines, we also give thanks to librarians at Howard University's Morland-Spingarn Room in Founders Library, Washington, DC; librarians at the famed Schomburg Library in New York City; and librarians at the Julia Davis Library in St. Louis.

Furthermore, we express our appreciation for the efficient service rendered to us by our typists Ladoris Puryear, Caroll "Neise" Jolley, Jeanne Morris, Travis Henson, Alice R. Williams, Marsha Williams, Lashonda Gabriel, and Linda Whittaker. They went through many drafts of some of the best handwriting (that of Joanne Martin) and the worst handwriting (that of Elmer Martin) that ever was. Thanks to you also, Mr. Frank Myers, for transporting so many drafts of the manuscript across town from our home to our typists.

We wish to acknowledge as well the great help we have received from our colleagues in the helping profession: first, Mr. Cottrell Wesson, a professor of social work at Morgan State University who took care of many of Elmer Martin's academic and administrative responsibilities, thus affording him the time to prepare this work (we regard Mr. Wesson as one of the best social work educators in America and see him as a role model); second, Mr. Gary Ware, for constantly pointing out to us relevant Afrocentric literature that we might have overlooked, literature that has significantly strengthened our thoughts; third, Dr. Salima Siler Marriott for providing us with deep insights into the historical and contemporary plight of black women as helping professionals and as clients; Dr. Maurice St. Pierre for sharing his profound sociological analysis of the black family and community; Dr. Rosetta Graham, for reading the manuscript with a critical eye that helped to strengthen the practice part of black experience–based social work and also for sharing her experiences and practice wisdom gained from working with inner-city Baltimore children traumatized by homicide; and Mildred McKinney for her encouragement.

And above all, we give thanks to the Creator and to our ancestors whose blessings made this work possible.

CHAPTER 1

A Historical and Theoretical Overview

$\int$ ocial work literature seldom treats black individuals as a unique people with unique cultural and historical experiences. Instead, the literature tends to lump black people together with Hispanic, Asian American, and Native American people in an attempt to create a social work practice with "people of color"; to put black people in the same "minority group" category as it puts people with disabilities, older people, women, homeless people, and even Vietnam veterans; to treat traditional and mainstream social work methods as if they are applicable to all people and all problems without alteration; and, worst of all, to pretend color blindness.

Yet almost a century ago pioneering black social workers issued a call for social work to view the black experience as a unique historical and cultural entity. The black social worker E. Franklin Frazier (1940) said that just because black people wear the same clothes and speak the same language as the white Americans, this does not mean that they have not gathered from "the totality of [their] social experience" their own "peculiar social definitions and meanings" and their "own social evaluations and distinctions" (p. 277).

As varied as the lifestyles of black people are, black individuals have in many ways a shared experience stemming from a common effort to survive, live, and solve problems in a perennially hostile environment. Moreover, the various vestiges of black people's African background add to and set these experiences apart from those of any other racial or ethnic group.

Feeling that blackness is a unique experience and has its own peculiar social definition, meanings, evaluations, and distinctions, the students in Morgan State University's Department of Social Work challenged us to lay the foundation for a social work knowledge base that is rooted in the black experience. This work is a response to their challenge. Our goal was first to determine whether black history, black culture, and black life (all of which we put under the rubric "the black experience") have anything to offer social workers today. We certainly had no desire to deify or romanticize past black experiences or assume that tradition is naturally of intrinsic worth. From our own previous scholarly work, we had found aspects of the black experience quite functional for social work practice, and after more extensive research, we were more convinced than ever that there is much that social workers of all colors, races, and nationalities can learn from the black experience that will help them significantly in their work with black people. Our next task, then, was to begin the arduous work of isolating, validating, systematizing, and legitimizing certain elements of the black experience and incorporating these salient features into a social work practice with black people.

Our desire in this book is to create a black identity or a black presence in social work that is sorely lacking despite current calls for greater awareness of racial, cultural, and ethnic diversity. By creating such a presence we hope that this book will enhance social workers in their effort to help black people regardless of the social work practice methods that social workers decide to use. This book is a supplement to and not an alternative to traditional or modern mainstream social work approaches. It is a synthesis of the black helping tradition and mainstream social work, not an antithesis. The aim is to provide social workers with an approach that will help them focus more keenly on the important features of the black cultural and historical experience, features that might aid them in their effort to help black people. Thus, when we speak of the "black experience," we are speaking primarily of the black helping experience.

PIONEER BLACK SOCIAL WORKERS

This book particularly focuses on the experience of pioneer black social workers during the first four decades of the 20th century as these social workers attempted to transform the lives of newly arrived black migrants to the urban North from the rural South. We highlight specifically early black social workers who worked in the National Urban League because these were the leading, most advanced black social workers, and their beliefs and thoughts were representative of black social workers on the whole. This book also focuses on the helping tradition of the migrants who journeyed to the cities. So significant was the rural-to-urban migration of black people that it became known to history as the "Great Migration." We deliberately target this transitional time period in black history because the professionalization of black social work and the problems of the black migrants mark a significant break from traditional black caregiving systems and an effort to apply the scientific method to black problem solving.

Furthermore, the period is significant because it brings black tradition face to face with urban modernity as the old ideas that shaped black rural life were seriously challenged by new ideas of success, race pride, and a social gospel-type religiosity. As social workers of the first few decades were promising to transform lives, their own lives were being transformed by the new thoughts and outlooks that were serving to usher in what black intellectuals of that time called "The New Negro." More important, the earlier experiences of black social workers with the black newcomers have profound implications for social work with black people in contemporary society.

Our thesis is that pioneering black social workers were presented with a great opportunity to incorporate salient elements of the black helping experience into social work practice, but they opted to take on the middle-class or bourgeois outlook of the dominant society and to challenge, even to wage war against, black folk culture rather than to learn from it. Furthermore, our thesis is that many of the important issues that pioneering social workers failed to resolve in the past because they did not rely on the cultural apparatus of the black masses are still with us in contemporary society, leaving us with much of the same distorted view of black life, culture, and history and with the same ineffectual instruments of social change. What we are saying, in essence, is that if black social workers had incorporated primary features of the black helping experience into their work, they would have enhanced the power of social work to effect change in the black American condition.

For a brief historical overview, it is significant to recall that the entry of black people into the social work profession began at the turn of the century when pioneering black social workers issued a call for the training of black social work professionals to help the thousands of rural black peasants trekking cityward, seeking refuge from acute poverty, powerlessness, and racial terrorism. These leaders thought that traditional black helping systems, such as extended families, churches, fraternal orders, benevolent societies, and women's clubs, were ill-equipped to help the urban black newcomers. George Haynes (1911), who was trained at the New York School of Philanthropy as one of the first black professional social workers, wrote that the problems confronting the migrants were too massive and complex to leave in the hands of "inefficient and inexperienced enthusiasts" (p. 387). He argued that "the conditions affecting Negroes in cities can best be improved by those of their own race whose latent capacity has had superior training directed toward social service" (p. 384).

Haynes became the leading advocate for the recruitment of black social workers. After becoming the founder and first executive director of the National Urban League, Haynes placed the college training of black social workers at the top of the league's agenda. Haynes himself was instrumental in establishing the first undergraduate social work program at a black college, Fisk University, in 1911. Howard University and Payne College soon followed Fisk University's lead in establishing undergraduate social work programs. By 1922, the first black graduate school of social work had been established at Morehouse College in Atlanta, Georgia, and was called the Atlanta University School of Social Work. Its first director was Garry Ward Moore. With Haynes as the founder of the first undergraduate program of social work at a predominantly black college and Moore as the first director of the first graduate school of social work at a predominantly black university, we see the growing interest of black men in the social work profession, a profession once considered to be exclusively women's work.

THE EMERGENCE OF SOCIAL WORK

In her analysis of this evolutionary stage in the field of social work, Ross (1978) stated that "the foundation for the professional training of blacks as social workers administering to the social welfare concerns of the urban black community were laid in the . . . historical period, 1896–1915" (pp. 422–423). At the turn of the century there were only four known black professional social workers. Social work as a profession was in its infancy for both black and white people. The training for social workers moved from "learning by doing" to the presentation of one or two courses on charity, philanthropy, or social economy in academic departments of philosophy, sociology, and economics. At the 1897 meeting of the Conference on Education for Social Work, social workers finally decided that it was necessary for those who had long been in the field to pass on their knowledge and skills to those entering it so that the same mistakes would not be repeated in the process of "learning by doing." In the summer of 1898, The New York Charity Organization Society opened a summer session in social work for social work practitioners. By 1909 this session had been expanded to one full academic year and, in 1910, it was expanded to two academic years. Other schools of social work, following the two-year academic curriculum, came into existence throughout the country to provide formal academic training for the profession. Concerned with the widespread migration of black people to the cities, Haynes and other National Urban League officials felt that it was imperative to get as many black people trained professionally in social work as possible. By 1930, Haynes and these officials were crediting themselves with helping to bring into existence approximately 1,500 black social workers, a third of whom had received college training. Yet, they were calling for more. In 1930, Charles S. Johnson (1938) of the league held that there was "a ratio of one [black] social worker to every 11,456 Negroes" and that "ratio suggests the need for larger numbers in this field" (pp. 268–269). The response of black people to this call was outstanding because previously the only two major professions readily open to black people—meaning professions that would not raise the ire of racist white people—were teaching and preaching.

Although Northern cities offered black people broader economic opportunity as cheap, unskilled manual laborers and domestics, Southern corporations stifled the development of independent black enterprises, leaving most black businesses with a segregated black clientele and little or no access to a wider market in the dominant society. Professional associations were highly effective in frustrating the careers of black scholars, physicians, managers, nurses, teachers, and lawyers by denying them avenues for training and education, licenses to practice, and the social connection or access to the "buddy system" or the "good old boy network" necessary for success, power, and influence. Even when black people scored high on civil service "merit" examinations, they were systematically denied government jobs. The system was so rigged against them that any black person who received even a token political patronage job for having delivered to some white politician the "Negro vote" was viewed as a race leader and a symbol of black progress. Under these circumstances, social work promised a new and exciting career opportunity for black people. It promised to open up to them a professional career that was every bit as respectable as that of teaching and preaching while simultaneously allowing them to make a living, enjoy professional status in the black community, and satisfy their desire to be of service to the race. Furthermore, in the area of racial uplift, social work promised to be a more effective and efficient method than the traditional helping techniques that were born in black churches and fraternal orders where formal or academic training in helping was practically nonexistent. In fact, professional training in social work promised to set black people apart from these traditional black caregivers who relied largely on sentimental goodwill, common sense, moral exhortation, and religious emotionalism. To black social workers at the turn of the century, it was the scientific method that distinguished social work from traditional black caregiving systems.

SCIENTIFIC METHOD

In the late 19th century, social workers, as members of an emerging profession, met as a constituent part of the American Social Science Association under the section on social economy. Social work and the social sciences held onto the prevailing belief that the objective study of society and the application of rational intelligence were crucial to solving the mounting social ills of the time. Social workers had high hopes for the dawning of a new era of scientific enlightenment. To black people pursuing careers in the promising new profession, the scientific method involved a more systematic investigation of social phenomena and a step-by-step process of matching problems to methods of intervention. The scientific method was based on empirical and objective observation, not on opinion, mother wit, instincts, trial and error, mysticism, tradition, or faith. E. Franklin Frazier (1924), a leading black social work educator before being driven out of the profession and becoming an acclaimed sociologist, held that the scientific method moved black people beyond their traditional dependence on "good will" and "sentimentalizing" and maintained that "only the properly trained colored social worker can impress upon the community the value of the scientific method" (p. 252). Forrester B. Washington (1926), another distinguished black social work educator of the time, maintained that the scientific method provided social workers with "a knowledge of human frailties" and "a process by which social change takes place." He also believed that social workers were not equipped to handle the problems of the black migrant until they had gained training in the scientific method. In other words, these pioneer social work leaders felt that the scientific method provided a knowledge base that was lacking in traditional black helping systems. As deans of the Atlanta School of Social Work (Washington served for nearly 30 years), both Frazier and Washington passed their outlook on to many first-generation black social workers.

Armed with the scientific method, black social workers during the first two decades of the 20th century had strong faith in the transformative powers of social work. One leading black social work practitioner wrote that social work would "raise the level of intelligence" of black people, "give them a stronger economic foundation," help them gain "a better appreciation of social values," "develop competent and dependable leadership," bring "closer cooperation" between black and white people, and "remove from the Negro masses the feeling of . . . inferiority" (Jones, 1928, p. 293). Overall, Jones held that social work "will help to produce a healthy race, a self-contained group, a resourceful people" who will make "special contributions to the welfare of man" (p. 293) and earn the respect and confidence of the entire nation. It did not matter to black social workers at that time that the black migrants brought to them difficult, complex, multifaceted problems. Black social workers still saw social work as a kind of panacea.

BLACK SOCIOLOGY

Viewing social work as a cure-all, early black professional social workers also relied heavily on sociology to provide them with a knowledge base derived from the scientific method, not the typical racist sociology of the time but sociology written by black people. Many of the leading black social workers during the first few decades of the 20th century (for example, George Haynes, E. Franklin Frazier, Forrester B. Washington, Ira de A. Reid, R. R. Wright, Jr., and Walter B. Chivers) held degrees in both sociology and social work. Most social work programs at black colleges and universities were housed in sociology departments. For example, Morgan State University's program of social work did not "liberate" itself from sociology until the 1960s. As Ross (1978) pointed out, pioneering social workers drew heavily from the sociological analysis of sociologists such as Monroe R. Work, W.E.B. DuBois, and Charles S. Johnson and later from sociologists such as Oliver C. Cox. She held that both the black sociologists and the black social workers needed to be hailed as pioneers of black professional social work. Both black sociologists and black social workers believed that sociological studies of black life and racial relations provided them with a theoretical, analytical, and scientific knowledge base superior to the traditional ways of black knowledge gathering. A problem with this is that although sociology helped black social workers gain a profound understanding of society's race relations, class relations, and social problems, such as poverty, poor health care, and racial discrimination, it left many social workers without insights into the culture and psychology of the black migrants, an insight that was necessary for a fuller definition of the problems of this population. This lack of insight caused social workers to focus almost exclusively on broad societal or structural problems such as integrating black people into the industrial economy instead of making extensive use of all the tools social work offered them to deal with problems on the individual, group, community, institutional, and societal or structural levels.

Equipped with the scientific method and deep sociological insights into society from leading black sociologists, black social workers expected to do what America's democracy, the black church, the Civil War, and reconstruction had failed to do: transform former slaves into full, first-class American citizens. This meant that the faith that black social workers had in social work was also a faith in black people, a faith in their ability to rise from degradation to self-reliance, and a faith in their capacity to adopt new ways of viewing the world and new techniques of uplift and survival. However, this faith was rife with ambivalence. For although pioneering black social workers had faith in the ability of black people to rise, they had little or no faith in the old helping tools black people used to give themselves some measure of psychological and emotional security and integrity during slavery and during the semislavery rural conditions after emancipation. Black social workers sought to apply, with little modification, the social work knowledge base they had gained from white social work educators, practitioners, and theoreticians, often giving it a black bourgeois flavoring. They had little use for the folklore, humor, religion, and music that the masses of black people used to cope with living constantly on the edge of despair and doom. Black social workers seemed to have been so blinded by their own faith in social work to empower black people that they could not see that social work also needed to be empowered by the cultural–historical experiences of black people and that this synthesis promised to make social work the kind of potent force pioneering black social workers thought it could be.

DISILLUSIONMENT WITH THE PROFESSION

It was during the Great Depression of the 1930s that the enthusiasm black people had for the power of social work and its scientific method waned to the point of widespread disillusionment. The Great Depression exposed the limitations of social work in handling basic survival needs that were massive and stark. It also created relief agencies that were callously unkind to black recipients, causing them to turn their ill feelings back on social workers, especially the black ones who generally worked with them as a result of segregationist practices in the social welfare workplace.

At the dawning of the 21st century we find that many black social workers are still disenchanted with the ability of social work to bring about desired social change, particularly in the black community. Despite the call of the social work profession for more "minority group" content in social work curricula and for emphasis on cultural diversity, cultural awareness, and ethnic-sensitive social work practice, few professions, as Solomon (1976) pointed out, are held in greater contempt by the black masses than social work. The attitude of black people toward social workers makes it difficult to recruit black individuals for the profession and to have them answer the call issued nearly a century ago. However, what is even more problematic is that many of the issues that confronted black social workers in the past remain unresolved today. For example, issues of how best to define problems confronting black people, what methods to use, and how to deal with the sensitive matter of gender, class, and race confronted pioneering social workers and are still profoundly relevant in contemporary social work practice. Most significant, social workers still have not figured out how to make effective use of black history, black culture, and the overall black experience for the maximum development and well-being of black people. When contemporary social workers do examine the black experience, they tend to take a surface, ahistorical, idealistic look at the role of the black church and the black extended family as helping institutions. Without a historical context in which to view these institutions, social workers fail to see the tensions, conflicts, and contradictions these institutions have suffered over time. They also fail to see the trends showing the conservative tendencies in these institutions that at times have caused them to be antithetical to the very helping tradition that they helped spawn. Modern social workers also make a great fuss over so-called black communication styles. They concentrate fatuously on "expressive" rapport, "rap," slang, "street talk," or "black English" as if these communication patterns were the most important cultural traits with which social workers should be concerned. An in-depth probe into the richly communal and deeply emotional content of the black experience as expressed in the spirituals, work songs, blues, folk narratives, gospels, sermons, dance styles, humor, folk tales, jazz, and oral history is practically nonexistent in social work. Yet it is this content that forms the soul of black people.

BLACK EXPERIENCE–BASED SOCIAL WORK

These unresolved issues of the past and the lack of black presence in social work not only create a problem of bringing black people into the field but also a problem of retaining them once they are recruited. The dropout rate of black students in departments and schools of social work across the country is high. Even at Morgan State University, which is a predominantly African American university in Baltimore, Maryland, we have found that we have had to make a concerted effort to maintain the early enthusiasm our graduates had for social work. After graduating and working a few years in the social work field, some black social workers express deep disappointment, and a few drop out of the profession altogether. As much black experiential content as we incorporate into our social work curriculum, our former students still call for more systematic attempts in this area so that their social work practice with black people will be even more grounded in black reality. As our undergraduates go off to graduate and even to postgraduate schools of social work, they find that the knowledge and practice content they receive often has such little basis in black reality as to many times render their work with black people ineffective. What they have called for is a black identity in social work; they want to see some reflection of themselves in the social work knowledge base other than as pathological objects to be observed or problems to be solved. They want to draw from a social work emphasis on black experiences, black values, black perspectives, and black methods of problem solving.

Our belief is that many of the issues raised and many of the lessons learned by black pioneer social workers in their work with black migrants are still relevant and applicable to social work today. It is this belief that prompted this book. What those pioneers did and what they failed to do both have tremendous importance to contemporary social work practice with black people. Although the times are different, the black situation then is similar to the black situation now because black people are still trying to find their niche in the American social order. They are still beset with the problems of racism, family instability, poverty, and all the attendant social ills. They are still confronted with a racist, reactionary mentality that views them as intellectual inferiors, social deviants, and economic parasites, outcasts who should be locked up, controlled, or contained. They are still in a place in time where their lives are precarious and their future destiny is fraught with agonizing uncertainty.

Drawing from the challenges, struggles, examples, and lessons of traditional black caregivers and first-generation or pioneer professional black social workers, this book seeks to establish a black presence in social work by laying the foundation of a social work approach we call "black experience–based social work." The theoretical perspective that guides this book is that black people in traditional Africa, slavery, and rural life after emancipation—in other words, before black people turned cityward during the Great Migration—had their own ways of identifying problems and their own tools of intervention. We hold that their traditional helping approach could have benefited greatly from professional social work as a science and as a helping art form. Also, the traditional black caregiving systems would have been more effective and efficient if they had developed the administrative, organizational, and service delivery skills of professional social work. Professional social work, in turn, could have been humanized, spiritualized, and radicalized by the black helping tradition, making the masses of black people view it less as an instrument of social control and containment and more as a potent force for social change.

The theoretical perspective that underlies black experience–based social work relies heavily on the historical method. A basic premise of this approach is that it is crucially important for social workers with black clients to gain a basic understanding of black history. This goes for black social workers as well because it cannot be assumed, given the kind of education black students generally receive in America, particularly in schools of social work, that black people automatically know black history. Social workers will never understand black life as long as their information is derived largely from a statistical count and recording of current black pathologies. Even if they lack thorough knowledge of black history, social workers should at least have historical knowledge of the black helping tradition, particularly the kind of issues and problems that confronted first-generation professional black social workers as they attempted to solve the "Negro problem."

Admittedly, it is not easy finding information with respect to the black helping or caregiving experience. We had to dig deeply just to uncover scanty and little-known information in this area; fortunately, we were able to find a few rare eyewitness accounts by earlier black social workers that allowed us to view them close up as they used social work skills to solve problems facing black people throughout the first four decades of the 20th century.

BLACK CULTURE

Black experience–based social work also draws heavily from black culture. As we made an in-depth excursion into the history and tradition of the black helping experience, we found ourselves deep in the territory of black culture as well because black history and black culture are inextricably connected. Black culture brought us face to face with black music, dance, folk tales, humor, and religion, many basic nonmaterial features of black life that black people used to soothe troubled souls. Black experience–based social work sees the interconnectedness of black history and culture particularly in terms of how the black masses have sought to solve problems and gain some mastery over their situation. As Pinderhughes (1989) remarked, "What clients and patients see as a problem, how they express it (i.e., whether it is somatic, behavioral, or affective), what specific symptoms they use, whom they seek out for help, what they regard as helpful, and the strategies they prefer" (p. 13) are all determined by their culture.

Drawing from the deep well of black culture, we particularly turned to that distinctly black musical form known as the spirituals and to that unique black musical form known as the blues. (All of the spirituals quoted are documented in Lovell's, 1972, *Black Song,* and all of the blues songs quoted can be found in Titon's, 1977, *Early Downhome Blues*.) We concentrate on the spirituals and the blues primarily because they are much more than musical art forms. They are the voices of the black past, of the ancestors, articulating their suffering, joy, and wisdom to the current generation. The spirituals and the blues encompass so broadly the philosophy, emotional expression, and social striving of black people. Thus, when pioneering black social workers confronted the black migrants, they were confronting a people of the spirituals and the blues. What these first-generation black social workers failed to grasp is precisely what contemporary social workers still do not know: that no matter how precise, scientific, and quantitative their instruments of research, assessment, and diagnosis, they will never fully understand the masses of black people until they understand the cultural experiences that have shaped them. The spirituals and the blues address these experiences more profoundly than any other cultural art form. They speak of that raw black material that has made for black survival and black sanity in a white society bent on destroying black people's mind, body, and soul.

Black literary artists of the first few decades of the 20th century understood the need to focus on black folk material more so than social workers then or now. For example, the black literary giant Richard Wright (1978) called on black writers decades ago to use their own folk tradition and culture to lift black people to a new level of aesthetic awakening, racial awareness, and political consciousness:

> *Blues, spirituals, and folk tales recounted from mouth to mouth; the whispered words of a black mother to her black daughter on the ways of men; the confidential wisdom of a black father to his black son; the swapping of sex experiences on the street corners from boy to boy in the deepest vernacular; work songs sung under blazing suns—all these formed the channels through which the racial wisdom flowed.* (p. 40)

Another black literary giant, Ralph Ellison, who transformed black folklore into a literary art form, held several decades ago that black leaders would never be accepted by the black masses and never fully grasp the problem facing them until they became "aware of the psychological attitude and incipient forms of action which the black masses reveal in their emotion-charged myths, symbols, and . . . folklore (quoted in Neal, 1989, p. 41). He too held that "only through a skilled and wise manipulation of these centers of repressed social energy will Negro resentments, self-pity and indignation be channeled to cut through temporary issues and become transformed into positive action" (p. 41). He warned that "without this knowledge, leadership, no matter how correct its program, will fail" (p. 41).

MOANING, MOURNING, AND MORNING

Taking the lead from Wright, Ellison, and other black literary figures, we found three basic concepts derived from the spirituals and from the blues that seem to capture the philosophical essence of black experience–based social work: (1) moaning, (2) mourning, and (3) morning. In both the spirituals and the blues "moanin'" refers to black pain, suffering, and grief. Through moanin', or crying or shouting out, black people sought to bring deep-seated pain to the surface for collective affirmation of its reality. "Mournin'" in the spirituals, and to some extent the blues, pertains to a collective effort to overcome grief. It involves a collective process of identification, empathy, and catharsis, whereas "mornin'" in the spirituals represents a significant breakthrough, the arrival of a brighter day, a new beginning, a transformation, or a change. So important are these concepts to the spirituals that they are often used interchangeably, emphasizing their interrelatedness. For example, a line in a spiritual that says, "Oh what a mornin' sister (or brother)" could just as easily say, "Oh what a moanin'" or "Oh what a mournin'." We thought about including these concepts in the title of this book but found that because they sound so much alike, we would have spent too much time spelling each word out so that people would know the distinction.

Because each of these concepts signifies a different (but related) emotional or situational state, a different philosophical outlook, and a linear progression from suffering (moaning) to collective healing and support (mourning) and finally toward an ideal state of health, happiness, and transformation (morning), we saw these concepts as significant in helping us to connect the black experience to the social change process. This meant that we had to operationalize these concepts in ways that would make them functional for social workers. Hence, in black experience–based social work, moanin' indicates the definition of the problem, because nowhere are the trials, troubles, and tribulations of black people better articulated and emphasized than in the blues and the spirituals. In other words, the problem that caused black people the most pain was the one they were most likely to moan, groan, or cry over in their music.

Whereas the moanin' concept helps to highlight what the problem is, the mournin' concept involves a problem-solving process. Slaves, particularly when they were engaged in religious worship and in singing the spirituals, referred to themselves as fellow "mourners." As Lovell (1972) indicated, "a mourner was a fellow sufferer" who needed to be helped, and "saving him was an act of benevolence, but also one of great joy" (p. 278). Slaves acknowledged that they were all sufferers and all in need of group sympathy, healing, and support and that they were in a constant state of mourning.

Mourning then among the slaves involves a problem-solving process with four stages:

1. a collective empathy with the suffering of a fellow mourner
2. an effort to relieve suffering through emotional catharsis or through shouting, singing, praying, dancing, and crying the pain out
3. an inculcation of hope and faith or instilling in the sufferer the belief that one day soon his or her troubles would be over
4. a keen focus on reality or objective conditions so that the mourners would not become disillusioned if their biggest hopes and dreams failed to materialize.

We sought to operationalize the concept of "mourning" to mean a problem-solving process of empathy with the client, a collective effort to seek alternatives to solve the problem, collective encouragement and reinforcement, and a constant testing of reality.

Mornin' in the spirituals meant to black people a day of joy when they would see the light or achieve hoped for, dreamed of results after being in the storm so long. In the spirituals the desired result or ideal state was always centered around closeness to God and salvation. It was a feeling of being filled with the Holy Spirit; of heightened self-assurance, security, and confidence; and of being in tune with the "old-time religion" of the ancestors. It was truly a joyous feeling of being "born again" but this time in a world where the holy had touched and transformed the profane. This pleasure, this joy, this great morning was just a sample on earth of what black people expected to receive in full measure once they were in heaven with lost loved ones. When the spirituals got too carried away with utopianism, idealism, and mysticism, the blues became a stark reminder that this desired pleasure or outcome was not guaranteed, that hard times and rough roads were still lurking over the next mountain, and that black people had better not get too content or complacent or stray too far too long from reality. We operationalize the concept of morning to mean seeking to achieve the desired goal of strengthening black people individually so that they can face their problems, avoid the pitfalls designed for them by a racist society, and take responsible action for solving their problems and therefore put themselves in a position where they can work collectively with other black people for economic uplift, social justice, and political empowerment and find self-realization in a collective struggle for social change.

Although all three of these concepts reflect the philosophical orientation and theoretical outlook of black experience–based social work, the concept of mourning takes on added significance. We hold that a crucial problem that keeps black people from uniting to seek solutions to common problems is that as black people became increasingly urbanized, they began to lose their traditional ability to mourn with one another (that is, to identify with, affirm, and empathize with one another's suffering), lend each other support in overcoming pain and grief, and encourage and inspire one another to keep struggling against the tremendous obstacles confronting them. This inability to mourn was evidenced by growing divisiveness and mistrust in the black community that still stifle black people's sense of community, hamper their commitment to uplift and

social change, and leave them unable to stop the increasing antiso-
ciality that further thwarts stability and development in the urban
black family and community. Not since thousands of black people
participated in selling their own kin to European slave traders has
the inability to mourn been as pronounced in black history as it is
in the contemporary black experience. We hold that a social work
practice modality that draws from the black experience must
include creating a helping method and process that will help black
people regain their ability to mourn. This is key to ending much of
the moaning and ushering in the promise of morning, or the coming of a brighter day.

In drawing from black history and black culture, we sought not
to recreate the past but to use the past experiences of black people
as the foundation for creating a new social work approach relevant
to today's issues and problems. Hence, we did not rely solely on a
study of the past. We also relied significantly on "social experiments" with our students, drawing information from approximately 500 students and former students over a 12-year period
(1983–1995). In doing so, we were keeping with black tradition.
According to the black social work educator and historian Edyth L.
Ross, black social worker educators have a tradition of enlisting students for social experimentation. She held that W.E.B. DuBois started the "social experiments" with black students at Atlanta
University at the turn of the century. He enlisted their help in the
scientific study of the "Negro problem" as they "used the city and
urban environment as a sociological laboratory" (Ross, 1978, p.
423). Other professors of social science and social work at Atlanta
University continued this tradition of instruction.

We started this work in the early 1980s in a social work course
on the black family at Morgan State University. Initially the course
presented the history and examined major theoretical perspectives
of the black family and critically assessed social welfare policies and
programs. However, as popular as the course was, students wanted
more. They wanted not to just apply the black helping experience
to hypothetical family cases; they also wanted a practice compo-
nent to help them tackle their own individual and family problems.
Hence, the theoretical perspective and the practice modality of
black experience–based social work evolved with the invaluable

assistance of our students in a careful and painstaking but exhilarating process of refinement and preparation to extend it beyond the classroom setting. As a result, many of our former students are using black experience–based social work in whole or in part in their own social work practices. The aim of this work is to lay the foundation of black experience–based social work so that it has the opportunity for wider use and refinement and wider critical scrutiny.

Because we used primary black historical and cultural sources and social experimentation with our students to lay the foundation of a new social work approach, we organized this work around the three key concepts: (1) moaning, (2) mourning, and (3) morning.

Part 1 deals with the identification of the problem, or moaning. Chapter 2 examines the problem as pioneering black social workers viewed it, their faith in the power of social work, and their disillusionment with social work during the Great Depression; chapter 3 uses the concept of moaning with respect to the perception the black masses themselves had of problems confronting them; and chapter 4 explores social work and the moaning experience.

Part 2 takes up the concept of mourning. Chapter 5 explores the helping methods black people have traditionally used to solve problems; chapter 6 looks at the problem of collective amnesia and the inability to mourn; chapter 7 takes up the sensitive matter of race; and chapter 8 examines how class and gender matters hamper the ability of social workers to work and mourn with black people.

Part 3 revolves around the concept of morning. Chapter 9 outlines the major philosophical and theoretical principles underpinning black experience–based social work; chapter 10 deals with the kind of education that is needed for black experience–based social work; and chapter 11, relying on social experimentation with social work students, examines how social work practitioners can be trained to use black experience–based social work in their work with black people.

Overall, the chapters analyze the relevancy and applicability of black problem identification and problem solving in the past to social work practice today to seek a synthesis of the black experience and mainstream social work for the maximum empowerment of social work practice with black people Although the primary goal

of black experience–based social work is to help caregiving professionals, regardless of race, become more effective in their work with
black people, the subsidiary goal is to help social workers overcome
their disillusionment with the profession, to project a more positive
image of social work in the black community, and to restore the
faith that black social work pioneers had in the power of social
work to transform lives and to effect social change.

REFERENCES

Frazier, E. F. (1924, April). Social work in race relations. *Crisis, 27*(6),
    252–254.

Frazier, E. F. (1940). *Negro youth at the crossways.* Washington, DC:
    American Council on Education.

Haynes, G. (1911). Cooperation with colleges in securing and training
    Negro social workers for urban centers. In *Proceedings of the National
    Conference on Charities and Correction.* Fort Wayne, IN: Fort Wayne
    Printing.

Johnson, C. S. (1938). *The Negro college graduate.* Chapel Hill: University
    of North Carolina Press.

Jones, E. K. (1928, November). Social work among Negroes. *Annals of the
    American Academy of Political and Social Science, 140,* 287–293.

Lovell, J., Jr. (1972). *Black song.* New York: Macmillan.

Neal, L. (1989). *Visions of a liberated future.* New York: Thunder Mouth
    Press.

Pinderhughes, E. (1989). *Understanding race, ethnicity, and power.* New York:
    Free Press.

Ross, E. L. (1978). *Black heritage in social welfare: 1860–1930.* Metuchen,
    NJ: Scarecrow Press.

Solomon, B. B. (1976). *Black empowerment: Social work in oppressed
    communities.* New York: Columbia University Press.

Titon, J. T. (1977). *Early downhome blues.* Urbana: University of Illinois
    Press.

Washington, F. B. (1926, September). What professional training means to
    the social worker. *Annals of the American Academy of Political and Social
    Science, 228,* 165–169.

Wright, R. (1978). Blueprint for Negro writing. In E. Wright & M. Fabre
    (Eds.), *Richard Wright reader* (pp. 36–49). New York: Harper & Row.

PART 1

Moanin'

CHAPTER 2

Black Social Work Pioneers
and the Power of Social Work

A t the turn of the 20th century, the mechanization of agri-
culture, racial persecution, and the desire to better their lot
caused hordes of unlettered, unskilled, dirt-poor, black rural peasants to trek cityward. They left the deep southern states to face an
uncertain future in big midwestern, eastern, and northern cities.
Attracted by the lure and promise of work in industry, these
migrants wanted to gain a foothold in the American economy, fully
participate in the "American dream," and be treated as citizens and
human beings. As they crowded into the slums of the big cities,
they began to feel more and more like unwelcome intruders tres-
passing on someone else's territory. It was not long before an alarm-
ing rate of poverty, disease, and crime arose among them, and they
were soon being contemptibly dubbed by white city officials as the
"Negro problem," the primary threat to urban progress and stability. To make matters worse, even the black people who had a long
history of living in the city were often embarrassed by and ashamed
of these black newcomers. City-born and -bred black people viewed
their newly arrived country cousins as uncouth, unkempt, boisterous, and ignorant. They feared that the newcomers would reinforce
stereotypes of black people and stir up antiblack sentiments that
would have dire consequences for all black people, even for those
old city dwellers who had gotten along well with white people. One
black woman voiced the sentiments of many black people when
she stated,

*When the Negro started coming to Chicago, I didn't know what to
do. We had always been able to go where we pleased without any*

23

*thought of race and had our white friends who visited us and whom
we visited. I would get on the street car, for instance, and see a big
black man or big fat black woman come in the car and drop down
beside a white person. I would run to see Mr. X (a leading colored
man) and say to him X, what are we going to do with all of these
Negroes from the South coming in here. They look terrible. They sit
down on the street car beside white people and I am sure that there is
going to be trouble. He would always tell me that these were my
people but, I would always answer that I don't belong to any such
people. Moreover, he would tell me to be sympathetic toward them—
trying to show me that they had to make a living as any other
people. I would shake my head in disgust and leave his office.*
(Frazier, 1939, p. 82)

Mr. X's attitude was evidence that although some black people
were disgusted with the new black arrivals, others showed sympathy. Among the greatest sympathizers of the black migrants were
black social workers who seemed undaunted by the huge challenge
they faced. Their enthusiasm for social work and belief in its transformative powers were high, and their confidence in the ability of
black people to rise with the aid of social work seemed unshakable.

Black social workers believed that social work had the promise
and the power of lifting a perennially oppressed people from ultimate degradation to full first-class American citizenship. How did
black social workers gain this faith? And why did they become so
disillusioned with social work after having so much initial enthusiasm for it? Also, how did their growing disillusionment affect their
definition of the problem and their confidence in the ability of the
black masses to rise?

BLACK MIGRANTS AND WHITE IMMIGRANTS

The magnitude of the confidence pioneering black social workers
had in the ability of social work to help black migrants rise cannot
be fathomed without insight into the kind of world the migrants
were entering. Waves of European immigrants had already claimed
a stake. These European immigrants from southern and eastern
Europe had started coming to the big cities in droves in the 1880s,

nearly three full decades before the Great Migration. They too had started out the American dream in the nightmarish world of slums, poverty, and labor exploitation and faced the discrimination, anti-Semitism, and ethnic prejudice and persecution by Anglo-Saxons who sought to maintain racial purity and ethnic dominance. Their deplorable situation also caught the attention of social workers who sought to help them adjust to the American way of life. In the initial stages of immigration, between 1899 and 1909, organized American charity paid no official attention to the influx of immigrants, but when by 1920 more than 8.5 million European immigrants had migrated to America, their plight could no longer be ignored. White social workers, operating largely out of settlement houses, took up the cause. For example, Jane Addams, the settlement house pioneer, chose a neighborhood in Chicago in which to establish her Hull House precisely because "within a few blocks of the Settlement lived Italians, Russians (many of them Jews), Poles, Bohemians, Swiss, French, Canadians, Irish, Dutch, Germans, Scandinavians, and a few Greeks and Arabs, not to mention Englishmen" (quoted in Levine, 1971, p. 151). Although Jane Addams and other white settlement workers felt that the primary problem facing the immigrants was how to Americanize them, they realized that this was no simple task. They could see that the effort to assimilate the immigrants into Anglo-Saxon culture required waging a vigorous battle for better schools, better health care, better housing, better wages, and better working conditions. Jane Addams held that just as hard a task was getting the Anglo-Americans to respect the immigrants as people. Therefore, she went a step further than was common in most settlement houses by establishing in Hull House a labor museum to highlight the immigrants' traditions, customs, heroes, and contributions. Her hope was that exposing Anglo-Saxons to the culture of the immigrants would help them gain an appreciation for these European newcomers (Levine, 1971).

Despite the gravely serious problems that were encountered in the Americanization of the immigrants, few immigrants expressed the slightest doubt that they would be assimilated eventually, once they smoothed over the rougher edges of their old ways. The black migrants had no such assurance. They knew from experience that the avenues opened to white immigrants for upward mobility were closed to them; the white immigrants had easier access to capital, to the vote, to the political machine, to philanthropy, to education, to organized labor and even to organized crime as vehicles of uplift. Black migrants knew from more than 400 years of experience that the great American "melting pot" was meant for these European newcomers but not for them. Even if there were social class differences among the white people and even if the different white immigrants did not always get along with one another, they still had the common phenotypical trait, the same European background, and the common satisfaction of knowing that they were all white. For an interesting discussion comparing the plight of black migrants and European migrants, see the first two chapters in Stanfield (1985).

Black migrants were not in the city too long before they felt the weight of this enduring racial bond of whiteness. For example, although white people exploited both the white immigrant and the black migrant, they took specific advantage of the economic desperation of black people and often hired them mainly as cheap, dirty menial laborers to break strikes. This practice, of course, incurred the wrath of white organized labor and led to some of the worst urban race riots in the nation's history. So bloody were the race riots during the summer of 1919, for instance, that it became known to history as the "Red Summer." The black migrants were not long in urban America before they could see clearly that all the European immigrants felt that black people were inferior, lazy, immoral, and of extremely retarded intelligence; that all white people sought to move to residential areas free of these black savages; and that all black people, even those of the professional classes and irrespective of income or status level, were residentially confined, restricted, and circumscribed as the color line served to keep both the black urban newcomers and those who had a history of living in the city literally in their place.

In essence, black migrants were not in the city long before they experienced daily the deeply entrenched hatred and psychosexual fears that even the new white arrivals expressed toward black people. Yet, despite the hatred demonstrated daily to them by white people, black migrants kept coming in large numbers to the cities.

They wanted a home in America and realized that home could never be in the South again. Although Southern blacks had headed westward in the great "Exoduster" movement of the late 19th century, they understood too that they could never call the West home because the free land and opportunity given to homesteading white people were not offered to them. All hopes for seeking the American dream in the West ended during the 1922 Tulsa, Oklahoma, race riots with the unprecedented aerial bombing of black homes and the roundup and placement of black people in concentration camps. The big, dirty, noisy, sprawling cities of the North and the Midwest became the last hope for many of these rural southern sojourners, the last place to run. For, as Brown (1956) wrote, where could black people run when they were already in the promised land?

THE POWER OF SOCIAL WORK

The faith black pioneering social workers had in the power of social work had to be strong given the condition of the black migrants. If white social workers knew what a rough time they were in for in seeking to assimilate the white immigrants, then surely black social workers had to have realized that their task of transforming black people practically fresh out of slavery into full first-class American citizens would be even rougher. Anybody could see that the general naivete of the migrants made them easy marks for greedy landlords, businessmen, labor recruiters, and other vicious characters, both black and white. Anybody could see that the schools were not properly educating black children, that the police and judges treated black people like animals to be locked up in a zoo, and that public officials had little or no regard for the economic, recreational, health, housing, or safety needs of black people (Henri, 1975).

Despite the challenge of uplifting the black migrant, black social workers saw enough in the systematic way in which social work approached problems, its ability to marshal resources, its emphasis on social reform, and its advocacy on behalf of downtrodden people to believe that social work was superior to the traditional systems of caregiving. The black social workers felt that a basic weakness inherent in traditional black helping systems was that such systems tried to tackle too many massive social problems with too few resources. The black church, for instance, engaged in numerous helping activities beyond its traditional roles of feeding the hungry, clothing the naked, and giving counsel to those troubled in mind and spirit. Many black churches, especially the larger ones, sought to perform myriad social services functions such as seeking decent housing for poor families; looking for foster homes for abused, abandoned, and neglected children; organizing various recreational activities; seeking jobs for unemployed people; holding classes in cooking and sewing; and even teaching job skills.

Ross (1978) held that black professional social workers felt that the problems confronting the black migrants were so complex that they "required the attention of welfare specialists" and demanded "national attention and redress" (p. 335). Black professional social workers felt that specialization was required in the areas of family life, housing, health, sanitation, employment, poverty, crime, recreation, leisure, and education. These, they felt, were problems of the nation, beyond the capabilities, scope, and resources of local black self-help initiatives. Social work, they believed, had the power to provide the helping specialists the black community needed and to call to the attention of the nation how badly its black citizens were living while the rest of the nation prospered (Ross, 1978).

CONFLICT WITH THE BLACK CHURCH

In seeking to emerge as the leading caregivers in the urban black community, professional black social workers often found themselves in a conflictual situation with the dominant traditional black caregiving system, the black church. Jesse O. Thomas (1967), one of the founders of the Atlanta School of Social Work, contemptuously wrote that the black church's "conception of social service" is to have the pastor take up an "altar collection" or offering each Sunday and, "during his pastoral visits the following week, divide the amount among the shut-ins or those on the sick list" (p. 76). Thomas predicted that the "new conception of social work," one supplying "a more scientific approach" was destined to make "social service departments" in churches disappear (p. 97). E. Franklin Frazier (1924) wrote that "churches . . . have scarcely anything to ameliorate conditions. They are still more interested in getting Negroes into heaven than in getting them out of the hell they live in on earth" (p. 252). Frazier hoped that social work as "a new force at work . . . [would] transform the churches" (p. 252).

Another leading social worker of the time, Eugene Kinckle Jones (1928), attacked black churches on two grounds. He held that they seldom assessed the needs of the people to whom they dispensed services, that they, in effect, provided the same services to clients regardless of how different their needs were, and that they were not accountable in how they handled or dispensed funds for social services.

The tension between the professional social workers and the black ministers was often so intense that social workers were seen by ministers as usurping their counseling and almsgiving roles. Many black professional social workers sought peaceful coexistence. Realizing the power that ministers wielded in the black community, some black social workers sought a division of labor, turning over to ministers social services work concerning religious and spiritual development while leaving for themselves the more complex secular social issues and problems, sort of their own rendition of rendering unto Caesar that which belongs to Caesar and to God that which belongs to God. However, despite the compromises, pioneering black social workers were indeed taking a bold step in demanding that black churches step aside and make room for the new, scientific social work approach. When one understands that in the black community, especially at that time, the black church was looked on as a sacred institution that was beyond criticism, one can fully grasp how confident pioneering black social workers were in the power of social work.

EMPHASIS ON INDUSTRIALIZATION

Black social workers felt that social work was the chief weapon for turning black migrants into skilled, unionized industrial workers and fully integrating them into the urban political economy. They believed that the future of the black race in America depended on the extent to which black people became industrialized (Parris & Brooks, 1971). In this respect, they were following the lead of

Booker T. Washington, whose philosophy of success was very popular during the first two decades of the 20th century when black
social workers were groping to find a philosophical basis for social
work practice. Like Washington, black social workers began to
become interested in the material well-being of the race and to
measure success by the ownership of land, homes, businesses,
union membership, and bank accounts. Washington (1967) himself
said,

> *One farm bought, one house built, . . . one man who is the largest*
> *taxpayer or has the largest bank account, one school or church*
> *maintained, one factory run successfully, . . . one patient cured by a*
> *Negro doctor, one sermon well preached, one office well filled, one life*
> *cleanly lived—these will tell more in our favor than all the abstract*
> *eloquence that can be summoned to plead our cause.* (p. 364)

Although black social workers were influenced by the Progressive
era's emphasis on social, industrial, and municipal reform, they put
industrial education, training, employment, unionization, and
inclusion at the front of their agenda. The National Urban League,
the leading black social work organization of the time, believed, for
example, that if the American industrial workforce would fully
absorb the migrants, who were considered to be the most impover-
ished, uneducated, unskilled, and culturally backward members of
the race, then the race problem in America would be virtually
solved. Hence, National Urban League black social workers went
about assessing the needs and defining the problems of black
migrants in terms of job training and placement and in terms of
pleading with industry to open its doors.

The potential for the kind of industrial democracy that Urban
League members dreamed of looked promising during World War I
because the severe shortage of white labor led the war industry to
relax its traditional antiblack practices and to use black workers by
the scores. The league had every reason to believe that it was making headway, especially because it was experiencing unprecedented
success in finding industrial jobs for black workers (although mainly in menial and semiskilled capacities). Also, like Booker T.
Washington, Urban League black social workers had hitched their

future to the goodwill of the white ruling capitalist class, depending on an alliance with white philanthropy and white capital to uplift one of the poorest and least-powerful groups in America. The contradiction of seeking to absorb black workers into labor unions while turning to the capitalist class for their own bread and butter presented no problem to Urban League social workers. It was not until capital took an extreme turn for the worse that they shifted their attention from private capital to government intervention as a means for solving the "Negro problem." Black social workers shifted focus when something happened that even the leading economists of the time with all their precise indicator charts and predictor graphs could not foresee: the Great Depression of the 1930s. Just as pioneering black social workers were beginning to gain confidence that black people had a chance of becoming an integral part of the American industrial order, the bottom fell out of the economy, leaving the American citizens with the most catastrophic depression in the nation's history and black social workers with waning beliefs in the power of social work to effect massive social change.

THE GREAT DEPRESSION

The attitude of black social workers toward social work did not immediately change during the initial stages of the Great Depression because they found that as hard as times were for black people in general, the Great Depression opened up for black social workers new avenues of employment. Before the Great Depression, black social workers found employment in agencies such as the National Urban League; they even found administrative roles in segregated YMCAs and YWCAs and took jobs in "Negro sections" of the criminal and juvenile systems, the health field, and the educational system. Black social workers basically worked with dysfunctional, poor black families, many of whom had caught the attention of the courts or private charities. With the coming of the Great Depression black social workers managed, despite pervasive racism, to find employment in New Deal direct and work relief programs. This marked a significant step in their professional development but, unfortunately, also a major step in their disillusionment with the power of social work to transform lives. They discovered that finding jobs for black workers in a relatively stable economy was one thing; working with poor black people in relief agencies during a time when resources were scarce and needs so desperate was another.

The rare eyewitness account of Anna Hedgeman, a depression-era social work supervisor for New York City's Emergency Relief Bureau with 40 workers under her charge, gives an idea of what black social workers in general were up against. Hedgeman recalled that the migrant black people during the Great Depression were like a swarming, hostile hive. They were "cut off from former home relationships" and did not find "the understanding which they had expected in the North" (Hedgeman, 1964, p. 70). In New York City alone, more than 10,000 black people lived in cellars and basements that had been converted into makeshift flats. Hedgeman reported "that packed in damp, rat-ridden dungeons, they existed in squalor not too different from that of the Arkansas sharecroppers" and "were forced to pay exorbitant rents to landlords who flagrantly violated the city building and sanitary codes" (p. 56). Face to face with homelessness and starvation, New York black people by the thousands, she said, "turned sadly to welfare" (p. 57), where they received from the Home Relief Bureau only eight cents a meal for food, forcing black men, women, and children to forage with cats and dogs for food in garbage cans.

The situation of the black migrants during the Great Depression was so bleak, according to Hedgeman (1964), that the black social workers who serviced them felt overburdened and exhausted. She wrote that most of her workers had nothing in their professional training to prepare them to meet the raw needs of desperate black clients as they came for clothes and food or money for rent, gas, and fuel, what Hedgeman referred to as elemental needs "of the starkest kind" (p. 56). Moreover, nothing in their training had prepared black social workers for the huge caseloads and the scarce and grossly inadequate resources they were working with to meet the monumental, multilayered needs of desperate people. Hedgeman wrote that social workers were expected to use scanty resources to work the miracles of fighting evictions, securing suspension of rent claims, seeking employment even when there was mass unemployment (not to mention mass job discrimination against black people), and finding milk for babies, food for starving families, and fuel and shelter to keep people from going homeless and freezing to death. So inadequate were the resources to address the monumental needs of urban black people, both native and migrant, that Hedgeman had no choice but to order her workers to "give aid to the worst emergencies" only, but those workers reported to her that "everything looks like an emergency" (p. 57)

Soon these emergencies began to take an emotional, physical, and spiritual toll even on Hedgeman's most dedicated workers. They were caught up in a seemingly never-ending crisis situation, and the numerous emergencies kept them on the job far beyond the requirements, making their weekends as busy as their weekdays. What was worse was that many of Hedgeman's workers "had come from the relief roles themselves" and their great identification with and compassion for their clients often prompted them to investigate clients by day and help organize them by night, Hedgeman lamented, "to demand more than we could give" (Hedgeman, 1964, p. 61).

Although Hedgeman stated that her four years of dedicated relief work gave her "basic insight into the needs of the exploited at every level" and taught her to find creativeness despite bureaucratic sterility, acceptance despite apathy, and hope despite desperation, she too became "tired of the problems of the multitude and desperately needed rest" (Hedgeman, 1964, pp. 69–70). Like many other black social workers during the Great Depression, Hedgeman threw in the towel and went in search of a less stressful, less overwhelming, less limited profession.

BECOMING SOCIAL ACTIVISTS

Black social workers who stuck it out found that they had to play a role larger than just dispensing handouts. Many concluded that if change was going to take place at all, they would have to become social activists and advocates. Already they were so close to the problems of the black migrants and the equally down-and-out native urban black people that they could see firsthand that whatever Roosevelt's New Deal intended, it only amounted to the usual raw deal for thousands of black people. They could see that black people constantly were not receiving their fair share or equal treatment in the New Deal programs and would not receive fair treatment and equality unless black social workers themselves escalated the struggle from public almsgiving to higher political levels of social action. Therefore, black social workers targeted their attention on local white business leaders and politicians who controlled the relief programs. Although Harry Hopkins, the national head of the Federal Emergency Relief Administration had formally decreed that there was to be no discrimination in relief programs on the basis "of race, religion, color, noncitizenship, political affiliation," or because of "membership in any special or selected group" (quoted in Kurzman, 1974, p. 129), local relief was dispensed according to the whims, egos, and political agendas of local white power brokers. These petty welfare despots were meticulous—indeed, practically artful—in making sure that the segregated social services doled out to black people amounted to a disproportionately small amount of the total community welfare budget. They made certain that when black people sought help from nonsegregated relief agencies, they would find that the prevailing attitude toward them would be that no black person should receive food, fuel, clothing, rent money, or public work so long as there was one white person still in need. When black people did come to these agencies they were treated with the utmost disrespect and contempt. As one black woman from Georgia complained, "When I go to [white relief officials] they talk to me like I was a dog" (J. Jones, 1985, p. 223).

So angered and humiliated were black relief applicants that their numerous letters to the National Urban League prompted Urban League social workers to monitor relief programs and demand justice, launch investigations, and hold public hearings on wrongdoing in relief agencies. One report summed up the plight of both black relief applicants and black social workers:

First—Negroes are suffering to a greater extent than others. Second— as the last persons hired and the first fired, they have been longer exposed to unemployment than others and as a consequence have used up all surpluses or resources they may have accumulated. Third—there are employers who are discharging them in order to make room for white workers. Fourth—the Negro unemployment situation is too often incidental in our emergency set-ups when because of the very nature of the factors involved, their problems should have a larger place and more sympathetic treatment. Fifth— Negroes with leadership qualities, social service training, and general knowledge of problems affecting their people are not being used to the extent that they should by the various relief agencies throughout the country. (Parris & Brooks, 1971, p. 220)

FIGHTING IDEOLOGICAL BATTLES

When black social workers were not seeking fairness, equality, and justice from local relief agencies, they found that another major battleground was along ideological lines. Local white business leaders, politicians, and relief officials had inherited the Poor Law mentality in maintaining that poor people should be required to prove beyond a shadow of a doubt that they possessed the traits of honesty, industriousness, sobriety, thrift, and worthiness to receive relief. They felt it necessary in cities and towns across America to wage a vigorous campaign to detect "chiseling" and to conduct client eligibility studies, particularly in the black community. The hidden agenda was to remove as many black people from the relief rolls as possible to open up more slots for white people. These welfare detectives propagated the notion that is still very much prevalent today: Black people had developed a "relief habit" that caused them to seek a handout rather than a job.

Black social workers found themselves expending considerable energy countering such notions. For example, the eyewitness account of Thyra Edwards (1936), a black relief worker, suggested that she took seriously her role in combating welfare stereotypes of black and poor people. Edwards said that she had personally witnessed scores of black men and women begging for relief work assignments, even when the wage offered was a mere equivalent of their relief budgets, and that she had seen black men going to work relief jobs "so poorly clad that they could hardly do the outdoor jobs assigned to them" (p. 214). This inadequacy of clothing, she said, caused some waiting rooms in relief stations to display "a gruesome exhibit of crisping, cracked, frozen ears, bleeding hands and swollen, frost bitten feet" (p. 214). Edwards upheld the rights of black people, like white people, to relief and expressed doubt that there was any "virtue in the gesture of pacing the sidewalks in the futile search for jobs that do not exist" (p. 214). Harry Hopkins declared:

> I am getting sick and tired of these people on the WPA [Works Progress Administration] and local relief rolls being called chiselers and cheats. It doesn't do any good to call these people names because they are just like the rest of us. They don't drink any more than the rest of us, they don't lie any more, they're no lazier than the rest of us—they're pretty much a cross section of the American people. (quoted in Kurzman, 1974, p. 158)

Despite Hopkins's dismay, the Poor Law mentality prevailed.

Edwards (1936) criticized white social workers for not doing more to address these stereotypes about black people. She felt that their daily experiences with and access to case records of black people put them in a unique position "to expose and explode these hairtrigger conclusions branding the unemployed as maligners, chiselers, and indolent and hopeless parasites" (p. 215). She asserted that "instead of the too ready indictment of the unemployed, condemnation should, it would seem, be directed against the political economy that creates these conditions of mass unemployment and its attendant malnutrition, disease, overcrowding, immorality, delinquency, and family disorganization" (p. 215).

DISILLUSIONMENT

As dedicated and as overzealous as many black social workers were in expanding their roles from mere dispensers of the welfare dole to social activists and social advocates, the Great Depression began to take its toll. E. Franklin Frazier (1932) wrote that even "the most optimistic social workers with the care of a hundred or more dependent and broken Negro families" (p. 84) were beginning to feel they were fighting a losing battle. Even the generally optimistic National Urban League social workers began to experience a sense of disillusionment. They could see that the state of the economy was such that their dreams of industrial democracy were far out of step with current realities. Instead of the millions of jobs they had envisioned for black workers in industry, they found a disproportionate number of black workers among the millions of Americans who were jobless. As Weiss (1974) pointed out,

> *The Depression effectively nullified the Urban League's work in*
> *industrial relations. . . . No longer could it plan its programs in terms*
> *of progress; rather, "it had to think grimly of bare survival." . . .*
> *When there were no jobs at all, arguments for new jobs for blacks*
> *became moot; even holding on to positions blacks already filled was*
> *more than the Urban League could possibly have accomplished.*
> (p. 250)

Eugene Kinckle Jones, the executive director of the Urban League during that time, once stated in speech after speech that it was only a matter of time before black people would move from rural peasantry to full industrialized workers. However, after the Great Depression gained momentum, and "numerous speeches and disillusionment later," Jones began to "narrow his subject" and started to wonder whether black people would ever grasp the elusive American dream (Parris & Brooks, 1971).

BLACK DISCONTENT

Not only were black social workers becoming increasingly aware of the limitations of social work under harsh economic circumstances, they also suffered from the fact that black people whom they had worked overtime to feed, had fought hard to help get a fair share, and had defended so vociferously against ideological attacks were beginning to turn against them as if black social workers were traitors to the race. The problem was that black people seeking relief assistance were so badly treated by some white relief workers and authorities that they started to identify all social workers, regardless of their race, as dirty workers and as a major threat to black survival. Black social workers were specifically targeted. They were the ones working directly with black clients because they were forbidden to work with white clients. It did not matter that black social workers did not make policy and that most did not promote the notion that black people were welfare chiselers. The resentment of black people toward "relief" or welfare workers became so deep-seated that it is still directed toward social workers today (Solomon, 1976). According to Piven and Cloward (1971), this is the case largely because four decades after the Great Depression, public welfare recipients were still subjected to insults and humiliation; still subjected to unreasonable searches, harassing surveillance, eavesdropping, interrogation, and fraud investigation; and still cruelly "branded as sexually immoral, as chiselers, and as malingerers" (p. 167). The Poor Law mentality had continued to show vigorous signs of life. According to Solomon (1976), contemporary black people have so come to associate social workers with an oppressive relief system that the only hope social workers have of improving their tarnished image in the black community is to call themselves by another name or to refer to themselves in terms of their specialty, such as child specialist, family specialist, or community development specialist.

LOSS OF FAITH IN BLACK PEOPLE

The larger problem was that as black people began to lose faith in black social workers, black social workers, unfortunately, also began to lose faith in the people they served. Black social workers had started out with tremendous faith in social work and tremendous faith in black people. As one prominent black social work pioneer stated at the beginning of the century, "one qualification for work with his own people which the colored worker possesses which surpasses all others [is] faith in the ultimate destiny of the Negro race" (Dexter, 1921, p. 440). However, now as they felt the cold resentment of black people toward them, black social workers were beginning to wonder also whether black people were actually ready for their rightful place in the sun. After all, had they not seen close up too many black people too many times failing to take full advantage of the few opportunities big-city living offered them?

As black social workers began to doubt their own capabilities in transforming rural peasants into fully industrial workers, they also began to have some doubt about the ability of black people to rise.

Charles S. Johnson (1943), the editor of the National Urban League's magazine *Opportunity,* voiced the sentiments of many black social workers when he lamented that even though the big city offered the black migrants far greater educational opportunity than they could ever hope to have in the rural Southern community, many of them still regarded "education beyond the elementary grades as unnecessary and useless" (p. 235). Although they were offered greater employment opportunities, Johnson said, many black people still "accepted their economic dependency on whites 'as normal' and would not develop their own skills and general ability without the white man's insistence" (p. 235). Even when urban life offered them greater room for political expression and black leaders urged them to become civically involved, many black migrants did not see the "race problem" as "an urgent issue" (p. 235). Johnson also maintained that even when black migrants had hundreds of other black migrants as examples of success, they had brought to the big city "an undeveloped appreciation of the professional abilities of their own race" (p. 235), even of members who had dedicated their lives to helping them.

Johnson made sure that *Opportunity* printed stories of black success to inspire the black masses to higher levels of achievement and excellence. In doing so, he was following a pattern set by black newspapers and journals in general of printing story after story about black people who had achieved against the odds. It did not matter how insignificant the achievement might have been in the eyes of the dominant society; black newspapers and journals such as *Opportunity* printed all kinds of stories about black people who had gained territory, regardless of how small, that was once the exclusive domain of white people. Black leaders such as W.E.B. DuBois, Marcus Garvey, and Carter G. Woodson also felt that one of their main tasks was to keep black people from falling victim to alienation and social apathy, from retreating or just simply accepting the status quo. Black social workers felt that with the advantages the big city offered over rural life and the constant inspirational urgings of black leaders, black people, despite setbacks caused by the Great Depression, generally should have pushed harder for material uplift than they did. Black social workers had once thought that black people had the potential to become a strong army of black unionized industrial workers who would turn America upside down; however, as the Great Depression wore on, black social workers were beginning to reexamine and redefine the "Negro problem."

REDEFINITION OF THE PROBLEM

Black social workers during the Great Depression were precisely where many social workers are today in identifying the problem confronting black people. Is it economic? Is it racial? Or does it have to do with something inside the "Negro's psyche?" Their culture? Their southern psychology? After all, hadn't these migrants not brought to the big city a servile personality that was ever dependent on white people? Didn't their isolated rural environment deprive them of the kind of sophistication it took for living in the rough world of the big city? Black social workers knew that the arguments offered by white racists were unacceptable: namely, that black people did not move upwardly, indeed, could not move forward, because of genetic inferiority. They knew that racism was still alive and well because the biggest battle of the civil rights movement at the turn of the 20th century was to convince Congress to adopt an antilynching bill. Furthermore, they knew all along what the Great Depression finally taught white people: There are economic forces beyond a people's control that can leave them destitute, and economic deprivation is not simply a matter of immorality, sin, genetic makeup, skin color, character defects, or the wrath of God. Yet, black social workers felt they could still detect something inside the souls of black people that caused them not to give a full effort to uplifting themselves.

Had black pioneering social workers been so blinded by Progressive-era liberal ideology that they truly believed that black people would rise as fast in the American political and economic arenas as European immigrants? Did they naively believe that black people were just as "meltable" as these groups were in the "great American assimilationist melting pot?" Did they really believe that the white capitalist class who threw crumbs their way would genuinely assist them in uplifting the black masses? It appears that in their sincere desire to help the black migrants find their rightful place in the American sun, pioneering black social workers had grown close to the value system of their wealthy white benefactors and to the virtues they felt had helped immigrants to rise.

Many of these social workers reached the conclusion that what was lacking in the black migrants was good old-fashioned American middle-class values. It appears that a common pattern among black social workers was that finding themselves burnt out and frustrated in trying to change the dominant system, they focused their attention on trying to change the character of the victims of the dominant system, helping them to cope better with their oppression.

Although they continued to attack racism, even National Urban League social workers were beginning to feel it necessary to instruct the black masses in "the most basic level of manners and morals," touching every aspect of "time-honored middle class virtues" (Weiss, 1974, p. 117). National Urban League officials were constantly instructing black migrants to "use the toothbrush, the hairbrush and comb and soap and water freely," "to avoid loud talking, and boisterous laughter on streetcars and in public places," and "to dress neatly and to wear clean clothes, to keep their homes clean, and to be punctual, sober, thrift, and civilized" (Weiss, 1974, pp. 118–120).

Weiss (1974) wrote that "this effort of the middle class to mold the behavior of the migrants in its own image was clearly a one-way process. There was never any hint that the black bourgeoisie had anything to learn from its newly arrived neighbors" (pp. 120–121). With the one-way communication style of social workers, there was little room for them to understand the culture and the psychology of the black migrants. In fact, it would not be until the 1960s that social workers would reach the conclusion that exploring a people's culture is probably a great tool for understanding them. Social workers had grown accustomed to telling black people what they needed and to tailoring their practice toward instilling bourgeois values in black people so that they could become in a sense sociologically white. Because social workers habitually treated black people in a pejorative, paternalistic, condemning manner with little respect for their history, life, and culture, social workers during the 1960s were called all manner of unflattering names, such as "overseers," "colonizers," "dirty workers," and "oppressors," by more militant black people (Burgest, 1973). This name calling suggests how far the black community has strayed from the belief in the transformative power of social work. The shift of black social workers from trying to wrest changes from the society to placing responsibility for change on the black people oppressed by society (currently, this process is called "blaming the victim") shows a significant decline in a belief in the power of social work. What is even more problematic is that the one-way process of bourgeois imposition caused pioneering black social workers to perceive the problem of the migrants through their own middle-class lenses. Acting as if they—the "experts"—knew exactly what was best for black people, early black social workers failed to look at how the black sufferers themselves had defined and solved problems. They failed to explore whether the definitions and solutions of the black migrants were useful to social workers, particularly to determine whether these definitions and solutions could be enhanced and made even more effective as tools of problem solving and change by the use of the highly valued scientific method and by the kind of social activism and social advocacy black social workers waged during the Great Depression. Early black social workers, themselves belonging to the middle class, bought heavily into urban America's philosophy of achievement and acquisition as defined by middle-class material standards. They were beginning to judge the progress of the black migrants by those standards, disregarding even the slightest hint that the black migrants might have had criteria of their own by which they defined success, progress, and worth. The social class differences between black social workers and black clients created a gulf between them that still has not been fully overcome.

As black people approach a new century, they find that they are still far from being fully absorbed into American political and economic society. Their poverty, joblessness, and poor health conditions and housing situations are not much better than those of black people during the Great Depression several decades ago. Social workers and social welfare policymakers are still baffled as to what to do with these people. These social welfare professionals realize that the American government has not committed itself to providing the resources necessary for structural changes and preventive measures, and the failure of the Great Society programs of the 1960s to meet the massive needs of urban poor people created a disillusionment in activist social workers that closely resembled what black pioneer social workers experienced during the Great Depression. Like many of the social workers then, modern social workers began to redefine the problem in terms they felt they could manage. Many retreated from social activist and advocacy roles, left the public sector of social services, and abandoned poor people altogether so that they could concentrate their attention on the neuroses and psychoses of middle-class clients who could pay. Others began to take up notions that it was not so much the social system itself that created the problem confronting black people and other poor American people as it was a so-called culture of poverty, meaning that there was something in the value systems of black people and in their own psyche and behavioral patterns that did not allow them to take full advantage of the opportunities available to them. What this amounted to was a situation similar to that of black social workers in the 1930s; that is, when present-day social workers felt powerless in reforming the social structure itself, they began to seek to impose their own bourgeois outlook on poor people. This bourgeois outlook of social workers allowed politicians to continue to use poor people as scapegoats; to castigate them as immoral and unambitious; and to pursue social control, social containment, and punitive policies toward them without organized protest from social workers. Like the black social workers then, present-day black social workers failed to examine black history and black culture for the ways in which black people themselves defined the problems to see whether the black experience can give social work the boost of humanized, spiritualized, and radicalized energy it needs to restore the faith that black social workers and the black community in general had in the ability of social work to work greater magic and perform greater miracles than even the preacher, the conjurer, and other traditional healers and helpers in the black experience.

REFERENCES

Brown, C. (1956). *Manchild in the promised land.* New York: Dutton.

Burgest, D. R. (1973). Racism in everyday speech and social work jargon. *Social Work, 18,* 20–25.

Dexter, R. C. (1921, June 25). The Negro in social work. *Survey, 46,* 439–440.

Edwards, T. (1936). Attitudes of Negro families on relief. *Opportunity, 10*(7), 213–215.

Frazier, E. F. (1924). Social work in race relations. *Crisis, 27*(6), 252–254.

Frazier, E. F. (1932). *The Negro family in Chicago.* Chicago: University of Chicago Press.

Frazier, E. F. (1939). *The Negro in the United States.* New York: Macmillan.

Hedgeman, A. (1964). *The trumpet sounds.* New York: Holt, Rinehart & Winston.

Henri, F. (1975). *Black migration.* Garden City, NY: Anchor Press/Doubleday.

Johnson, C. S. (1943). *Patterns of Negro segregation.* New York: Harper & Brothers.

Jones, E. K. (1928, November). Social work among Negroes. *Annals of the American Academy of Political and Social Science, 140,* 287–293.

Jones, J. (1985). *Labor of love, labor of sorrow.* New York: Basic Books.

Kurzman, P. A. (1974). *Harry Hopkins and the New Deal.* Fair Lawn, NJ: R. E. Burdick.

Levine, D. (1971). *Jane Addams and the liberal tradition.* Madison: State Historical Society of Wisconsin.

Parris, G., & Brooks, L. (1971). *Blacks in the city: The history of the National Urban League.* Boston: Little, Brown.

Piven, F. F., & Cloward, R. A. (1971). *Regulating the poor.* New York: Vintage Books.

Ross, E. L. (1978). *Black heritage in social welfare: 1860–1930.* Metuchen, NJ: Scarecrow Press.

Solomon, B. B. (1976). *Black empowerment: Social work in oppressed communities.* New York: Columbia University Press.

Stanfield, J. (1985). *Philanthropy and Jim Crow in American social science.* Westport, CT: Greenwood Press.

Thomas, J. O. (1967). *My story in black and white.* New York: Exposition Press.

Washington, B. T. (1967). The virtue of industrial education. In L. H. Fischel, Jr., & B. Quarles (Eds.), *The Negro Americans: A documentary history* (pp. 364–367). Glenview, IL: Scott, Foresman.

Weiss, N. J. (1974). *The National Urban League 1910–1940.* New York: Oxford University Press.

CHAPTER 3

Moanin' and the Identification of the Problem

*P*ioneering black social workers had two basic shortcomings in the identification of problems confronting the black masses: (1) they examined the plight of the black masses through their bourgeois outlook, and (2) they supported "the ideas of their white benefactors concerning racial and economic questions" (Frazier, 1957, p. 86). Black social workers in charge of black charitable institutions knew that they could not define the problem in a way that would offend the wealthy white patrons on whom they depended for their financial lifeblood. Walter J. Stevens (1946), a black social worker at the turn of the 20th century, said he was appalled at how "colored" charitable officials "often acted in undignified ways" (p. 161) to receive paltry donations from white contributors. Recalling one situation, he remembered:

A secretary of a colored social agency told me that he induced wealthy white people to contribute to his work by showing pictures taken of childbirth in the rural South under the most deplorable circumstances. A master showman, he would display these primitive pictures to them and then remark, "Isn't that horrible?" Because it is in the nature of many white people to like to see the horrible conditions under which some of the colored race live, they will generally dig down in their pockets and throw a handful of coins or perhaps a few dollar bills to Negro charitable agencies who are "helping the degraded and heathenish blacks." (p. 161)

As the head of an organized black charity, Stevens often found himself locking horns with the white people who controlled the funds. He had defined the problem of black people in terms of racism, labor exploitation, segregation, and political powerlessness and called for concrete economic, educational, and cultural services. However, he said, "All my employer wanted was to teach undernourished children and hard-working mothers how to turn somersaults on handle bars" and "to sing the spirituals as only colored people are supposed to sing them" (Stevens, 1946, p. 161). Stevens was forced to resign because his analysis of the problem and its solution was radically at odds with that of the white people who funded the project. E. Franklin Frazier (1924) held that some wealthy white philanthropists went so far as to put their cooks, butlers, chauffeurs, and maids in charge of "colored charities" to make sure that only conservative ideas regarding the race problem were entertained and propagated.

BLACK SOCIOLOGY

Social workers' identification of the problem was also shaped by early black sociologists, many of whom attended the University of Chicago. They were brought there to a large extent by the white sociologist, Robert Ezra Park, who created at the University of Chicago what became known as the Chicago School of Race Relations. Many of the most prominent black sociologists in American history—such black sociological giants as Monroe Work, Charles S. Johnson, E. Franklin Frazier, Ira D. A. Reid, and Oliver C. Cox—received degrees in sociology from the University of Chicago. The careers of E. Franklin Frazier and Charles S. Johnson were meticulously guided by Park, and their views on race relations, which were also highly influenced by him, were to have the greatest impact on early black social work thought.

Park's own views on race relations were developed while working as the secretary of Booker T. Washington at Tuskegee Institute. He became a fervent believer in Washington's ideology of racial accommodation and a staunch defender of Washington's ideas on industrial education. So wedded was he to the Tuskegee program of accommodationism that he became the ghostwriter for many of Washington's books, speeches, and articles (Stanfield, 1985). After leaving Tuskegee for the University of Chicago, Park further sharpened his ideas on race relations and continued to advocate the Tuskegee type of nonconfrontational, gradualist program of racial adjustment. By dressing old "Booker T.-ism" in new sociological garments, Park is recognized for his race cycle thesis that proposed that through a natural evolutionary process black American people would gradually move from stages of conflict and accommodation to stages of acceptance and assimilation. Although his views were opposed to the old biological, deterministic views that bluntly and tenaciously held to notions of black genetic inferiority, he advanced a cultural deterministic perspective that also justified the maintenance of a Jim Crow society. In this respect, Stanfield (1985) wrote,

> *Cultural determinism in the justification for Jim Crow took two forms: natural historians [such as Park] optimistically stressed the benefits of allowing race relations problems to be resolved without state intervention. They believed that although racial groups in America had problems to work out due to social and cultural misunderstanding and divergent economic interests, the biracial organization of society was not to be tampered with. . . . Sociocultural evolutionists argued that Jim Crow was an unfortunate evil whites and blacks had to put up with as they learned step by step how to get along.* (p. 9)

Although E. Franklin Frazier's association with Robert Ezra Park and other white faculty at the University of Chicago helped to gain him prominence as a black sociologist, it was Charles S. Johnson's ideas, not Frazier's, that had the deepest influence on the thoughts of early black social workers. Frazier's thoughts tended to be too critical for white patrons of black social work to push. Johnson, however, would make Park's ideas of racial relations the dominant perspective guiding black social work thinking and practice.

Park had started to have an impact on black social work thought even before he had made Johnson his favorite student. Park's reputation as "the father of modern research on the Negro problem in sociology" earned him the presidency of the Chicago Urban League, one of the largest of the league's local branches (Stanfield, 1985). It was as president that Park brought Johnson on board as the first research director of the Chicago Urban League. Park also brought Johnson along with him as a researcher for the Chicago Race Relations Commission. Fortunately for Johnson, the commission was highly financed by the Julius Rosenwald Foundation, which recognized Johnson's skills in collecting and presenting empirical data on the "Negro problem." Other major funding services such as the Laura Spelman Rockefeller Memorial, the American Missionary Association, and the Julius Rosenwald Fund also supported Johnson's work. Stanfield (1985) stated that "Johnson's attractiveness to philanthropists and foundations can be attributed to the Parkian ideas he espoused" (p. 55). Park also saw to it that Johnson's work was published by the prestigious University of Chicago Press and the American Journal of Sociology.

White foundations, philanthropists, and publishers made Johnson the most prominent and influential black sociologist in the country during the 1920s, 1930s, and 1940s. They did so not only because Johnson was considered to be a "safe" black person advocating a "safe" position on race relations but also because of Johnson's dedication to collecting empirical data on the "Negro problem." Johnson's rich collection of facts blended perfectly with the racial ideology of these funding sources. The factual descriptions of myriad pathologies in black family and community life implied the need for black "adjustment" to the status quo. Johnson's race relations facts were, in essence, ahistorical, atheoretical, apolitical, and nonideological and therefore nonthreatening. Black sociologists such as Johnson understood perfectly well that powerful white philanthropists were not going to fund black scholarship that challenged the power of the white ruling elite. Johnson learned this lesson firsthand when he tried early in his career to get a few of his more-critical and power-oriented works funded only to find that his white patrons assigned these works to sociological oblivion. He could also see that black scholars who documented oppression to advance a politically assertive program of social change were shunned by white foundations and viewed as intellectual deviants, mavericks, and misfits. For example, when the black sociologist Oliver C. Cox (1948) had the gall to use his own money and effort to present a study on race relations that was critical, radical, historical, and political—in which Cox even had the audacity to present a powerful, incisive critique of the sociology of Park and other sacred icons of sociology—foundations, mainstream publishers, social sciences circles, and sociologists around the country tried to relegate him to a sociological dung heap.

By the time Johnson moved from his job as research director of the Chicago Urban League to his position as editor of *Opportunity* at the National Urban League headquarters in New York City, he had already done significant work in making the Parkian idea of race relations the dominant approach of Urban League black social workers. With this approach the National Urban League became recognized for viewing the black migrant through the eyes of the league's white patrons and for constructing social welfare programs in ways that would not rock the boat.

BLACK FOLK CULTURE

E. Franklin Frazier (1924) was the first prominent black pioneer social worker to hold that social work would "not perform any miracles" and that industrial inclusion did not provide "the solution to the so-called Negro problem" or the "panacea for racial conflict" (p. 252). Frazier was also the first among the early black professional social workers to believe that social workers would never fully grasp the situation of the black migrants until these social workers had some basic understanding of black culture. He wrote that after reviewing social work case records during the 1930s, he was not "able to get from these records data which threw light on the cultural situation" (Frazier, 1932, p. 165). Although these records gave meticulous descriptions of desertion, illegitimacy, nonsupport, crime, delinquency, and family disorganization, Frazier stated that they made only "sporadic inference" concerning the migrants' "inner lives, their attitudes, and conception of life" (p. 188). Frazier felt that the key to understanding the black migrants was an understanding of "folk culture" as expressed by folk music (the spirituals and the blues) and as structured in institutions such as the rural black church. He believed that as tools to explain the situation of black people, the philosophy implicit in black folklore was infinitely superior to "the opportunistic philosophy of Negro intellectuals who want to save their jobs and enjoy material comforts" (Frazier,

1973, p. 56) and "infinitely superior in wisdom and intellectual candor to the empty repetition of platitudes concerning brotherly love and human dignity" (p. 60) of black social workers.

Frazier implied that the conditions that made black migrants "sing the blues" and moan spirituals such as "Sometimes I Feel Like a Moaning Dove" and "Nobody Knows the Trouble I Sees" were at the core of the problems that the black masses felt were facing them. Frazier was one of the first black social workers to suggest that instead of black social workers relying so heavily on the "facts," they might also theoretically examine black culture for what the black masses themselves might teach them concerning their own perception of the problem. Frazier, then, can be viewed in a sense as having laid the first major premise of black experience–based social work, that is, the need to study the culture of the people to gain their own identification of the problems concerning them.

What could Frazier possibly have seen in black folk culture that would assist scientific-minded social workers in the identification of the problem? An examination of Frazier's work indicates that he knew clearly that when one undertakes to study such crucial elements of black culture as the spirituals and the blues, he or she will find that these songs are more than just musical expressions; they are definitions of the problem confronting black people during their most difficult hour. As L. Jones (1963) stated, "The most expressive music of any given period will be an exact reflection on what the Negro himself is" (p. 137) and the kind of problems he suffers at that particular time. As one author pointed out, "The spirituals are the spontaneous expressions of the soul in search of comfort and escape from physical and mental turmoil. The Negro poured his sorrow and frustrations into song and uttered his turbulence with an all-consuming feeling. . . . The theme of spirituals is troubles, trials, and tribulations" (Johnston, 1954, p. 41). Ellison (1964) gave a similar perspective in his eloquent, classic definition of the blues. He wrote, "The blues is an impulse to keep the painful details and episodes of a brutal experience alive in one's aching consciousness, to finger its jagged grain, and to transcend it, not by the consolation of philosophy but by squeezing from it a near-tragic, near-comic lyricism. As form, the blues is an autobiographical chronicle of personal catastrophe expressed lyrically" (pp. 78–79).

MOANING

It is significant to note that black people did not just sing the spirituals or the blues; they "moaned" them. This moaning indicated that they were expressing deep, painful emotions, that they were crying out the accumulated hurt in their lives. Moyd (1979) defined moaning or crying in the spirituals as meaning "those verbal and nonverbal expressions which include weeping, groaning, moaning, humming, chanting, singing and praying individually or in a communal setting, both ceremonial and nonceremonial" (p. 107). He said that the concepts of crying, groaning, and moaning, concepts used interchangeably, were such a basic part of black spiritual life that the black church became the chief institution where black people could cry or moan collectively. Preachers then not only preached, they moaned; the choir not only sang, they moaned; the congregation not only prayed, they moaned.

> *I love the Lord*
> *who heard my cry and*
> *pitied every groan.*

Rural black people preferred the "moaning" preachers over the more sophisticated, rational, and intellectual ones because the moaning preachers helped them to define, articulate, and affirm their suffering. In the spirituals, when black people cried "I'm rollin through an unfriendly world" or "I'm a-trouble in the mind," or "Sometimes I feel like a motherless child," they were articulating feelings and giving definitions to emotions that they all understood, given their common oppression. In the blues, when black people moaned phrases such as the following, they were not just expressing sadness but bringing to surface and redefining a complexity of emotions, including joy, emotional ambivalence, and protest.

> *Mm hear my weep and moan*
> *Mm mm hear my weep and moan*

Won't you hear me pleading, hear me grieve and groan

Mm mm mm mm mm mm
Mm mm mm mm mm mm mm
Mm mm mm mm mm mm mm mm mm
Mm mm mm mm mm mm mm mm mm

The "moaning" theme of the spirituals and the blues indicated that the worst thing that black people could do was to keep inside even the deep pain that they wanted to hold to themselves. Thus, when black people sang "I got the blues, but I'm too damn mean to cry" or "Got the blues so bad, it hurt my feet to walk; Got the blues so bad, it hurt my feet to walk; It wouldn't hurt so bad, but it hurts my tongue to talk," they were expressing the need to bring these feelings before an audience so they could be fully absorbed, reexamined, redefined, rethought out, and reassessed. This was black folk culture's type of social work and its way of identifying the problem.

THE PROBLEM OF SEPARATION AND LOSS

Both the spirituals and the blues cover a wide range of problems, but a central, recurring, dominant, and pervasive theme of both is the problem of loss and separation. In the spirituals, this problem is highlighted by the emphasis slaves placed on "reunion" with loved ones in heaven. Raboteau (1978) said that the repeated references of the spirituals to "reunion" with loved ones in heaven was "a devout hope for slaves who had seen parents, sisters, brothers and children sold away with no chance of reunion in this world" (p. 262). Thurman (1975) wrote that "we are not surprised to find in the spirituals a great emphasis on reunion. There was nothing more heartrending in that far-off time of madness than the separation of families at the auction block. . . . The issue of reuniting with loved ones turned finally on the hope of immortality" (p. 133). Slaves themselves understood how deeply the spirituals expressed their moaning over separation and loss. For example, describing a parting scene in which he himself was a participant, Jacob Stroyer wrote,

> *Those who were going did not expect to see their friends again.*
> *While passing along many of the Negroes left their master's field and*
> *joined us . . . some were yelling and wringing their hands, while*
> *others were singing little hymns that they had been accustomed to for*
> *the consolation of these that were going away such as*
>> *When we all meet in heaven,*
>> *There is no parting there;*
>> *When we meet in heaven,*
>> *There is no parting there.* (quoted in Raboteau, 1978, p. 262)

The black educator Charlotte Forten Grimké who worked with the newly emancipated black people on the Sea Islands of Georgia and South Carolina, said that nowhere was the suffering of black people more mournfully articulated than when they sang spirituals about separation and loss. She wrote that when they sang,

> *"I wonder where my mudder gone, sing, O graveyard! Graveyard*
> *ought to know me, Ring, Jerusalem! . . .," they improvise many more*
> *words as they sing. It is one of the strangest, most mournful things I*
> *ever heard. It is impossible to give any idea on the deep pains of the*
> *refrain, "Sing, O graveyard!" In this, and many other hymns, the*
> *words seem to have but little meaning; but the tones—a whole*
> *lifetime of despairing sadness is concentrated in them.* (quoted in
> Forten, 1969, pp. 76–77)

Grimké said that the singing of spirituals brought out her own feelings of grief in respect to the death of her mother, feelings she had never expressed or knew existed.

Although the expression of pain was on a more personal, secular, visceral, and sensual level, the blues also expressed moaning over loss and separation. Blues songs are replete with themes of being betrayed by "a cheating-hearted woman" or a "no-good man," being on the chain gang, missing the loving arms of a husband who had been lynched, and other secular, worldly themes of loss and separation.

Black people sang such lyrics as

Yeah, I hear my hamstring a-poppin, my collar cryin'
Lord, I hear my hamstring a-poppin, baby, and I hear
my collar cryin'.
Now how can I stay happy, Lord, when my baby's down the line.

or

Sometimes I wonder why don't you write to me
Sometimes I wonder why you don't write to me
If I been a bad fellow Lord knows, I did not intend to be.

or

How long baby how long
Has that evenin' train been gone
How long how long baby how long
Here I stood at the station watched my baby leavin' town
Blue and disgusted nowhere could peace be found
For how long how how long baby how long.

These and thousands more were moaning songs of loss, separation, and the need to be reunited.

Certainly, the problem of separation and loss was not the only pressing problem confronting black people. Black people at the turn of the 20th century lived constantly in a state of crisis from an accumulated abundance of problems. However, this problem of separation and loss was a core one. Thus, we will follow this problem throughout this book because it remains a central problem among black people in contemporary society.

Unfortunately, this problem was not explored by other pioneer black social workers. Moreover, few of them were inclined to believe that there were ways of problem identification other than by the collection of bare facts. The collection of empirical data could shed light on how many black "illegitimate babies" the black migrants brought to a given city, how many black men were in jail and how many black women were on welfare, and even, if the collector of the facts dared risk disturbing the funding source, tell how many black people were lynched. However, dry statistics on slices of black life could never give full insight into the deep emotional and psychological hurt and spiritual anguish of black people, and without such insight, social workers were not likely to ever gain a full identification of the problem.

BLACK NARRATIVES AND THE PROBLEM

Even if pioneering social workers were skeptical in terms of the reliability of black music in portraying accurately the feelings and experiences of the black masses, they still could have looked to folk narratives and, thus, gained a firsthand account from the people themselves. They would have been astonished to find that the spirituals and the blues were keenly accurate in reflecting the same insights provided in folk narratives. For example, no theme is more recurrent in the folk narratives than the theme of separation and loss. The ex-slave Tom Jones (1854) captured the feeling of many slave men and women when he wrote,

> *My dear wife and my precious children were seventy-four miles distant from me, carried away from me in bitter scorn of my beseeching words. I was tempted to put an end to my wreched life. . . . A deep despair was in my heart, such as no one is called to bear in such cruel, crushing power as the poor slave, severed forever from the object of his love.* (p. 32)

Slave narratives reveal that black people separated from loved ones never quite overcame the pain of the experience. For example, George White (1810) recorded in his narrative that after learning that his mother was still alive, his yearning to see her became an obsession. He bothered his master so much about seeing her and became so obstinate that his master finally relented:

> *As my mother knew not what had become of me, the reader will easily imagine the affection, nature and circumstances of the scene of the first meeting, of a parent lost, and a child unknown; and both in a state of the most cruel bondage, without the means or even hope of relief. But our joyful interview of mingling anguish, was of but short duration; for my condition, as a slave, would not permit of my*

prolonging the visit beyond the day appointed for my return; there we were obliged to undergo the painful sensations, occasioned by a second parting; and I, to return to my former servitude. (pp. 5–6)

For many former slaves, even after being 70 years or more removed from slavery, their most vivid memory was their moaning over loved ones from whom they had been separated. For example, when officials of the Federal Writers Project under the New Deal administration recorded the narratives of former slaves 70 years after the ending of slavery, they found many testimonies such as the following:

I seen children sold off and the mammy not sold, and sometimes the mammy sold and a little baby kept on the place and give to another woman to raise. Them white folks didn't care nothing 'bout how the slaves grieved when they tore up a family. (quoted in Botkin, 1945, p. 106)

The narratives of the Federal Writers Project revealed that slaves lived on the edge of panic in regard to their dread of loss. One ex-slave recalled

I remember well the grief this [separation from loved ones] caused us to feel, and how the women and the men used to whisper to one another when they thought nobody was near by, and meet at night, or get together in the field when they had an opportunity, to talk about what was coming. They would speculate, too, on the prospects they had of being separated; to whose lot they and their children were likely to fall, and whether the husbands would go with the wives. The women who had young children cried very much. My mother did, and took to kissing us a great deal oftener. This uneasiness increased as the time went on, for though we did not know when the great trouble would fall upon us, we all knew it would come, and were looking forward to it with very sorrowful hearts. (Brown, 1855, pp. 5–6)

BLACK HISTORY

It is true that oral information can be distorted because it relies on the reconstruction of memory. Also, people can romanticize their lives and leave out significant episodes of their experiences. Nevertheless, even if pioneering black social workers could not have questioned the reliability of the spirituals and the blues or the authenticity of folk narratives, they still could have turned to black history for information and insight on black people, instead of taking an ahistorical approach. If they had taken this route they would have found that black history confirms the findings in the spirituals and the blues and the folk narratives in recognizing separation and loss as a primary problem confronting black people.

The black historian and Africanist scholar Chancellor Williams (1987) pointed out that even before the Atlantic slave trade that was a monument to black loss, the continuous invasions by relentless Arab invaders before the coming of the European invaders inflicted loss and separation on black people unceasingly for more than 5,000 years as they sought control over Africa's greatest civilization—Egypt (known to the black people who ruled it as Kemet). The 400-year slave trade compounded the problem, instilling in black people a fear of loss and separation that generations of them would never forget. Conservative estimates hold that more than 15 million black people died (whereas more-liberal estimates have the count as high as 100 million) during the infamous "middle passage" with its horrors of stench, heat, sickness, forced feedings, suicides, beatings, rapes, torture, and lack of food, water, and fresh air. Before black people were forced to board these death ships, thousands were killed in the raids on African villages, raids that made hundreds of African ethnic groups extinct. Thousands died during marches from the interior of Africa to the slave pens on the African coast in what were called "slave coffles." Williams (1987) said that the slave coffles were often slowed down by "the trampling and stumbling over the skeletons and rotting bodies of Africans who had died before them on the trails" (p. 256). Thousands died in the slave pens and forts while awaiting the arrival of the slave ships.

When black people arrived in the New World, the separations and losses continued from the auction block to the slave plantation. Blassingame (1979) wrote that there was no question that in the minds of the slaves, separation and loss were still the problem they dreaded most:

> *To be sold away from his relatives or stand by and see a mother, a sister, a brother, a wife, or a child torn away from him was easily the most traumatic event of his life. Strong men pleaded, with tears in their eyes, for their master to spare their loved ones. Mothers screamed and clung grimly to their children only to be kicked away by the slave trader. Others lost their heads and ran off with their children or vainly tried to fight off overseer, master, and slave trader. Angry, despondent, and overcome by grief, the slaves frequently never recovered from the shock of separation. Many became morose and indifferent to their work. Others went insane, talked to themselves, and had hallucinations about their loved ones. A few developed suicidal tendencies. (p. 297)*

To avoid the pain of loss and separation, African people—even before African American black people turned cityward centuries later—often were forced to take flight in search of an environment that promised them greater security. Williams (1987) said that before the slave trade, the Arab and European invaders kept African people constantly on the run, making them become splintered-off refugee groups caught up in a permanent crisis situation. Driven from the great African kingdoms, these African people sought survival on the cliffs of mountains, in the swamps, the forest, the desert, and in caves, anywhere they could find a haven that allowed them to recuperate and regroup. Slave hunters coming along years later could determine the various routes of flight by "the bones of . . . thousands who . . . die in flight . . . [now] buried forever under the tons of sand and rocks" (Williams, 1987, p. 191). Williams wrote that the slave trade made black people a "people forever migrating, forever on the move, forever in flight from threats to survival; a new location found, sighs of relief and thanksgiving for a new breathing spell, and new efforts at reunification and state-building all over again" (p. 220).

VERSATILITY AND THE PROBLEM OF LOSS AND SEPARATION

History shows that when black people were not taking flight to avoid loss and separation, they were mastering other techniques to deal with this core problem. Even slaves, with their circumscribed environment and their limited room to maneuver, wanted to be versatile enough to minimize the threat and reality of loss and separation. Being versatile often meant accommodation or learning the art of being patient and steadfast and, most importantly, of behaving themselves in a manner suitable to the white master. If they behaved themselves, then perhaps the master would spare them the awful separation from their loved ones. Although this survival technique was necessary, it was generally doomed to failure because it depended on the capricious whim and goodwill of the slave master. Frederick Douglass (1883) wrote that in the case of his grandmother, "she had served my old master faithfully from youth to old age"; nevertheless, "she saw her children, her grandchildren, and her great grandchildren divided like so many sheep, and this without being gratified with the small privilege of a single word as to their . . . destiny" (p. 92).

When accommodation seemed to fail to achieve the desired results of softening the heart of the slave master, slaves often resorted to role playing, that is, pretending to be docile and obedient while never revealing to their oppressors their inner self-aspirations. An old slave folk saying goes, "got one mind for white folks to see, another for what I know is me." The black bard Paul Laurence Dunbar captured the essence of role playing when he wrote, "We wear the mask that grins and lies. It hides our cheeks and shades our eyes" (Martin & Hudson, 1975, p. 306). Slaves felt that their survival depended on how well they engaged in a ceremony of servile bows and counterfeit smiles—how well they wore the mask. One ex-slave, Lunsford Lane (1842), wrote that "even after I entertained the first idea of being free, I endeavored so to conduct myself as not to become obnoxious to the white inhabitants, knowing as I did their power, and their hostility to the colored people" (p. 31). Another former slave, Josiah Henson (1849) wrote, "The objects I pursued . . . were to be the first in the field, whether we were hoeing, mowing or reaping, to surpass those of my own age, or indeed any age . . . to obtain the favorable regard of the petty despot who ruled over us" (pp. 7–8). Still another ex-slave, Henry Bibb, held that "the only weapon of self defense I felt comfortable in relying upon was that of deception" (quoted in Osofsy, 1969, p. 95). It was through their music, their folktales, their humor, and their religion that black people could reveal their true inner self to one another and often in disguised form to the white oppressor. It was in their music and other areas of their cultural life too that they could affirm their own worth as human beings.

If they were versatile enough to accommodate when necessary and role play when necessary, then perhaps the opportunity might come for freedom. Thus, the truly versatile slaves were in constant preparation, preparing mentally and emotionally to muster up the courage to take the risk of taking flight. Frederick Douglass (1883), for example, said that he had grown tired of "putting one over on old massa" and had a deep desire "to act as well as to think and speak" (p. 153) his true inner feelings. He wrote, "I became not only ashamed to be content in slavery but ashamed to seem to be content. . . . [Therefore,] I drove from me all thoughts of making the best of my lot and welcomed only such thoughts as led me away from the house of bondage" (pp. 153–154). Douglass held that although to other slaves the spirituals may have been a balm to calm their fears and frustrations in slavery, to him they "were tones, loud, long and deep, breathing the prayer and complaint of souls boiling over with the bitterest anguish" (p. 194). He wrote that to him "every tone was a testimony against slavery, and a prayer to God for deliverance from bondage" (p. 195). The truly versatile slaves sought to become as literate and master as many work skills as they could so they could remain versatile once they were free.

Fleeing slavery necessarily involved the blues because just as staying ultimately meant facing the loss of loved ones, leaving also meant being separated from loved ones. Douglass (1883) wrote that "thousands more would have escaped slavery but for the strong affection which bound them to their families, relatives, and friends" (p. 195). The dread of leaving his friends behind was Douglass's own "strongest obstacle to running away" (p. 195) and it was not without much agonizing that he finally did. William

Still, an underground railroad conductor, said that even when black slaves successfully escaped bondage, the uppermost thing on their minds was the loved ones many had had to leave behind. Still (1871/1970) wrote that sometimes those who aided in the escape of slaves advised fugitives to "never think of writing back," to forget their kin, to not "fret about . . . [their] wife and children" (p. 189), and to concentrate on taking care of themselves. However, Still conceded that despite such advice, "one of the most gratifying facts connected with the fugitives, was the strong love and attachment that they constantly expressed for their relatives left in the South . . . forty, fifty, or sixty years in some instance elapsed, but this ardent sympathy and love continued warm and unwavering as ever" (pp. 189–190). The spirituals and the blues helped black people develop spiritual toughness in the face of loss and separation, maintain psychic balance and emotional stability, explore to the fullest the limited options open to them, and stir up and direct their energies toward the hard task of survival.

CONTEMPORARY ORAL HISTORIES

Even if early social workers did not examine the black history of the past for insights, they should at least have taken an in-depth look into the migrants' current experiences to find out from the migrants themselves why they had left the South and what they perceived as their most pressing needs. We suspect that had the black social workers conducted current oral histories on the migrants they would have found that the thousands of black people who migrated from the rural South during the first four decades of the 20th century did so for the same reasons that fleeing African people and slaves did: to find refuge, to seek greater control over their lives, and to afford greater protection to their loved ones. Recognizing this ancestral connectedness, the prominent black psychiatrists Grier and Cobbs (1968) asserted that the challenge of the black newcomers was not so much their poverty or their urbanization, it was "a latter day version of the problem faced by the slave family. How does one build a family, make it strong, and breed from it strong men and women when the institutional structures of the nation make it impossible for the family to serve its primary purpose—the protection of its members?" (p. 84). Rural black people could clearly see that even though they were said to be "emancipated," the mob, night riders, gangs, terrorist organizations such as the Ku Klux Klan, and activities such as muggings, kidnappings, incendiarism, whippings, bombings, lynchings, and blackmailing still ruled the day.

Lynching

Lynching was the chief reminder to black migrants that any white man, let alone a white mob, could destroy their property and take their lives without any fear of legal reprisal. Any black man, woman, or child could be lynched for such apparent trivialities as "acting uppity," talking back, questioning one's pay, forgetting to address a white person as "mister" or "ma'am" or for using a toilet or water fountain marked "for whites only." Between 1882 and 1901 an average of 150 lynchings a year took place as the South became a gruesome theater of lawless violence against black people. Lynching was a vicious, murderous, cowardly, extralegal mob activity that entailed the grisly practice of roasting black people alive, riddling their bodies with bullets, snapping their necks with a rope, and dismembering body parts in a frenzied rush for souvenirs and trophies.

The Chain Gang

The convict lease system, known to black people as "the chain gang," was also a stark reminder to black people of their inability to protect their loved ones. Because the convict lease system was a profitable venture to politicians and prison officials who leased so-called convicts out to private mining and railroad companies and to farms and industrial operations, all black people, even women and children, were in danger of being brought up on trumped-up charges and placed on the chain gang. As Marable (1983) wrote, "Black women who were chained together in straw bunks at night were often raped by white guards. Their children were also confined to the penitentiary with them" (p. 112). Black people knew that once their loved ones were placed on the chain gang, they were in grave danger of never being seen again. Marable wrote,

The annual death rate for Black convicts ranged from 11 percent in Mississippi to 25 percent in Arkansas in the 1880's. One 1887 grand jury study of a Mississippi prison hospital declared that all convicts bore marks of the most inhuman and brutal treatments. Most of them have their backs cut in great wales, scars and blisters, some with the skin peeling off in pieces as the result of severe beatings. They were lying there dying, some of them on bare boards, so poor and emaciated that their bones almost came through their skin, many complaining for want of food. We actually saw live vermin crawling over their faces, and the little bedding and clothing they have is in tatters and stiff with filth. (p. 112)

Rape

Although black men were generally lynched on the pretext that they had raped a white woman, the raping of black women became a daily way of life for southern white men. Although black people were reluctant to talk about rape, it became a primary factor in the migration of black people from the South. L. Jones (1963) stated, "Significantly, black men mentioned the degraded status of their womenfolk as one of the prime incentives to migrate" (p. 157). Faced with lynchings, chain gangs, and the constant sexual brutalization of black women, not to mention the day-to-day insults, kicks, cuffs, slaps, and threats, it was crystal clear to migrants why they were in search of a place they could really call home. Some migrants were so eager to leave the South that they left with hardly more than the clothes on their backs. Raper and Reid (1941) recorded,

One black family left on bus tickets from the sale of their few bushels of sweet potatoes, a peck of peas, fourteen cans of fruit, a shotgun, a cook stove, and two bedspreads. By some strange alchemy the two mattresses had been transformed into a half dozen bundles, which various members of the family lugged on the bus. The only other packages they had were a bulging cardboard suitcase and a securely tied shoebox which contained cherished remedies for their ailments. (p. 71)

Even when the economic status of black people remained wretched, few wanted to return to the rural South and put their lives solely back in the hands of vicious white people. For example, when one migrant who had not fared well economically in the big city was asked why he had not returned to his rural home, he replied,

After twenty years of seeing my people lynched for any offense from spitting on a sidewalk to stealing a mule, I made up my mind that I would turn the prow of my ship toward the part of the country where the people at least made a pretense at being civilized. . . . When a man's home is sacred; when he can protect the virtue of his wife and daughter against the brutal lust of his alleged superiors; when he can sleep at night without the fear of being visited by the Ku-Klux because of refusal to take off his hat while passing an overseer—then I will be willing to return to Mississippi. (quoted in Henri, 1976, p. 129)

THE INTELLECTUAL DEBATE

Although black migrants were clear why they had fled the night-marish psychological and physical traumas of living constantly under a system of intimidation and terrorism, black intellectuals were locking horns debating the cause of black migration. Summarizing the two sides of the debate, the black historian Carter G. Woodson wrote,

Some say that they left the South on account of injustice in the courts, unrest, lack of privileges, denial of the right to vote, bad treatment, oppression, segregation, or lynching. Others say that they left to find employment, to secure better wages, better school facilities, and better opportunities to toil upward. (quoted in Adero, 1993, pp. 1–2)

Taking sides in this debate himself, Woodson said that scholars were "wrong in thinking that the persecution of the blacks has little to do with the migration" (Adero, 1993, p. 2). He held that "it is highly probably that the Negroes would not be leaving the South today, if they were treated as men although there might be numerous opportunities for economic improvement in the North" (p. 2). In any case, Woodson concluded that the answer to the cause of migration lay in "what the migrants themselves think about it" (p. 1).

Although Woodson stressed the negative factors causing migration, early black social workers, ever conscious of how their remarks might be perceived by their white patrons, generally stressed the positive factors. For example, Charles S. Johnson held that even though persecution played a part, "the Negroes who left the South were motivated more by the desire to improve their economic status than by fear of being manhandled by unfriendly whites. The one is a symptom of wholesome and substantial life purpose; the other, the symptom of a fugitive incourageous opportunism" (quoted in Adero, 1993, p. 44). Johnson said that these black people, "like all others with a spark of ambition and self-interest" (p. 44), took flight in search of a better life.

Johnson was expressing the sentiments of many social workers of the day. Those sentiments fit well with the emphasis social workers placed on economic development and were strategically more suited to attracting the aid of white philanthropists and northern industrialists. As Johnson stated, "The thought of flight from persecution excites little sympathy either from the practical employer or the northern white population among whom these Negroes will hereafter live. Every man who runs, is not a good worker" (Adero, 1993, p. 47).

Other powerful black social reform-minded leaders took a similar stance. For example, Mary McLeod Bethune acknowledged that, although "the desire for protection impelled many a rural dweller to move into or nearer the city" (quoted in Adero, 1993, p. 111), the main reason they came was to improve their economic status, to enjoy greater educational opportunities, to have decent housing, to improve their health, and to have a more wholesome recreational life. She said it was "the mission" of social workers and organizations like the National Urban League to make "militant efforts in these directions" and to make these problems of economics, education, housing, health, and recreation "national in scope and purpose" (quoted in Adero, p. 112). Because Bethune was an adviser to President Franklin Roosevelt and the director of the Negro youth division of Roosevelt's labor department, she could not emphasize such negative factors as lynching as a chief cause of black migration, particularly when the National Association for the Advancement of Colored People was urging Roosevelt to pass an antilynching law. He never did for fear of losing the southern vote.

BLACK EXPERIENCE–BASED SOCIAL WORK

Black experience–based social work holds that political expediency, class outlook, and monetary concerns should not figure in the equation of the identification of the problem. It argues that gathering empirical data should not be the only method used for assessing the situation of black people. It holds that there are other methods of gaining insights into black life as well, insights that are drawn directly from black music, black folktales, folk narratives, black history, contemporary oral histories, and even fictitious works such as black poetry, short stories, and novels. Black experience–based social work is not antithetical to gathering raw, empirical, so-called hard data. It simply rests on the notion that the aim is also to capture the mood, the feelings, and the soul of black people, something that cannot be done by providing mere statistical descriptions of the "facts."

In capturing the mood, feelings, and spirit of people, black experience–based social work seeks to produce the "massive concentration of black experiential energy" (Henderson, 1973, p. 44) that powerfully affects the meaning of black life as expressed in black song, black speech, black dance, black thoughts, and black spiritual and social striving. Early black social workers did not seek a synthesis of empirical data collected through the scientific method and black folk culture's use of subjective emotions, art, and even spiritual revelation to identify the problem. If they had done so, they would have realized that there is no great differentiation between the secular and the sacred in the black experience. As the black historian Lerone Bennett (1964) wrote of the spirituals and blues tradition,

The Negro tradition, read right, recognizes no such dichotomy. The blues are the spirituals, good is bad, God is the devil and every day is Saturday. The essence of the tradition is the extraordinary tension between the poles of pain and joy, agony and ecstasy, good and bad, Sunday and Saturday. One can, for convenience, separate the tradition into Saturdays (blues) and Sundays (spirituals). But it is necessary to remember that the blues and the spirituals are not two different things. They are two sides of the same coin, two banks, as it were, defining the same stream. (pp. 50–51)

Most significantly, black experience–based social work, taking a cue from the ancestors, recognizes loss and separation as a core problem of black life, not only in the past but also in contemporary society. The ancestors recognized that to be black in America is to be grossly, continuously, and disproportionately exposed to traumatization on many different levels. For example, we were surprised to learn that the traumatic effect of loss and separation was just as widespread and intense in the lives of our on-campus black college students as it was among our prison inmate black students. The major difference was that the on-campus college students had explored more options and fewer self-defeating and destructive paths; in other words, they were more versatile in handling traumatization.

Black experience–based social work holds that no social work practice method, therapy, or problem-solving instrument is likely to be successful in working with black people unless it is highly sensitive to the traumatization effects of loss and separation in the contemporary black experience and unless it explores ways of helping black people develop the cultural versatility necessary to minimize the danger and maximize control over their own lives.

REFERENCES

Adero, M. (Ed.). (1993). *Up south.* New York: New Press.

Bennett, L., Jr. (1964). *The Negro mood.* Chicago: Johnson.

Blassingame, J. W. (1979). *The slave community.* New York: Oxford University Press.

Botkin, B. A. (1945). *Lay my burden down.* Chicago: University of Chicago Press.

Brown, T. (1855). *Slave life in Georgia.* London: M. W. Watts.

Cox, O. C. (1948). *Caste, class and race.* New York: Monthly Review Press.

Douglass, F. (1883). *Life and times of Frederick Douglass.* Secaucus, NJ: Citadel Press.

Ellison, R. (1964). *Shadow and act.* New York: Random House.

Forten, C. (1969). Life on the Sea Islands. In L. C. Lockwood (Ed.), *Two black teachers in the Civil War* (pp. 67–86). New York: Arno Press and New York Times.

Frazier, E. F. (1924). *Social work in race relations.* Crisis, 27(6), 252–254.

Frazier, E. F. (1932). *The Negro family in Chicago.* Chicago: University of Chicago Press.

Frazier, E. F. (1957). *Black bourgeoisie.* New York: Collier Books.

Frazier, E. F. (1973). The failure of the Negro intellectual. In J. A. Ladner (Ed.), *The death of white sociology* (pp. 52–67). New York: Vintage Books.

Grier, W. H., & Cobbs, P. M. (1968). *Black rage.* New York: Basic Books.

Henderson, S. (1973). *Understanding the new black poetry.* New York: William Morrow.

Henri, F. (1976). *Black migration.* New York: Anchor Books.

Henson, J. (1849). *Life of Josiah Henson, formerly a slave, now an inhabitant of Canada, as related by himself.* Boston: Arthur D. Phelps.

Johnston, R. F. (1954). *The development of Negro religion.* New York: Philosophical Library.

Jones, L. (1963). *Blues people.* New York: William Morrow.

Jones, T. H. (1854). *The experience and personal narrative of Uncle Tom Jones.* New York: G. C. Holbrook.

Lane, L. (1842). *Narrative of Lunsford Lane published by himself.* Boston: Hewes and Watson.

Marable, M. (1983). *How capitalism underdeveloped black America.* Boston: South End Press.

Martin, J., & Hudson, G. H. (Eds.). (1975). *The Paul Laurence Dunbar reader.* New York: Dodd, Mead.

Moyd, O. P. (1979). *Redemption in black theology.* Valley Forge, PA: Judson Press.

Osofsky, G. (Ed.). (1969). *Puttin' on ole massa: The slave narratives of Henry Bibb, William Wells Brown, and Solomon Northup.* New York: Harper & Row.

Raboteau, A. J. (1978). *Slave religion.* New York: Oxford University Press.

Raper, A. F., & Reid, I.D.A. (1941). *Sharecroppers all.* Chapel Hill: University of North Carolina Press.

Stanfield, J. N. (1985). *Philanthropy and Jim Crow in American social science.* Westport, CT: Greenwood Press.

Stevens, W. J. (1946). *Chip on my shoulder.* Boston: Meador.

Still, W. (1970). *The underground railroad.* Chicago: Johnson. (Original work published 1871)

Thurman, H. (1975). *Deep river and the Negro spiritual speaks of life and death.* Richmond, IN: Friends United Press.

White, G. (1810). *Account of life, experience, travels and gospel labours of an African.* New York: J. C. Tuttle.

Williams, C. (1987). *The destruction of African civilization.* Chicago: Third World Press.

CHAPTER 4

Social Work and Moanin'

*B*ecause early black social workers had no method of probing the inner lives of black migrants, they tended to define the problem almost exclusively in economic terms. Given the widespread abject poverty that was so characteristic of rural black life, this definition was not inappropriate except that the heavy concentration on broad-scale economic characteristics was often to the neglect of emotional, psychological, and cultural factors that were also crucial to understanding the migrants' situation. Even on the casework level, social workers at the turn of the 20th century tended to focus on economic issues. For example, Mowrer (1927) held that the casework records pertaining to the problem of desertion usually ignored all factors "other than economic factors" (p. 187). He wrote that the social worker handling this problem usually spent most of the time trying to get the man to assume economic support of his family and that so much attention was given to "elaborating the description of the financial situation from every angle possible," that the social worker paid little or no attention "to the genesis of the attitudes which receive superficial expression in the external behavior of the individual" (p. 187).

We have already spoken of the tendency of pioneering social workers to adopt the ideas of their funding source and to define problems in terms that would not offend their white patrons or in ways that would not jeopardize their own bread and butter. Economics loomed large in how early social workers defined the problems of black migrants.

TRIBELESS BLACK MEN

Using basically economic terms to define, describe, and explain the experiences of black people, social workers had extreme difficulty in understanding the kind of black man that E. Franklin Frazier (1949) described as "tribeless." Frazier depicted the tribeless black men as those migrants who avoided establishing close ties with anyone. These tribeless black men sought to sever all ties to rural social support systems, even the extended family, and to seek adventure and work as solitary wanderers. Frazier held that tribeless black men tended to form tenuous, temporary relationships with women mainly for sexual favors and for domestic services but would abandon these relationships once they became serious. In other words, these men were chronic deserters as they moved from one short-term relationship to another, leaving many abandoned children in their wake.

These tribeless black men were men of the blues. That is to say that they were men in deep pain because many had experienced painful losses and separations. Their fear of attachment was in essence a fear of experiencing the pain of losing again. Hence, blues lyrics such as the following defined them:

> I got something to tell you when I get a chance
> somethin' to tell you when I get a chance
> I don't want to marry just want to be your man.

Blues defined their roaming spirit:

> I'm sittin' here wonderin' will a matchbox hold my clothes
> I'm sittin' here wonderin' will a matchbox hold my clothes
> I ain't got so many matches but I got so far to go.

When the tribeless men sang the blues they were without question creating a mood by which shared experiences could be examined collectively. Hence, they moaned about what the central themes of their lives were: losing their women, being on the chain gang, being run out of town, and moving from place to place. An economic analysis might explain how hard they worked for so little, but the blues indicated a deeper emotional and psychological analysis, portraying men who had been cut so deeply emotionally that they tried to adopt an inner attitude of indifference to intimacy. The blues helped these men to overcome the dreaded sense of powerlessness that they faced as a result of their inability to protect loved ones from lynching, starvation, the chain gang, and rape— real, not fanciful, terrors. Through singing the blues, they could help one another overcome the loneliness, isolation, and unhappiness that tended to arise from their relationships.

Early black social workers felt that all they had to do with these tribeless men was to teach them skills and find them industrial work, and the men would be well on their way toward adjustment and assimilation. However, when these men began to not show up for appointments, seemed to want to "hang out" in the streets, and developed a high rate of absenteeism after social workers had gone through so much to find them work, social workers began to wonder whether the men could be helped to become productive workers. Because these tribeless men often blew entire paychecks on overnight gambling sprees or drinking binges, social workers began to classify them as irresponsible, charging them with wasting money that should have gone toward family survival. Watching tribeless black men work a few weeks and then quit decent jobs that paid decent wages confirmed to social workers that these men were irresponsible. Because these social workers had no grasp of the psychological and cultural life of tribeless black men, their first tendency, of course, was to resort to moralizing. This meant seeing the solution in terms of instilling middle-class values and constantly exhorting these men to be more ambitious; work harder; sober up; stay at home; save their money; and stop cursing, talking loud, and acting boisterous—niggerish, in other words.

Mowrer (1927) wrote that the sort of facts that caseworkers tended to select in regard to desertion cases involving tribeless men reveal "the lack of any comprehensive attack upon the problem" (p. 187). Lacking any understanding of the cultural, psychological, and emotional life of tribeless men, social workers, Mowrer stated, usually defined their problem in respect to the following moralistic and pejorative descriptions:

- laxity of ideals in relations with women
- laziness or shiftlessness
- intemperance
- intemperance combined with gambling or laziness or some other bad habit
- general worthlessness
- loss of interest in family
- unwillingness to share domestic difficulties
- a roving disposition
- a passion for gambling
- anger with wife
- morphine habit
- sexual immorality. (p. 187)

After a while, according to Mowrer, caseworkers would simply define the problem as "hopeless" and develop the attitude that the best course of action is not to help these men but to lock them up.

There is no question that the tribeless black men during the 1930s fit well the category of the hard-core unemployed described by sociologists in the 1960s and the black underclass described by sociologists in the 1990s (Glasgow, 1980). The moralizing continues, more prisons are built, and now not only is the situation of modern-day tribeless men viewed as hopeless, but these men themselves are seen as part of a "permanent" underclass, doomed to low-life existence forever.

THE PSYCHOLOGY OF CULTURAL SICKNESS

Both E. Franklin Frazier and Ernest Mowrer believed that the primary difficulty early social workers had regarding problem identification was that they often gave little or no attention to the personal and cultural background of their clients. Frazier held that if early social workers had undertaken a study of the culture and inner lives of the black migrants, they would have discovered that the problem was as much a psychological problem as it was an economic one. In many cases, Frazier (1924) held, the problem was "essentially psychological" (p. 252). Frazier wrote that the southern environment that black migrants left behind not only left them in economic distress but was also so repressive that it had a stifling effect on personality development. Frazier (1925) also wrote, "When supposedly civilized intellectual white men of the South still speak of a general massacre to rid the South of the Negro" and when black people have lived 50, 60, or 70 years under constant threats, fear, and terror, there is most definitely "an indisputable connection between the repressive environment and the mental health of the Negro" (p. 489).

Frazier (1925) identified one mental health problem among southern rural black people that he said was very difficult to describe. He could only refer to it as "the psychology of the sick" (pp. 489–490). (We call it "the psychology of cultural sickness" because it stems from the racism inherent in the dominant white southern culture.) Frazier said that black people showed symptoms of the psychology of cultural sickness when they acted as if they were sick when there was nothing actually physically wrong with them. This sickness was more than a kind of psychosomatic illness; it was part of the psychological survival mechanism of rural black people. For example, Frazier held that when southern white people asked black people how they felt, the standard answer was "right poorly," no matter how fit they were. They felt that survival depended on how well they presented to white people an image that they were too weak, vulnerable, and incapacitated to be a threat to white supremacy. Frazier (1925) explained that "a sick man is expected not to assert himself. Objectively considered, he will elicit pity rather than resentment from the dominant society" (p. 489). Survival even depended on presenting an image of being too sick to take responsibility for one's own life let alone to rise up. The psychology of cultural sickness was consistent with the image white people had of black people, that is, that they were childlike dependents ever in need of the care and authority of white paternalism.

Oliver C. Cox (1948), a leading black sociologist, acknowledged that the social system instilled in black people a psychology of the sick. He held that by impelling black people to rise in status individually as if the paradoxical restraints of color were nonexistent, "the system judges the colored person as if he were under no social handicap of color" (p. 383). Cox wrote that a rebuff because of their color puts black people "in very much the same situation of the very ugly person or one suffering from a loathsome disease," and the mental anguish that this engenders is often aggravated "by a consciousness of incurability and even blameworthiness, a self-reproaching" (p. 383) that tends to leave black people starkly aware that they are viewed and treated like the enemy—outsiders—in their native land.

Rural southern black people acknowledged the psychology of the sick when they constantly talked about how bad their "nerves" were and how "sick and tired" they were of being sick and tired. Lerone Bennett, Jr. (1962), the black historian, demonstrated what having "bad nerves" and "being sick and tired" meant to these black people:

> To work from sun up to sun down for a whole year and to end owing "the man" 400 dollars for the privilege of working; to do this year after year and to sink deeper and deeper into debt; to be chained to the land by bills at the plantation store; to wash away this knowledge with bad gin; to blot it out in an ecstasy of song and prayer; to sing, to pray, to cry; to bring forth a boy child and to be told one night that four thousand people are roasting him slowly over a hot fire and leisurely cutting off his fingers and toes; to be powerless and to curse one's self for cowardice; to be conditioned by dirt and fear and shame and signs; to become a part of these signs and to feel them in the deepest recess of the spirit; to be knocked down in the streets and whipped for not calling a shiftless hillbilly "Mister"; to be a plaything of judges and courts and policemen; to be black in a white fire and to believe finally in one's own unworthiness; . . . to not know where to go and what to do to stay the whip and the rope and the chain; to give in finally; to bow and to scrape; to grin; and to hate one's self for one's servility and weakness and blackness—all this was a . . . nightmare which continued for days and nights and years. (p. 238)

E. Franklin Frazier implied that when many of the migrants arrived in the city, they still had not shed themselves of the psychology of the sick. They still felt a need for dependency; they still feared being assertive; and they still felt feelings of inferiority and inadequacy and were lacking in confidence in their ability to rise. In other words, they had learned this defense mechanism so well and used it so often for so long that they did not feel safe giving it up. Urban League social workers merely told the black migrants that they would have to change their behavior and mannerisms and conform more to middle-class standards if they ever hoped to get jobs and to be acceptable in the eyes of white society. They did not address the core psychological needs of black people.

Caseworkers were confounded because they had no idea where this problem came from, so vague were black migrants in describing it. When black migrants told caseworkers that they did not show up for the job because they felt "sick and tired" and drained of energy, this of course meant to social workers that they were just simply "lazy" and "unambitious." When they told them that they blew a paycheck on liquor because their nerves were bad, this meant to social workers that they were simply "trifling" and "irresponsible." Because social workers were so accustomed to trying to figure out the particular problems of particular individuals, they could not possibly fathom that the problem that many individual black people brought to caseworkers were actually not individual problems at all but historical problems common to numerous black people. The psychology of cultural sickness was (and still is) a problem of accumulated black oppression, a deep psychological trauma black people inherited from their ancestors. As Freud (1949) stated,

> When we study the reactions of early traumas, we are often surprised to find that they are not strictly limited to what the subject himself has really experienced but diverse from it in a way which fits in much better with the model of a phylogenetic event and, in general, can only be explained by such an influence. (p. 157)

Southern rural black people were "sick" not only because they were facing daily their own personal nightmares but also because they were carrying the weight of historical oppression. Freud (1949) posited that "the archaic heritage of human beings comprises not only dispositions but also subject matter—memory traces of the experience of earlier generations" (p. 158). Bulhan (1985), writing on the psychology of oppression, held that "the millions of slaves lost in the middle passage, the ravages of tribal wars instigated to divide and rule, the ruthless exploitation of every human and material resource—all these still remain sedimented in social existence and in the deeper recesses of the psyche" (p. 253). Could it have been possible that the traumatic ancestral sediments were unfrozen to the point that migrants suffered the double fear of having memory traces of raided villages in Africa, slave forts, slave ships, and the "breaking" process during slavery along with the stark consciousness that their own lives and the lives of the ones they loved were constantly in jeopardy? If so, then it is no wonder that the psychology of cultural sickness left black people acting helpless and unmotivated and lacking in energy and spirit as they sought psychologically to bear the constant threat and reality of loss, separation, and death.

THE PSYCHOLOGY OF CULTURAL PARANOIA

If early social workers had used their scientific method to probe the inner lives of black migrants, they would have discovered patterns of the psychology of cultural sickness and also detected patterns of the psychology of cultural paranoia among rural black people. Freud (1929) explained that civilization is a thin veneer to keep in check primal sexual and aggressive urges that would be utterly shocking and disgusting to civilized people. When it came to black people, white people in the South could let loose their primal urges unchecked by law, religion, morality, or any civilized standard. Nothing indicated this more strongly than the kind of anger that a lynching engendered. The following 1920 report from *The Atlanta Journal Newspaper* of a black man accused of murdering a white woman is a chilling example:

> *After his body had been mutilated, while he was alive, the Negro was saturated with gasoline and burned, and while he was burning his body was literally riddled with bullets and buckshot. The mob numbered several thousand . . . and many thousands who were in the crowd literally fought to get close enough to see the actual details. Almost every person who had a firearm, and it seemed that every one carried a gun or pistol, emptied the weapon into the man's prostrate*

body. He was not shot until he had been mutilated and saturated with gasoline and with a match torched. The infuriated mob could hold itself in check no longer. One shot was fired from a revolver and it was the signal for a thousand shots which made mince meat of the body. Four young women from the crowd pushed their way through the outer rim of the circle and emptied rifles into the Negro. They stood by while other men cut off fingers, toes and other parts of the body and passed them around as souvenirs. After all of the ammunition had been used, more wood was piled on the remains and gasoline poured on the pile. Later the charred remains were tied to the limb of a tree left dangling over the road. (quoted in Ginzburg, 1962, pp. 132–133)

There were white people in the South during the era of the Great Migration who would not hesitate to burn any black person alive, rape a black woman, cut off a black man's penis and keep it in a pickle jar as a souvenir, and riddle black children with bullets and throw their bodies into rivers without any fear of legal reprisal or public outrage. To most southern white people, black people represented something uncivilized, savage, devilish, sinful, animalistic, and monstrous. As Fanon (1967) stated, for the Europeans, "The Negro has one function: that of symbolizing the lower emotions, the lesser inclinations, the darker side of the soul" (p. 190).

Viewed this way and treated as if they were something subhuman or inhuman, black people came to take on what the black psychiatrists Grier and Cobbs (1968) termed the psychology of "cultural paranoia," a profound, practically pathological distrust of white people. Rural black people developed the deep distrust because white southerners tricked, cheated, and took advantage of them on a daily basis. Rural black people knew well that it was not unusual for white people thirsting for excitement to try to trick black people into leaving themselves vulnerable to a beating or some other abuse. An elderly black man told one of the authors of this book how white men had tried to trick him into a lynching. He recalled that while he was walking across a field one day in Georgia, he came upon a group of white men. For sport, one of the men asked him didn't he think a white woman who lived on the hill was pretty. The old man said that he was doomed if he said yes and doomed if he said no. Both answers would have indicated that he had committed the atrocious crime of looking at a white woman. Having become adept in maneuvering around such tricks, the old man said he lowered his head, scratched his butt, and said in a slow, stupid drawl: "Boss man I don't know nothing 'bout no women, especially no white women's, and I's got sense enough never to know anything. All I knows is about mules and I'm on my way right now to get my old mule and plow this here field for Mr. Charlie." Such a remark left the white men laughing—that time.

Once black people became "citified," the psychology of cultural paranoia came not only to mean black people not trusting white people, but also to developing a projected self-hatred toward other black people. During the first few decades of the 20th century, black social workers were astounded that the black migrants did not trust them any more than they did white social workers. They could not see that this was a result of black migrants' viewing black social workers as representatives of white oppression or, more bluntly, seeing them as "white Negroes."

THE PSYCHOLOGY OF CULTURAL CLAUSTROPHOBIA

It was not just the constant sickly feeling or the paranoidal mistrust that drove thousands of rural black people cityward but also the anxious feelings of being hemmed in by a circumscribed environment and having to choke back one's true feelings and desires. William Pickens, a notable civil rights leader during the early decades of the 20th century, held that to him Jim Crowism was worse than lynching because although "lynching occasionally kills one man," racial discrimination and segregation "perpetually tortures ten thousands" (quoted in Adero, 1993, p. xvii). Pickens said that Jim Crowism tortures by keeping black people limited while crippling their ambitions and aspirations. Zora Neale Hurston, the novelist and folklorist, said that the repressive, immobilizing rural southern environment smothers the impulses, makes black people feel "crowded in on," kills their dreams and makes them feel restless, oppressed, and unstable, causing them to "cry inside" as if their souls were being tortured (Adero, 1993). She stated that this feeling of being hemmed in and bottled up was so agonizing and immobilizing that it made many black people act as if they were "slaveships in shoes" (Adero, 1993, p. 60).

THE PSYCHOLOGY OF CULTURAL AMNESIA

Along with wanting to flee persecution and to better their lot, many rural black migrants sought to move away from the stifling provincialism of the rural environment. The radio, the motorcar, the train, and the black northern tabloids were breaking down their cultural isolation and making them thirst for a larger worldview. They no longer wished to feel like sick men and women, handicapped by color, incapacitated by the inability to take full control over their lives, and treated like a social plague. They no longer wished to choke back their true, inner feelings and to feel hemmed in and thwarted. They wanted more space and more room to explore new horizons, broaden their vision, and realize some of the dreams that had been suffocating them. They wanted to forget, start fresh, and find their new bright morning in the New Jerusalem.

Once in the city black migrants began to feel less like a people living in sickly, stifling air; less like harbingers of dead dreams; and less like people who had to keep their guard up against tricks, bloodhounds, and lynch ropes. However, their desire to forget and to put their nightmarish experiences behind them caused them to develop a psychology that was unprecedented in their history. Jacoby (1975) called this new psychology that black people were adopting the "psychology of social amnesia," and Wilson (1993) called it the "psychology of historical amnesia" (p. 33). Borrowing from both, we call it the "psychology of cultural amnesia."

This cultural amnesia went beyond the denial and traumas and fears of oppression. Black migrants wanted to forget their entire rural way of life and rid themselves of every trace of the old ways of dressing, talking, acting, behaving, and thinking. Being citified meant to them that now their speech was no longer right, their drawl was a telltale sign of rural ignorance and backwardness, their clothes were too plain and gaudy—"country," and their religion was overly emotional and entailed too many theatrics. Even their music was either too sad or too "churchified." Now the new art form called "jazz" was more suitable to their cosmopolitan, urbane, and sophisticated taste. Now everything "country" had to be urban-ized, and everything backward had to be polished and refined.

This seeking of a conscious unremembrance was to have a dev-astating effect on black urban life, particularly on black youths. These youths, now alienated from the old rural ways, seldom had the chance to experience the social bonding and communalism of the rural experience and were highly susceptible to the individual-ism and materialism of urban life. To many black adults who had grown up in the rural southern environment, their past life was not worth remembering, let alone passing on. In light of where they had come from, the city was a great improvement over their rural existence. Many of the older black adults had come out of the rural environment starving for such items as spoons, forks, glasses, wooden floors (instead of mud floors), store-bought furniture, glass windows, shoes, decent clothing, running water, electricity, indoor toilets, and automobiles, and the big city gave them the chance to acquire these material things that their rural poverty constantly denied them. The big-city factories promised to put more money in their pockets than they could ever hope to make from plowing fields and picking cotton. No, city life was not so bad, many of the adult black migrants thought. For example, Raper and Reid (1941) wrote that when one black migrant "thought of the health needs of his family, the education of his children, the shabby house he lived in, his inability to buy clothes . . . and to support his church and lodge as he wished" (p. 69), he decided to try his luck up North. The authors stated that after the migrant had gotten settled, he found that he preferred "the city slums to the rural one he left—his house [was] no worse, a yard spigot and closet [were] less inconvenient or smelly than were the rural facilities. Despite occasional police bru-tality, he [was] not nearly in such great danger of mob violence. Then too, in the city there [were] hospitals and clinics, better schools, cash money when you [could] get a job, more folks, and bright lights" (p. 76). However, many of the younger generation had not known the hardships of rural life and had not found the progress in big cities that their parents and grandparents felt they themselves had found.

Brown (1956) explained that migrant parents had come to the big city "to say good-bye to the cotton fields, good-bye to 'massa

Charlie,' good-bye to the chain gangs, and most of all, good-bye to those sunup to sundown working hours" (pp. 7–8). However, their children and grandchildren had not felt the full measure of hardship, brutality, and suffering of rural life. Many had not known of these horrors at all because they either were born and bred in the city or had left the rural South at an age too young for them to remember. What these youths did know was that the "good life" was staring them in the face from every billboard and blasting their sensibilities with the notion that regardless of how far their parents and grandparents thought they had come, black people in general still had yet to achieve the American dream. Brown wrote that although the grown-ups saw the promised land, "the children of these . . . colored pioneers" saw a slum ghetto where there "were too many people full of hate and bitterness crowded into a dirty, stinky, uncared-for, closet-size section of the city" (p. 8).

Although the older black migrants felt less like sick patients, their children felt economically and socially handicapped; whereas the adults could let their guards down somewhat, the young felt a sense of endangerment—if not by white men, then by all of these desperate black strangers; although older black people felt less stifled and hemmed in, their children living in the urban slums not only felt trapped but imprisoned. Furthermore, unlike the adults in the rural environment, these youths did not have the supportive social bonds and the sense of shared oppression and shared hope; they did not have the spiritual toughness that stemmed from the spirituals and the collective facing of reality in all its rawness and brutality that stemmed from the blues.

The blues and the spirituals were based on the principle that problems, no matter how traumatizing, were to be brought out into the open and collectively affirmed, shared, and addressed. The cultural amnesia that the newly arrived migrants were taking on was antithetical to this principle. In both the blues and the spirituals, traumatic life events were cried over, moaned, hummed, and shouted out in the presence of others who were sympathetic. In the big city, black people began to privatize their troubles, to be silent sufferers, and to internalize their fears and their rage. This privatization of their troubles shut off the younger generation from the experiences of the ancestors, experiences that were indeed traumatic but nevertheless also filled with lessons of survival, endurance, and hope. The lessons of the past would have helped black youths overcome their alienation, bitterness, and despair. Black experience–based social work recognizes that in contemporary society it is extremely difficult for social workers to break through the silent treatment and cultural amnesia of many black people who have deep-seated emotional problems. It also recognizes that the modern urban culture has made a virtue of being stoic in the face of adversity. Also, the urban street world inhabited largely by tribeless black men and disillusioned black children advocated putting up a cool front of emotional indifference to mask fears and vulnerabilities. Both the principle of the dominant culture and the street ideology were radically at odds with the black moaning tradition.

In light of the current tendency of black people to privatize their suffering, to be secretive in their family affairs, and to put up fronts that all is well, black experience–based social work maintains that social work with black people demands developing methods of disclosure that black people are familiar and comfortable with. Most importantly, it is starkly aware that the danger of cultural amnesia—of black people cutting themselves adrift from their heritage and lineage—and the privatization of their problems can lead to the most destructive psychology of all, "the psychology of cultural terminal illness." For example, without the social support, spiritual strength, and survival art that rural black people developed to help them cope with the psychologies of cultural sickness, cultural paranoia, and cultural claustrophobia, many urban black youths began to develop a more dead-end psychology, one that grew out of their alienation from the group experience. Patterson (1982) referred to this psychology as the psychology of "social death." His reference was to slaves who were so dominated and depersonalized that they were spared physical death as long as they were instruments of utility to their masters. In exchange for physical life, they suffered a social death in three areas: (1) their personality, (2) their social relations with other black people, and (3) their culture. Social death of black people continued through the emancipation and the organization of black people. It became so intensive among early urban black people and so frightening among contemporary urban black people that we call Patterson's "social death" "the psychology of cultural terminal illness."

THE PSYCHOLOGY OF CULTURAL TERMINAL ILLNESS

Even when black adults wanted to tell their story to the younger generation, many did not know how, especially when it came to relating their powerlessness in the face of white oppression. They had to ponder whether their horror stories might do even greater psychological and emotional harm that not to tell the story. One black migrant, speaking of his need to pass on his experience to his son, stated,

> *Soon I feel I must have a talk with him and explain the whole nasty business but what shall I say? Where shall I begin? Shall I go back to slavery? . . . How can I tell all that needs to be told without producing just the effect that I have been so carefully avoiding? How can I reconcile what I have to say with the Sunday school notions that I have tried to translate into every day situations or with the salute to the flag that must be said each day at school? Can I keep my son from hatreds and reprisals without injury to his self regard? Can I prevent him from being suspicious that, after all, people and things colored are not so worth while, so honest, so effective, so admirable as people and things white? If I fail to say anything, will I not leave him to get such idea as he can from the ubiquitous and sometimes humiliating racial signs of the South? So far I have avoided what seems to me to be a fatherly duty to a young son, but just how can it be told?* (Robinson, 1930, pp. 144–145)

Black adults either did not want to tell the story or did not know how. Yet they felt their own powerlessness in providing their children with the materialistic trappings by which success and worth are defined in urban America. The grown-ups could see the differences in their children, and they began to fear losing their children. They no longer feared their children would be frantically standing alone before the fully uncovered teeth of the lynch mob. They feared instead losing them to disillusionment and despair. Richard

Wright (1941), the black literary giant, captured the feelings of many black adults of the time when he wrote,

We watch strange moods fill our children, and our hearts swell with pain. The streets, with their noise and glaring lights, the taverns, the automobiles, and the poolrooms claim them, and no voice of ours can call them back. They spend their nights away from home; they forget our ways of life, our language, our God. Their swift speech and impatient eyes make us feel weak and foolish. We cannot keep them in school; more than 1,000,000 of our black boys and girls of high school age are not in school. We fall upon our knees and pray for them, but in vain. The city has beaten us, evaded us; but they, with young bodies filled with warm blood feel bitter and frustrated at the sight of the alluring hopes and prizes denied them. (p. 136)

Not only did black adults notice that their children were different and hard to figure out, but they also noticed how touchy, defensive, and destructive their children were. If they, the elders, had grown "sick and tired" of white oppression, it seemed that these youths were "sick to death" of black people and their own blackness and, most troublesome, of life. They seemed eager to fight one another, to entertain death, to play with it, and to welcome it as a way of life. Again Wright (1941) spoke for many older black people of the time when he agonized that

it is not their eagerness to fight that makes us afraid, but that they go to death on the city pavements faster than even disease or starvation can take them. As the courts and morgues become crowded with our lost children, the hearts of the officials of the city grow cold toward us . . . [and] our lives and the lives of our children grow so frightful that even some of our educated leaders are afraid to make known to the nation how we exist. (p. 136)

HEALING AND HISTORY

Wilson (1993) wrote that "many of the murders, deaths, and much of the destruction that we see in our communities today are the result of people trying to escape history, and living their lives in terror and fear of their own history and reality" (p. 35). This great denial of history took place on an unprecedented scale when black people became an unwanted people in their urban experience at the turn of the century. Black experience–based social work maintains that current individual, familial, and communal problems are related to the historical wounds in the black experience. Black people in contemporary society have inherited and lifted to monstrous proportions the negative psychologies of cultural sickness, cultural claustrophobia, cultural amnesia, cultural paranoia, and cultural terminal illness of their past. A basic premise of black experience–based social work is that black people must heal these historical wounds before they can fully develop economically, politically, culturally, and socially as a people.

If early black social workers had conducted a cultural analysis of the oppression of the black masses, they would have discovered that black people simply cannot be understood outside the context of their history and culture. As Pasteur and Toldson (1982) explained, black "culture has its own methods of attending to griefs of the soul" (p. 7). They would have ascertained that the problems of the black migrants could not be defined solely in economic terms. It was their own fear of black history and reality that left these social workers grossly unaware of the psychological and emotional problems that underlay the economic and racial oppression of black people. Without such insight, there was no way for social workers to see that no individual black person had a problem that was not in some way related to black history on the whole. This meant that no individual black person had a problem that was not in some way shared by other black people.

The relatedness of individual problems and historical oppression is a basic principle of black experience–based social work. This is not in any way to deny the immediacy and urgency of the problems individuals bring to the social work table. It is merely raising doubts about whether social workers can help black people with problems by continuing their ahistorical approach. It should be clear from reading this chapter that pioneering social workers could never understand the tribeless black men and the disillusioned black children without an in-depth historical–cultural probe. Without this kind of assessment, early black social workers were not likely to ever understand the significance of rural black people moving from a psychology of cultural sickness to a psychology of cultural terminal illness; to ever grasp the impact of black people consciously trying to forget their traumatic experiences; or to ever understand the consequences of black migrants throwing out the cultural therapies that helped them cope with those traumas. As the black migrants found themselves taking on the individualistic and materialistic ways of the dominant urban culture, they found themselves more or less seeking to solve their problems as individuals, a community of one in a war against all. Pioneering black social workers had overlooked the culture and history of the black masses. Therefore, they could not see that "moanin'" the blues or the spirituals was actually an in-depth assessment of the problem. Without such an assessment, particularly as migrants were beginning to develop an acute case of cultural amnesia, pioneer social workers were bound to neither see the negative psychologies rural black migrants had brought to the city with them nor have any idea of what therapeutic tools they had left behind.

REFERENCES

Adero, M. (Ed.). (1993). *Up south*. New York: New Press.

Bennett, L., Jr. (1962). *Before the Mayflower*. Chicago: Johnson.

Brown, C. (1956). *Manchild in the promised land*. New York: Dutton.

Bulhan, H. A. (1985). *Frantz Fanon and the psychology of oppression*. New York: Plenum Press.

Cox, O. C. (1948). *Caste, class and race*. New York: Monthly Review Press.

Fanon, F. (1967). *Black skin, white masks*. New York: Grove Press.

Frazier, E. F. (1924). Social work in race relations. *Crisis, 27*(6), 252–254.

Frazier, E. F. (1925). Psychological factors in Negro health. *Journal of Social Forces, 3*, 489–490.

Frazier, E. F. (1949). *The Negro family in the United States*. Chicago: University of Chicago Press.

Freud, S. (1929). *Civilization and its discontents*. London: Hogarth Press.

Freud, S. (1949). *Moses and monotheism*. New York: Alfred A. Knopf.

Ginzburg, R. (1962). *100 years of lynchings*. Baltimore: Black Classic Press.

Glasgow, D. (1980). *The black underclass*. San Francisco: Jossey-Bass.

Grier, W. H., & Cobbs, P. M. (1968). *Black rage*. New York: Basic Books.

Jacoby, R. (1975). *Social amnesia*. Boston: Beacon Press.

Mowrer, E. (1927). *Family disorganization*. Chicago: University of Chicago Press.

Pasteur, A. B., & Toldson, I. L. (1982). *Roots of soul*. New York: Anchor Press/Doubleday.

Patterson, O. (1982). *Slavery and social death*. Cambridge, MA: Harvard University Press.

Raper, A. F., & Reid, I.D.A. (1941). *Sharecroppers all*. Chapel Hill: University of North Carolina Press.

Robinson, W. A. (1930, May). How can it be told? *Opportunity, 8*(5), 143–145.

Wilson, A. N. (1993). *The falsification of Afrikan consciousness*. New York: Afrikan World InfoSystems.

Wright, R. (1941). *12 million black voices*. New York: Viking Press.

PART 2

Mournin'

CHAPTER 5

The Social Context of Mourning

*W*hen pioneering black social workers failed to dig into the experience of black people, they failed to understand that black people had their own ideas about defining their situation and meeting their core needs. This meant that part of the clue to solving the problems was not so much what the black migrants were going to gain once they arrived in the city but what they had left behind in the rural, small-town southern environment. Did they indeed leave something behind that might have been helpful to early social workers in their effort to assist them? Was there something in their past rural lives—despite the trauma of loss and separation, the flight from persecution, and the agonizing repressive psychologies—that made for strength, healing, creativity, and endurance? In other words, did social workers then and do social workers now actually have to look backward to move forward? Pioneer black social workers soon found out that the problems facing the black migrants were more complex than finding jobs, decent housing, and wholesome recreation for the new arrivals. Yet, they had difficulty recognizing that many of the migrants had experienced nightmarish psychological traumas from living constantly under a system of terrorism, and that their emotional problems had to be addressed as well. The key question of this chapter is, What elements were there in the "folk" culture of rural black people that helped them combat the negative psychologies of cultural sickness, cultural paranoia, cultural claustrophobia, cultural amnesia, and cultural terminal illness?

We have already suggested that the music, folk narratives, and other elements of the culture of rural black people were key to the identification of problems confronting them. Already we have gleaned lessons from the black experience that should be helpful to contemporary social work practitioners in their work with black people in modern society.

- Contemporary social work practitioners should have learned from the black experience to be highly sensitive to the problem of loss and separation. This has been a recurrent theme in the lives of black people throughout their history in America. Black people in contemporary society still face this trauma to a significant and disproportionate degree on various levels in their lives.
- Social work practitioners should have learned from the black past that indeed they should focus on the economic problems facing black people, particularly given the widespread impoverishment of black people. But they should also examine the relationship between black economic underdevelopment and the emotional or psychological traumas suffered by black people as a result of being perenially victimized by continued racial oppression.
- Practitioners should have learned from the black experience that individual problems can actually be problems of history—unresolved problems that black people have collectively suffered throughout their sojourn in America. This insight demands that social work practitioners focus not only on black people in the present but seek an ancestral connection. It suggests that a mere collection of the facts on current problems is not enough.
- Contemporary social work practitioners should have learned that in the black experience great effort is put on having black people bring their problems to the surface for collective scrutiny, identification, and support. In the first part of this book, we focused on the moaning theme in the spirituals and the blues because these themes reflect the troubles, trials, and tribulations of black people during difficult moments of their history. Moaning was a method of affirmation as rural black people, following the tradition of the slaves, articulated to one another how heavy were the burdens they must bear, how hard were the roads they must travel, and how high were the mountains they must climb.

   The moaning theme symbolized an examination and reappraisal of many of the problems and concerns of the masses of black people. Although this theme in the spirituals basically dealt with the relationship of black people with God, it also reflected earthly concerns. Some spirituals, for example, were disguises, secret codes, to express the desire for earthly freedom. Although the moaning themes in the blues generally dealt with the relation of black people to one another and to the world, they also reflected Godly concerns, if only to express spiritual ambivalence, turmoil, and doubt. As one old blues song goes,

I could had religion Lord this very day
I could had religion Lord this very day
But the womens and whiskeys Lord won't let me pray.

The purpose of the moaning theme in the spirituals and the blues was to put black people in a mood that would allow them to bring internal individual pain to the surface so that suffering could be reaffirmed, reexamined, and redefined collectively. This was black people's method of identifying the problem. The mood signified that life is hard, painful, and a struggle but that one should not deny or seek to run away from these painful, inevitable struggles; suffering must be brought to the surface, examined, and confronted. Blues and spiritual stanzas such as, "I'm a-trouble in the mind," "I've got the blues deep down in my bones," or "I've been 'buked and I been scorned" give voice to an identification of grief, hardship, and the burdensome weight of oppression.

Because black people have gone through a period of cultural amnesia, urban culture advocates stoicism in the face of adversity and the privatization of troubles, and the street ideology calls for hiding problems behind a facade of cool, it is even more imperative that social work practitioners explore creative methods of disclosure in their work with black people.

• Already, contemporary social work practitioners should know from the black experience that cultural versatility is the goal of black people, not social adaptation to their limited environment or social adjustment to an oppressive society. Cultural versatility means being able to maneuver around the myriad societal traps and pitfalls designed to dehumanize, depersonalize, defeat, and destroy. For example, a slave who was adept in the art of role playing was more versatile than slaves who were not. A literate and skilled slave was more versatile than those who were not. The risk-taking slave was more versatile than those who were not. The spiritually tough and the communally based slave was more versatile than those who were not. The black experience suggests to social work practitioners that their challenge may be to explore what qualities are more suitable to making modern black people more versatile in overcoming the many societal traps, pitfalls, and barriers that immobilize them individually and that weaken their families and communities.

In this part, we will see what other lessons are in store for the social work practitioner as we examine the social context of mourning.

MOURNING

A general mood reflected in the blues and the spirituals was that black people should not keep dwelling on their pain, wallow in self-pity, or, using modern terminology, adopt a victim psychology. Once the spirituals and the blues created the mood in which pain could be reexamined, they moved from identifying the suffering to depicting the process of healing through collective empathy, collective support, and hope.

By endowing one another with the title "mourners" during the days of slavery, black people affirmed a sense of responsibility for one another's well-being. This title gave explicit recognition that if one was black, one was destined to mourn, not just over the dead but as a way of life. As mourners, black people were expected to identify with one another's suffering and to make one another feel that no one was facing a cruel world, bearing burdens, and walking lonesome valleys alone. In the spirituals, black people were encouraged to "walk together children" and don't "get weary." Slaves also referred to themselves as fellow "sufferers," but this had a connotation that was different from that of being fellow mourners. Referring to themselves as sufferers meant a recognition that they experienced a common suffering; however, to be referred to as a fellow mourner meant that black people were viewing themselves as part of the healing process and holding themselves responsible for one another's safety, sanity, and overall well-being.

If the moaning theme depicted trouble and woe, the theme of mourning depicted empathy, catharsis, healing, hope, and liberation. However, neither the moaning theme nor the mourning theme was rigidly dichotomous. These themes were the flip side of the same coin. Thus, a spiritual that begins "Sometime I feel like a moaning dove," reflecting the moaning theme, ends with the following stanza:

Sometimes I feel like
An eagle in the air
Spread my wings an'
Fly, fly, fly
Spread my wings an'
Fly, fly.

This last stanza suggests that the sufferers feel they have lifted themselves up from the ashes of despair and disappointment and have risen to new heights of self-expression and healing. The first stanza indicates the moaning theme, whereas the last one depicts the theme of mourning.

The mourning theme of the spirituals promised healing:

There is a balm in Gilead,
To make the wounded whole . . .
To heal the sin-sick soul.

It promised hope and the assurance that "troubles don't always last":

O Stand the storm, it won't be long
We'll anchor bye and bye.

Furthermore, it promised deliverance:

Didn't my Lord deliver Daniel, deliver
Daniel, deliver Daniel,

An' why not-a every man!
He delivered Daniel from the Lion's den,
Jonah from the belly of the whale,
The Heaven children from the fiery furnace,
And why not every man!

Although both the spirituals and the blues are viewed as sorrow songs or songs of melancholy and woe, the mourning theme of these musical forms represents an effort on the part of black people to transcend their oppression and rise above it. Over and over again, the word "transcendence" is used to explain the major function of the spirituals and the blues. Locke (1969) wrote that the spirituals "transcend emotionally even the key experience of sorrows out of which they were born" (pp. 48–49). Lovell (1972) held that the spiritual "transforms" the individual "physically and mentally" and "gives the individual new strength, new direction, new motives and occupations, new capacity for wrestling with life, and above all a new sense of grandeur" (p. 103). Smith (1994) believed that "The Blues songs serve to transcend negative experiences and feelings of recapitulating or reprising the negative but precisely in such a way (ecstatically) that they transform the negative" (p. 123). We have already given Ellison's (1964) classic definition of the blues as "an impulse to keep the painful details and episodes of a brutal experience alive in one's aching consciousness . . . [in order] to transcend it" (p. 78).

Slaves gave the philosophical word "transcendence" concrete meaning. To them transcendence meant being so enveloped in an emotional and religious ecstasy that they experienced renewed energy, a heightened sense of belongingness, and an expanded sense of internal freedom. In numerous slave narratives, black people said that their music and religion lifted their spirits to the point that they "got happy," felt they were "filled with the holy ghost," and felt "uplifted" as if they were "flying."

This feeling of transcendence gave slaves such a surge of energy that they no longer felt like sick people, incapable, incapacitated, weak, helpless, and inferior. One black man who remembered the spiritual tradition being carried on after emancipation wrote,

*Those who have never heard these songs in their native setting can
have no conception of the influence they exert upon the people. I
have sat in a gathering . . . where the preacher strove in vain to
awaken an interest; I have heard a brother or a sister start one of
these spirituals, slowly and monotonously; I have seen the
congregation irresistibly drawn to take up the refrain, I have seen the
entire body gradually worked up from one degree of emotion to
another until, like a turbulent, angry sea, men and women, to the
accompaniment of the singing, and with shouting, moaning, and
clapping of hands, surged and swayed to and fro.* (quoted in
Barrett, 1912, p. 238)

Slaves and rural black people after emancipation often would get
so full of the spirit that other slaves had to calm them down lest
they carry their turbulent energy beyond the secret meeting place.
One ex-slave, Richard Carruthers, recalls that some of his fellow
mourners used to get "so joyous they starts to holler loud and we
had to stop up they mouth. I seen niggers get so full of the Lord and
so happy they drops unconscious" (quoted in Webber, 1978, p.
125). Sometimes the spirit got such a powerful hold on the mourners that some even had trouble restraining themselves before white
people. The ex-slave Fannie Moore said that one day while her
mother was plowing in the cotton field, "All sudden like she let out
a big yell, den she sta't singin' an' a-shoutin, an' a-whoopin; an' a-
hollerin'. Den it seem she plow all de harder" (Webber, 1978, p.
125). When Fannie Moore's mother got in from the field, the master admonished her for all her whooping and yelling, saying "We
put you there to work and you sho' 'bettah work, else we git the
overseeah to cowhide yo' old black back" (Webber, 1978, p. 125).
Moore said,

*My mammy Jes grin all over her black wrinkled face and say: 'I's
saved. De Lawd done tell me I's saved. Now I know de Lawd will
show me de way, I ain't gwine grieve no more. No matter how much
yo' all done beat me an' my children de Lawd will show me de way.
An' some day we never be slaves.* (quoted in Webber, 1978,
p. 125)

According to Moore, even after the master grabbed the cowhide and slashed her mother across the back, her mother never yelled. "She jes go back to de fiel' a singin" (quoted in Webber, 1978, p. 125).

This feeling of exaltation helped slaves overcome the psychology of cultural sickness, and it even made them overcome the psychology of cultural paranoia, feeling that if they trusted in God they no longer had to worry so much about trusting in the white man. They sang,

> No fearin, no doubtin
> While God's on our side
> We'll all die er shoutin
> De Lawd will provide.

Because the ecstatic feeling was created in a socioemotional context, it made black people trust one another more, even if wisdom and reality told them to continue their mistrust of white people.

Most significantly, the spirituals in their rightful context of dancing, shouting, praying, and feeling the spirit of the Lord deep down in the soul helped slaves break free of that smothering feeling of cultural claustrophobia. In the context of their music and religion, slaves could express their inner emotions and have their inner pain affirmed by others and lifted to another joyous level of reality. Slaves did not want to share their feelings with white people; they dared not share them. It was crucial to slaves that they meet and worship among themselves and be able to express the full range of their rage and the deepest level of their desire to be free.

Pasteur and Toldson (1982), two modern black psychiatrists, wrote that the spirituals, the blues, and other aesthetic forms helped black people overcome the psychology of cultural claustrophobia by helping them "to not be burdened by a massive unconscious area" (p. 16). Pasteur and Toldson wrote,

> Modern psychology, spurred by the thinking of Sigmund Freud, generally compartmentalizes human awareness into three areas: conscious, preconscious, and unconscious. The unconscious contains censored thought hidden from awareness. These exiled thoughts are

imprisoned by repressive defenses: denial, repression, rationalization, intellectualization, and others. The black/African mind appears not to be affected because of the propensity to use song, dance, oratory, painting, sculpture, etc., to expel urging impulses that ordinarily become the content of the unconscious in the Western-oriented mind. (p. 16)

MOURNING WORK

What is important to see is that although we are discussing the spirituals and the blues a great deal, this is not an analysis of black music per se. What we are saying is that embodied in the music, as well as the religion and other aspects of black folk culture, is the only social therapy and social work that black people in a given time period knew. In other words, music is not just something that one sings; it is a philosophy of life and it is a helping practice, a healing art form. It is social work because even though individuals can sing the blues and the spirituals as a kind of therapy of the self, the greatest power of these musical therapies is not realized until they are done in a social context. The spirituals and the blues are communal art forms expressed in a communal context, whether it is the church, the family, a honky-tonk, or an open field. The spirituals and the blues were vehicles by which black people could transcend the negative experiences and the immobilizing psychologies of their environment. These musical forms were the instrument by which black people could carry out their mourning work, which, in essence, was social work or at least the only social work they knew. This mourning work (translated as the social work of black folk culture) sought transcendence through empathy with one another's suffering, collective healing and catharsis, and the inculcation of hope.

COLLECTIVE IDENTIFICATION AND EMPATHY

The mourning work of slaves and rural black people after slavery had its origin in traditional African culture. African people emphasized collective identification and empathy above all else. Their ties to the ancestral spirits were designed to bring the living and the

dead into a harmonious relationship of group solidarity and identity. This tradition of collective identification was carried on during
the mourning work of black people through the spirituals and the
blues. For example, when one ex-slave was questioned about how a
particular spiritual song originated, he stated:

> I'll tell you; it's dis way. My master call me up and order me a short
> peck of corn and a hundred lash. The friends see it and is sorry for
> me. When dey come to de praise meetin' dat night dey sing about it.
> Some's very good singers and know how; and dey work it in you
> know; till dey git it right and dat's the way. (quoted in Raboteau,
> 1978, p. 246)

This statement indicates that the slaves felt that the suffering of
their individual fellow slaves was worthy of being expressed in song
and worthy of the confirmation and empathy of others. It also
implies that through singing about their suffering, or shouting or
moaning it out, slaves were seeking to take up the individual's burden as their own. As Lovell (1972) wrote, slaves believed that
"standing the storms of life as a group is much easier than standing
them as an individual" (p. 276).

The blues also developed out of the identification of black people with one another's suffering. The blues worked best when they
were sung in a context in which black people could feed off of one
another's emotions. As one blues singer stated,

> It's a sort of thing that you kinda like to hold to yourself, yet you
> want somebody to know it. I don't know how you say that two ways:
> you like somebody to know it, yet you hold it to yourself. Now I've
> had the feelin's which I have disposed it in a song, but there's
> something that has happened to me that I wouldn't dare tell, not to
> tell—but I would sing about them. Because people in general they
> takes the song as an explanation for themselves—they believe this
> song is expressing their feelin's instead of the one that singin' it.
> They feel that maybe I have just hit upon somethin' that's their lives,
> and yet at the same time it was some of the things that went wrong
> with me too. (quoted in Neal, 1989, pp. 114–115)

This statement suggests that even when one person sings while others listen, the singer is not only expressing his or her own emotions but reenacting the emotional experience of others. The singer reaches others and makes them cry, shout, or moan because they have experienced similar hurt and disappointment or, in blues vernacular, have "paid [similar] dues" or "gone through the same changes." By identifying with the suffering of the individual, the group seeks to bring the individual into harmony with the group. This is the essence of traditional African culture in practice. As Mbiti (1970) wrote, the traditional African view is that "the individual does not exist except corporately. He owes his existence to other people, including those of past generations and his contemporaries" (p. 141). Mbiti wrote,

> *Only in terms of other people does the individual become conscious of his own being, his own duties, his privileges, and responsibilities toward himself and toward other people. When he suffers, he does not suffer alone but with the corporate group; when he rejoices, he rejoices not alone but with his kinsmen, his neighbors and his relatives whether dead or living.* (p. 141)

MOURNING WORK IN TRADITIONAL AFRICA

The mourning work of traditional African culture entailed the same philosophical and practice orientation as the mourning work of the slaves and the rural black people after emancipation. As far back as 1909, the sociologist–social worker Monroe N. Work held that much of the African work of mourning was also geared toward the problem of loss and separation. Work (1909) stressed, for example, that the explorer and missionary Stanley Livingstone had discovered among African captives what to Livingstone was "the strangest disease" he had ever encountered; the disease of "broken-heartedness" (p. 434), an illness that proved fatal. Work wrote that Livingstone mentioned an instance of a large number of captives who "endured their chains until they saw the Lualabo River roll between them and their free homes. Then they lost heart. Many of them died within three days after crossing" (p. 435). Livingstone recalled that African "children for a time would keep up with wondered endurance, but it happened sometimes that the sound of dancing and the merry tinkle of the small drums would fall on their ears when passing a near village. Then the memory of home and happy days proved too much for them. They cried and sobbed, the broken heart came on, and they rapidly sank" (quoted in Work, 1909, p. 435).

In traditional Africa, mourning over lost loved ones was a highly ritualized healing art form and an extremely emotional experience. Even in contemporary Africa, the mourning work is more than just an individual or family event; it is a public ordeal. For example, Somé (1994) showed that mourning work among the Dagara people of Burkina Faso in 1994 was not different in the slightest from what Work described in 1909. Somé held that at Dagara funerals, the members of the immediate family are always accompanied by the group to help them purge their grief. He related that it is not individual or familial grief but public grief. Somé wrote that "unlike people in the West, the Dagara believe it is terrible to suppress one's grief" and that "only by passionate expression can loss be tamed and assimilated into a form one can live with" (p. 57). He found that "the Dagara also believe that the dead have a right to collect their share of fears" and maintained that "without music and chanting there is no funeral, no grief, no death" (p. 57). Somé wrote,

> The chanters, standing behind the musicians, began their mournful songs, piercing the hearts of the crowd with sorrow. It was their job to provide structure for the crowd to release their pent-up feelings. Each doleful phrase was followed by a huge howling, begun by the men and concluded by the women. It takes millions of tears to produce a flood capable of washing the dead to the realm of the ancestors. . . . Rhythm and chanting crack open that part of the self that holds grief under control. But grief unleashed without the help of ritual drummers, musicians, and chanters runs the risk of producing another death. (p. 57)

After spending days, sometimes even weeks, grieving and properly sending the dead to the ancestors, the mourning work increasingly becomes a celebration as the general atmosphere turns festive, indicating that the mourning work is complete. After the group work of mourning is done, mourning follow-up work is turned over to the family who must continue to pay homage to the deceased person by pouring libation, offering ritual sacrifice, and other means of retaining memory. It is only after group work and family work fails that the individual feels compelled and is even urged to move from traditional African group and family work to traditional African casework. For example, if the grief of an individual is prolonged and becomes pathological, that is, jeopardizing his or her mental health and affecting social relations, he or she could turn to traditional caregivers such as medicine men, witch doctors, root doctors, mediums, diviners, and sorcerers for assistance. However, even on a casework-type basis, any physical, emotional, or spiritual misfortune or calamity the individual might suffer is generally seen by these African clinical-type social workers in respect to the group or collective experience. This means that even the individual problems are perceived in respect to the individual's moving away from or violating the traditions of the group as sanctioned and handed down by the ancestors. The emphasis traditional African people placed on the collective identification with one another's suffering, public grief, music as a crucial form of emotional release, and group problem solving was carried over into the slavery experience. This identification was indicated, for example, by what slaves called "the ring shout."

THE RING SHOUT

The circle ceremonies of western African societies, where most American slaves originated, were used to carry out important group functions such as weddings, communion with the ancestors, and, most important, the burial ritual. The circle symbolized the unbroken unity of birth, life, and death and functioned to maintain group solidarity and cohesiveness. According to Stuckey (1987), the circle ceremony provides the key to understanding the means by which the many different African people brought to America on slave ships achieved oneness.

The slaves called the circle ceremony "the ring shout." The ring shout was a religious ceremony in which they gathered at the grave site of their dead and at other clandestine places; formed a ring and, moving counterclockwise, called on God and on the ancestral spirits; danced; sang; moaned; and "shouted out" their misery, pain, and grief. The use of the grave site as their common meeting place indicated an ancestral connectedness and a historical empathy with the suffering of past generations. As fellow mourners, they conducted the mourning work of collective catharsis and healing as the ring shout provided the context in which mourning work could take place. During the ring shout ceremony, it did not matter what tribe or ethnic or national group slaves had come from in Africa; because the circle ceremony was such a prominent feature of African culture, the ring shout was a religious practice with which most African people could identify. Thus, when someone took to the center of the ring and sang "Sometimes, I feel like a motherless child, a long way from home" or "Deep river, my home is over Jordan," he or she was articulating an emotion that all black people lamenting their broken ties to their spiritual and cultural roots could understand and identify with. The rhythm, the group precision, the group solidarity, and the emotionalism of the ring shouts alone were enough to help black people feel that even though they had lost their African home and ways, they were still a part of a family, a clan, and a loving black nation. The ring shouts were an original African tool of self-expression. White people could only observe. One white witness of a ring shout observed,

Three or four standing still, clapping their hands and beating with their feet, commence singing in unison one of the peculiar shout melodies, while the others walk round in a ring, in single file, joining also in the song. Soon those in the ring leave off their singing, the others keeping it up the while with increased vigor, and strike into the short step, observing most accurate time with the music. This step is something halfway between a shuffle and a dance, as difficult for an uninitiated person to describe as to imitate. At the end of each stanza of the song the dancers stop short with a slight stamp on the last note, and then, putting the other foot forward, proceed through the next verse. . . . They will often dance to the same song for twenty or thirty minutes. (quoted in Webber, 1978, p. 199)

GROUP ONENESS

These ring shouts, similar to the circle ceremonies in traditional Africa, were designed to promote group solidarity or group oneness. The spirituals, which were designed to bind black people together psychologically and emotionally, grew out of the ring shouts, and together these cultural forms provided slaves a social context in which they could avoid trying to deal with the harsh, cold realities of their existence alone. Frederick Douglass (1883) held that group solidarity among his fellow slaves was so strong that "no band of brothers could be more loving. . . . We never undertook anything of any importance which was likely to affect each other, without mutual consultation. . . . We were generally a unit, and moved together" (p. 153).

The slaves did not have many options in respect to their reactions to slavery. They could accommodate, role play, fight back (basically a suicidal act), or take flight (an extremely perilous and risky undertaking). It was only natural that they would band together for group solidarity and survival. It was also natural that the black extended family on the slave plantation would become the model for group solidarity and oneness. Slaves formed tightly knit fictive kinship ties and referred to one another as "brother," "sister," "auntie," "uncle," and "granny," whether they were related by blood or not. These ties were cemented by social obligations and mutual reciprocity. As one ex-slave explained, when someone got sick, even nonrelated slaves would come over to help with the children, cook the meals, wash the clothes, and do other necessary chores:

It wasn't like it is today when everybody seem like they trying only to git the dollar. Women would come over jus' to sit a spell an' sing an' pray 'roun' the sick bed. Nobody was lef' to suffer alone. Sometimes a man or woman with a healin' touch would brew a herb tea, mix a poultice, or apply peach tree leaves to fevered brow, to help the sick git well. All of this lovin' care cheer' up the trouble' soul, whether he got well or died. (quoted in Stuckey, 1987, p. 39)

Because slaves saw one another as fellow mourners and fellow sufferers, it was not a stigma to have a problem or ask others for help. Slaves sought to emphasize the commonality of their suffering. Hence, they frowned on individuals they called "tattlers" or "black Judases" who threatened group survival. They also harbored disdain for slaves who had become so brutalized by white oppression that they became indifferent to the suffering of others. Some slaves were so debased that they taunted slaves who were punished, whose relatives were sold, or who failed at attempts to escape. Slaves hated black people who had achieved some status or success but used it to further the oppression of other black people. In this category were those black slave drivers who were just as cruel to black people as white slave drivers were. For example, one black slave driver whipped his own wife so severely for stealing food from the master's house to help feed the driver's own children that she never recovered (Van Debury, 1979). Also in this category were black slave owners who treated their slaves as brutally as any white slave owner and black slave catchers and bounty hunters who tracked down fugitive slaves and brought them from freedom back to slavery.

Slaves held in high regard black people who were able to maintain close, lasting, mutually rewarding ties to loved ones, kin, neighbors, and friends without harming other black people in the process. They had high regard for black people who identified with the suffering of other black people, sought to relieve it, and sought to reinforce in the sufferer that a better day was coming. They made folk heroes of black people who could maneuver around any trap set for them by the white oppressor. The ring shouts, the spirituals, and the group identification and oneness helped them overcome the self-hating psychology of cultural paranoia directed against black people and helped them develop an ability to mourn.

That slaves sought to bring deviant black people back into the fold of the group does not mean that they did not allow for individual self-expression. We have already indicated that the ring shout allowed each individual to take a place in the ring to give testimony to personal suffering and joy. Slaves generally felt that the group did not restrict individual expression but enhanced it. Lovell (1972) wrote,

The community role did not substitute for the individual role, nor did it encroach upon the individual role. Yes, you had to walk the lonesome valley for yourself, but from another standpoint, when you combined with your "band" or with your relatives and friends, you could get more and different things done. You could also have experiences that gave you a different slant and insight from those of the individual alone. (pp. 275–276)

The work of mourning carried out by the slaves not only gave the individual a sense of security and strength and the recognition and reassurance of the group, but in many cases, it helped the individual preserve his or her true inner self. By viewing individual problems as common problems, slaves overcame individual feelings of stigma and shame. By working collectively to solve problems, they relieved the individual of the emotional and psychological pressures and tensions of trying to deal with one's burdens alone. The emphasis the spirituals and other elements of their culture placed on faith, hope, and uplift kept many black individuals from succumbing to defeatism, alienation, despair, and fatalism and gave them hope that they would realize true self desires or play a crucial role in helping others to do so. If it were not for the spirituals, the ring shouts, and other collective expressions of mourning, the individual would not have survived the emotional and psychological damage of slavery by attempting to go it alone. He or she would have been hopelessly marred and immobilized by oppression and overwhelmed by the emotionally constricting psychology of cultural claustrophobia.

THE INSTITUTIONALIZATION OF MOURNING

After emancipation, ring shouts gave way to the institutionalized black church, but black people did not give up their mourning work. They were still under the yoke of racial oppression, and they still needed the psychological and spiritual healing, therapy, and support necessary for overcoming their oppression. Thus, instead of giving up their mourning work, they took it a step further and institutionalized it in their churches, their extended families, and even their schools. Black people after emancipation knew that mourning work was still necessary not only to promote group solidarity and provide group therapy but to combat spiritually and emotionally the genocidal acts of aggression waged by white society against black people.

THE RURAL BLACK CHURCH

The black church became the primary mourning institution as the ring shouts were transformed into praise houses and praise houses developed into full-blown black churches. The mourning bench of the black church replaced the cemetery where the ring shouts usually took place. The black church became the chief place where black people could still give their own individual testimonies while simultaneously shouting until the glory in their souls turned night into day.

> *O shout, O shout, O shout away*
> *And don't you mind*
> *And glory, glory, glory in my soul.*

In the black church, black people could continue to express themselves with the most fervent emotionalism. Johnston (1954) held that just like the slave religion, the rural black church still "provided two psychological functions: first, catharsis, ridding the personality of strain and stress, second, concentration upon Heaven, providing a prospect and hope for an after-world of happiness" (p. 41). Just like in the ring shouts, the spirituals in the institutional black church were viewed not just as music to be entertained by but social therapy necessary for the group's spiritual and material advancement.

Few authors have captured the spirit of the black church's mourning as well as the black writer James Baldwin (1985) when he wrote,

> *The church was very exciting. It took a long time for me to disengage*
> *myself from this excitement, and on the blindest, most visceral level,*
> *I never really have, and never will. There is no music like that music,*

no drama like the drama of the saints rejoicing, the sinners moaning,
the tambourines racing, and all those voices coming together and
crying holy unto the Lord. . . . I have never seen anything to equal
the fire and excitement that sometimes, without warning, fill a
church, causing the church, as Leadbelly and so many others have
testified, to "rock." Nothing that has happened to me since equals
the power and the glory that I sometimes felt when, in the middle of
a sermon, I knew that I was somehow, by some miracle, really
carrying, as they said, "the Word"—when the church and I were one.
Their pain and their joy were mine, and mine were theirs—they
surrendered their pain and joy to me, I surrendered mine to them—
and their cries of "Amen!" and "Hallelujah!" and "Yes, Lord!" and
"Praise His name!" and "Preach it, brother!" sustained and whipped
on my solos until we all became equal, wringing wet, singing and
dancing, in anguish and rejoicing, at the foot of the altar. (pp.
345–346)

Baldwin described mourning work at its essence, when the pain and
the joys of the black fellow mourners become one.

THE BLACK EXTENDED FAMILY

Mourning work in the black extended family started in slavery and
continued in the rural black extended family after slavery. Because
being separated from loved ones was a persistent part of the slave
family existence, slave families had many losses to mourn. Hence,
they carried their mourning work from ring shouts in the fields and
the secret meeting places to their homes. For example, an ex-slave,
Mose Hurley, recalled that the mourning work in his slave family
made a deep impression on him:

On Sundays they had meetin', sometimes at our house, sometimes at
nether house. . . . They'd preach and pray and sing—shout too. I
heard them git up with a powerful force of the spirit, clappin' they
hands and walkin' round the place. They'd shout, "I got the glory. I
got that old time 'ligion in my heart." (quoted in Raboteau, 1978,
p. 221)

We stated in another book that the mutual caregiving or therapeutic thrust in the black experience evolved from the extended
family and was extended via fictive kinship, religious consciousness, and race consciousness to the entire black community (Martin
& Martin, 1985). One former slave lends credence to our observation:

> *At night, especially in the summertime, after everybody had eaten*
> *supper, it was a common thing for us to sit outside. The old folk*
> *would get together and talk until bedtime. Sometimes somebody*
> *would start humming an old hymn, and then the next-door neighbor*
> *would pick it up. In this way, it would finally get around to every*
> *house, and then the music started. Soon everybody would be gathered*
> *together, and such singing! It wouldn't be long before some of the*
> *slaves got happy and started to shouting.* (quoted in Raboteau,
> 1978, p. 221)

E. Franklin Frazier (1949) wrote that the black extended family
after emancipation gave black people such a sense of nurturance,
security, and belongingness that sometimes even the tribeless black
men had become so disillusioned with big-city life that they had
"memories of the secure affection and sympathy of the wife or children they left behind" (p. 277) and "a hidden longing for the secure
affection of families or an abiding attachment of an illegitimate
child that had been left along the way with extended family kin"
(p. 289). However, Frazier said, these longings for a sense of family
and community were usually only temporary because the deep fear
of losing would inevitably trigger the dominating force in their
lives: the fear of getting too close.

Most rural black people still clung tenaciously to their extended
families. They knew that although the selling, buying, and trading
of their loved ones was banned by law, black people were still confronted with a brutal racism that had myriad ways of breaking or
destroying black families. They knew that they could still turn to
their kin for material support and emotional therapy when they
could turn to no one else. They knew that the black extended family, not the church, was the primary caregiver in the black community and that it was the most significant black institution "for the

economic and emotional well-being of countless numbers of blacks over the generations" (Martin & Martin, 1978, p. 29).

INSTILLING HOPE

So important was the instillation of hope in the mourning work of slaves that they brought the weight of their entire culture—their folktales, humor, secular music, dance, and religion—to be used toward this end. Without hope, slaves sensed that they would die spiritually and emotionally and become the mindless, docile imbeciles the slave holders sought to mold. Therefore, their singing and shouting and sharing and caring were not just to ease the hunger, the cold, the beatings, and the separations so they could just endure slavery. They wanted to endure it because they had hopes that they would receive a better life and hopes that their children would one day know a better life.

Solomon Northup, a free black man who was kidnapped and sold into slavery, said "Had it not been for my beloved violin, I scarcely can conceive how I could have endured the long years of bondage. Often, at midnight, when sleep had fled . . . and my soul disturbed with the contemplation of my fate, it would sing me a song of peace" (quoted in Osofsky, 1969, p. 334). Dancing was also a key tool of relieving stress as indicated by an ex-slave's comment that his slave master could not understand how he could be seen dancing shortly after receiving 200 lashes:

They say slaves are happy because they laugh, and are merry. I myself and three or four others, have received two hundred lashes in the day, and had our feet in fetters; yet, at night, we would sing and dance and make others laugh at the rattling of our chains. Happy men we must have been! We did it to keep down trouble, and to keep our hearts from being completely broken. . . . I have done it myself— I have cut capers in chains. (Thurman, 1975, p. 17)

Religion, dance, song, and humor were all rolled up into one indispensable cultural tool for helping black people endure so that they would one day know freedom. Without hope of a better life on this earth and in heaven there was no reason for slaves to want to endure. Without hope, suicide would have been viewed as an option, given the pain, misery, and degradation of the slaves.

The black extended family and the black church were basically black survival institutions, even institutions of accommodation, helping black people adjust to their oppression. However, in their mourning work, rural black people used these institutions to instill hope. The black church continued the collective empathy with suffering and continued to be a sacred forum for sending out profound messages of hope. Living under semislavery-type conditions, rural black people after emancipation still found it difficult to keep from succumbing to alienation and despair and giving up on life all together. They realized that their prospect for a life free from the burdens, hardships, and trials of being black in a hostile white-dominated society were not much better than the prospect slaves had for a better life. This dim prospect made it difficult to keep hope alive and to hold fast to dreams that they would one day be able to protect their loved ones, break out of the stifling confines of their inner selves, and take full control of their destiny.

The black church might have provided a means for expressing feelings of being "done with this troubled world," and hence advancing a spirit of resignation, but black people also sang "we'll run and never tire," which is a spirit of hope, endurance, and overcoming. The black church was often an institution of accommodation, even escapism, because it often overemphasized the afterlife, but it was also an institution of transcendence. As Thurman (1975) pointed out, the preacher of the black church was often an accommodationist but he also "gave the masses of his fellow men a point of view that became for them a veritable Door of Hope. He told them in many ways: 'You are not slaves, you are not niggers, you are God's children'" (p. 17). Oliver C. Cox (1948) wrote,

> *Probably no one who has seen the Negro preacher in his cabin in the South, marching triumphantly over the King's English amid great surges of "Amen! Amen!!" And "Yes, Lord!" Lifting his congregation in repeated affirmation of faith and hope, could fail to realize that these people are far from being resigned in spirit. Their spontaneous songs of freedom and courage in the face of great trial . . . are not*

unlike in emotion the spirit of liberty which has everywhere in Christendom moved men to action. (pp. 441–442)

Lovell (1972) wrote that "the message of such songs as 'Hold out to the End' and 'Keep Your Hand on the Plow, Hold on' . . . sounded like a religious or an other wordly song to others (but) . . . often the songs which mentioned or implied heaven were created to encourage the group to look upward, to reach for high goals in this life" (p. 277). The rural black church sought to instill hope by getting black people to believe that God was a just God and that God would see them through the storm. In these black houses of worship, singing and praying went hand in hand in helping black people to believe "There's a better day a-coming, fare you, well, fare you well" when all their "troubles would soon be over." They sang:

Keep prayin
I do believe
We'll git home
Bye and bye.

Frances Grimké wrote "Praying was their only weapon at that time, and how mightily did they wield it" (quoted in Woodson, 1942, p. 279). "Every day, every night, almost every hour in the day, the cry of their bleeding hearts was poured into the ears of heaven" (p. 247). Prayer gave them hope that one day a just God would hear their fervent cries and set them free.

Extended families in rural black life were basically survival institutions concerned mainly with keeping family members together and alive and extending that invitation to the wider black community. Extended families also adopted the mourning theme of instilling hope. For the protection of their young people, families had to teach them the etiquette of race relations, that is, how to get along with white people; this often meant teaching them deference and obsequious behavior. A black father in the 1940s related how he used his own experience to instruct black children:

When I go to a white man's house I stands in the yard and yells, and he comes to the door. If he tells me to come then I goes up to the door to talk to him, and I don't go in unless he tell me. If he tell me,

then I goes in, but I don't set down lessen he tell me. And I don't
talk to white folks direct like I does to colored. I lets him do the
talking, let him take the lead. That's what he wants, and if he says
something to me that I don't like, I says, "now Mr. so-and-so, don't
you think I oughta do such and such a thing," and then mos' likely
he say yes, but you better not go straight at the thing with a white
man, he'll think you're smart. Yes, suh, I tells any chillen to do lak
that. That's the way to get along. (quoted in Johnston, 1954,
p. 247)

Although there is no doubt that black parents and grandparents, concerned with protecting their children in a dangerous and hostile environment, instilled in them their own old accommodation ways and habits, black extended family members nevertheless sought to give their children a sense of personal worth, tried to prevent them from developing feelings of inferiority, and attempted to give them a dignified conception of themselves and their place in the world. Hence, the spirit of uplift, hope, and transcendence extended from the church to the black extended family. Faced with bitter, vengeful white people, extended family members did indeed encourage their children not to rock the boat, but they also were the first to give children a sense of their worth in a world that thought them to be worthless except as cheap labor. They were generally the first to tell them they were beautiful in a world that viewed them with ugly contempt, and they were usually the first to tell black children that despite the hardships, it was possible for them in this life "to make a way out of no way." Langston Hughes brilliantly captured the black family's uplift mood in his poem "Mother to son":

So boy don't you turn back.
Don't you sit down on the steps
'cause you find it's kinder hard.
Don't you fall now—
for I'se still goin' honey
I'se still climbin'
And life for me ain't been no crystal stair.
(cited in Rampersad, 1986, pp. 43–44)

In the rural South after emancipation, black schools also inherited the mourning spirit of hope. Grossly underpaid black teachers in shady backwoods and segregated schools often encouraged accommodation as a survival mechanism because they knew that even a trifle such as speaking "good," clear, and correct English could get a black person lynched. They knew that being "uppity" was one of the gravest crimes a black person could commit. They knew that white society valued the black laborer more than it valued the black professional. Nevertheless, black teachers were successful in convincing thousands of rural black students that a "nigger's place" existed only as a figment of the white man's mind, made black people feel that they were not only capable of learning but worthy of a better life, and gave them a vision of a worldview beyond tobacco and cotton fields, lynch ropes, and chain gangs. To give black people confidence in their ability, to inspire them to higher levels of achievement, to help them to trust in the guidance of the elders, and to broaden their outlook, options, and alternatives to become more versatile were the black masses' own way of combatting and overcoming the negative psychologies of cultural sickness, cultural paranoia, and cultural claustrophobia.

EARLY BLACK CAREGIVERS AND MOURNING

Early black lay caregivers, meaning those who were not academically trained specifically for social work, had no problems drawing from the mourning work of the black masses. They incorporated the mourning tradition in their own social services delivery systems. They did not need W.E.B. DuBois (1969) to call for a "talented tenth" of black people with special ability, talent, superior intellect, training, and education to help elevate the submerged 90 percent of black people. They were already under the influence of black mourning institutions, such as churches, schools, and extended families, that obligated them to identify with and mourn with their people. Janie Porter Barrett, an early black social welfare worker, indicated how vigorously inculcated in black youths was the idea that educated black people had to "be a credit to the race" (quoted in Neverdon-Morton, 1989, p. 105). In 1909, she recalled that during her college years at Hampton Institute "I did not love my race! I didn't want the responsibility of it. I wanted fun and pretty things. At the institute we were always hearing about our duty to our race, and I got so tired of that! Why, on Sundays I used to wake up and say to myself, 'Today, I don't have to do a single thing for my race!'" (quoted in Neverdon-Morton, 1989, pp. 105–106). However, she recalled that the message soon got through and before long she truly believed. Barrett's commitment to black advancement was so strong that she established the Locust Street Social Settlement in Hampton, Virginia, one of the first efforts of black people at settlement work.

Barrett made it clear that not only was her settlement house built around a race identification but also around what she called "the spirit of Christ." Black social settlement workers like Barrett warned social workers that although they were extolling the scientific method, they should not rule out the role of spirituality and religiosity in their clients' lives.

THE EXTENDED FAMILY AS A MODEL

Although early black caregivers were motivated by religious feelings and incorporated spirituals, prayers, and a belief in the power of God into their caregiving systems, the black extended family, not the black church, was their ideal model. They were not romanticizing the black extended family, because everyone knew that some families had stronger ties than others and that relatives did not always get along. What they recognized was that vital elements of the black extended family, such as mutual aid, male–female equality, social class cooperation, and the prosocialization of children, could be carried over into social services institutions. Indeed, these elements were carried from the extended family via fictive kinship, racial consciousness, and religious consciousness to the wider black community (Martin & Martin, 1985). As a result, when early black caregivers established old folks' homes, orphanages, women's clubs, settlement houses, and benevolent societies, they modeled their caregiving institutions after the black extended family, organizing them around basic extended family values.

At the turn of the 20th century, black women emerged as the leading caregivers in the black community. They organized themselves into women's clubs that carried out myriad caregiving functions in the black community, outdistancing the black church in this regard. Black women were the leading caregivers in the black extended family, and the women's clubs represented an extension of their caregiving roles. The primary concentration of the women's clubs was on black women who had to bear most of the burden of caring for ill people, indigent people, people with disabilities, people who were mentally ill, older people, dependent children, and other needy black people within their own extended families. These women were overburdened with caring and suffered in a sense a caring overload. The women's clubs helped to relieve the family burden of individual black women as they sought collectively to solve basic family matters. The chief target of their efforts were those black people who had lost a sense of family and community, people such as orphaned and delinquent children, "wayward girls," old black people without families, and convicts. Their concern was not with a so-called deserving poor, but a deep need to pay particular attention to black people who were torn from family and community ties. We reiterate, black families have had a historical dread of and sensitivity to separation and loss and had been stressing communal obligations and group solidarity as far back as traditional Africa.

When black women built caregiving institutions, most of these resources were designed to bring stranded elements of the black community under a type of extended family security and caring. For example, Janie Porter Barrett's Locust Street Social Settlement was modeled after the extended family because it concentrated on needy older black people and black children. When Amelia Perry Pride founded the Dorchester Home for the Elderly in Lynchburg, Virginia, in 1896 she stated that she did so because she was "appalled by the deplorable conditions in which elderly black women who did not have family to care for them were forced to live" (quoted in Neverdon-Morton, 1989, p. 109). In 1898, Carrie Steele founded the Carrie Steele Orphanage in Atlanta, Georgia, because she was "intimately acquainted with the hardships endured by orphans because, born a slave, she [herself] was orphaned at an early age" and she had witnessed black orphans, half-orphans, and neglected and dependent black children being used as servants to serve the white orphans, "waiting on them hand

and foot" (quoted in Neverdon-Morton, 1989, pp. 143–144). In 1908, Lugenia Burns Hope founded the Neighborhood Union in Atlanta, Georgia, after learning that one woman was found dying alone without her neighbor's knowledge of her suffering (Neverdon-Morton, 1989). Hope knew that in the past, black neighbors looked after one another as if they were family and that such a tragedy would not have happened. The union was formed to help black people teach other black people once again how to mourn the suffering of their neighbors.

Black male caregivers also modeled caregiving institutions on the extended family's emphasis on family togetherness. John H. Smythe, a black reform leader at the turn of the century, was concerned about the tendency of white judicial officials to put delinquent white boys and girls in reformatories while placing delinquent black boys and girls in jails and penitentiaries. This concern led him to seek a more family-type atmosphere for young black offenders. In 1897, Smythe became the head of the Virginia Negro Reformatory in Richmond, Virginia; the reformatory was funded almost solely by black people. Smythe was so adamant in his fight to keep black youths out of prison that he held that "it would be better to kill the unhappy children of my race than to wreck their souls by holding them in prison with common and hardened criminals" (quoted in Pollard, 1978, p. 103). Throughout the nation, it was not unusual to see black boys and girls as young as six, seven, and eight years of age with the regulation prison stripes on and fighting for survival among vicious seasoned adult prisoners. Smythe's reformatory became a model for other reformatory work among black people across the country.

Reverend Daniel Jenkins's Orphan Aid Society, founded in 1891, also became a model institution. Although uneducated and penniless, Jenkins raised enough money to purchase a farm on the outskirts of Charleston, South Carolina, that became the leading institution in the state for caring for orphans, half-orphans, and neglected black children (Pollard, 1978). Jenkins's society grew from four children in 1891 to 536 children in 1896. Another black male caregiver, Reverend B. J. Bridges, gathered up "the young idle independent orphans and blacks from the streets, alleys and gutters of the towns and cities of Georgia" (Pollard, 1978, pp. 104–105) and brought them under extended family–type care in the Georgia Colored Industrial and Orphans' Home, which he founded in 1900.

Given this tradition of viewing the black extended family as an ideal social service model, it is no wonder that in contemporary society the code of ethics of the National Association of Black Social Workers (1995) includes the pledge to "adopt the concept of a black extended family and embrace all black people as my brothers and sisters, making no distinction between their destiny and my own."

CLOSENESS TO THE BLACK MASSES

By using the extended family as a model and by incorporating religion and black music into their caregiving practices with black people, early black caregivers enjoyed a closeness to the black masses that would be the envy of social workers today. Because they had some insight into black culture and black needs as black people defined them, early black caregivers were less moralistic and paternalistic in their view of black people. This does not mean that they accepted black culture uncritically or incorporated all aspects of it. However, by having some insight into the people's lives, they knew what cultural elements to keep and what to discard. For example, when Amelia Perry Pride, the founder of the Dorchester Home for the Elderly, found that old black people at the turn of the 20th century had a habit of wearing layers of old dirty clothes and not bathing in the winter, she could have interpreted this behavior in a number of ways (Pollard, 1978). She could have easily adopted the racist notion that was so pervasive during that time and held that the people did not bathe because black people basically are an inferior, filthy, smelly race. She could have even held that they wore dirty clothes and did not bathe because they had not had middle-class virtues instilled in them; after all, "cleanliness is next to Godliness." However, because she understood the cultural background of these black people, Pride also understood that black people generally had such poor housing in the rural South—shabby huts and rundown shacks that were often extremely cold in the winter—and rural black people, especially older ones, felt that many layers of clothes would keep them warm and that a bath in the winter, especially in a cold hovel, would prove fatal (by leading to pneumonia). Thus, instead of judging and condemning these old black people and taking on an air of class superiority or applying popular racial stereotypes to them, she convinced them that the nursing home was warm, that they no longer lived in cold shanties and shacks, and that bathing periodically would add to their longevity and health and not put them in their graves. Even then she said that breaking this old habit was no easy matter because it took quite a bit of convincing to keep some of the older people from putting clean gowns on over their layers of rags.

We generally tell social work students that if social workers do not explore black culture they will never be able to discern what traditions are functional to black people. Pride understood that the cultural habit of not bathing in the winter was one that had to go; but she would not dare throw out their spirituals and their religious worship with the bathwater. These she would definitely retain because as social work moved from reform to repression, these old features of black culture were still the best psychological or therapeutic tools that the black masses had for soothing troubled souls and for being able to face another day.

BLACK PROFESSIONAL SOCIAL WORK AND MOURNING

It should be clear that by the time helping became professionalized in the black community, there was already a foundation for the development of a black experience–based social work practice. Black people had already developed their own methods for the identification of the problem. They had already developed a philosophy of helping geared toward maintaining the solidarity, identity, and survival of the group; a concept of normality and deviancy; a social context for helping; and a social work practice modality emphasizing collective empathy, collective oneness, and collective hope. Within the black practice paradigm, group and community work did not necessarily take precedence over casework, but there were no clear lines between them because the individual was first expected to try to solve his or her problem within the group context and, only after failing on that level, see a casework or clinical specialist such as a witch doctor or conjurer or engage in a one-on-

one counseling session with a wise elder or preacher. Black people had already perfected a healing or therapeutic art form, using music, humor, and every aspect of their culture in the therapeutic process, and they had already institutionalized the black helping tradition. More significantly, earlier black lay caregivers had already incorporated elements of black folk culture into their practice techniques, using the black extended family as a model.

Black traditional healing and helping forms did much to stave off the general feelings of inferiority, alienation, and depersonalization that stem from the psychologies of cultural sickness and cultural claustrophobia. However, as the migrants sought to forget the old ways, their old helping techniques were less effective before the onslaught of urban individualism and racial exclusion. The old black methods of mourning needed to be synthesized with the new "scientific" methods of the professional social worker.

Black professional social workers did not turn, however, to the history and culture of the black masses. They did not incorporate relevant elements of the black experience into social work practice. If they had, they would have forged a helping tool with which the masses could identify, but one more advanced and effective. If they had synthesized the old with the new, they would have enjoyed closer contact with the black masses and would have been viewed as fellow mourners with the expertise to enhance mourning work among black people. The expert help of trained social workers would have led to significant improvement in homes for older people, orphanages, reformatories, and settlement houses run by lay black people with little knowledge of administration, organization, fundraising, and treatment of serious mental disorders. Even the more successful black caregiving institutions run by highly educated and talented black people often operated largely out of faith and a strong desire to help. Few had a systematic, planned program of social healing and social change. If black professional social workers had incorporated pertinent aspects of black culture, they would have been in a better position to help these institutions in their mourning work and to help black people take the initiative in creating the healing-developing community, that is, a community that has to heal the psychological and emotional wounds of its history before it can rise to its highest height.

What black professional social workers discovered was that with all of their "science," and even with all their advocacy and activism on behalf of black people, it appeared to the black masses that they were selling foreign ideas. When black social workers began to find employment in social welfare settings that were set up primarily for social control and social containment purposes, they distanced themselves further from the black masses. They came to be viewed as black people who were incapable of helping to carry out the work of mourning and, worse, as black individuals themselves who lacked an ability to mourn.

REFERENCES

Baldwin, J. (1985). The fire next time. In J. Baldwin (Ed.), *The price of the ticket* (pp. 333–380). New York: St. Martin's/Marek.

Barrett, H. (1912). Negro folk songs. *Southern Workman, 41,* 238–245.

Cox, O. C. (1948). *Caste, class and race.* New York: Monthly Review Press.

Douglass, F. (1883). *Life and times of Frederick Douglass.* Secaucus, NJ: Citadel Press.

DuBois, W.E.B. (1969). The talented tenth. In B. T. Washington et al. (Eds.), *The Negro problem* (pp. 54–61). New York: Arno Press.

Ellison, R. (1964). *Shadow and act.* New York: Random House.

Frazier, E. F. (1949). *The Negro family in the United States.* Chicago: University of Chicago Press.

Johnston, R. F. (1954). *The development of Negro religion.* New York: Philosophical Library.

Locke, A. (1969). The Negro spirituals. In A. Gayle, Jr. (Ed.), *Black expression* (pp. 48–49). New York: Weybright & Talley.

Lovell, J., Jr. (1972). *Black song.* New York: Macmillan.

Martin, E. P., & Martin, J. M. (1978). *The black extended family.* Chicago: University of Chicago Press.

Martin, E. P., & Martin, J. M. (1985). *The helping tradition in the black family and community.* Silver Spring, MD: National Association of Social Workers.

Mbiti, J. S. (1970). *African religion and philosophy.* Garden City, NY: Anchor Books.

National Association of Black Social Workers. (1995). *Code of ethics.* Washington, DC: Author.

Neal, L. (1989). *Visions of a liberated future.* New York: Thunder Mouth Press.

Neverdon-Morton, C. (1989). *Afro-American women of the South and the advancement of the race, 1825–1925.* Knoxville: University of Tennessee Press.

Osofsky, G. (Ed.). (1969). *Puttin' on ole massa: The slave narratives of Henry Bibb, William Wells Brown, and Solomon Northup.* New York: Harper & Row.

Pasteur, A. B., & Toldson, I. L. (1982). *Roots of soul.* New York: Anchor Press/Doubleday.

Pollard, W. (1978). *A study in black self-help.* San Francisco: R. & E. Associates.

Raboteau, A. J. (1978). *Slave religion.* New York: Oxford University Press.

Rampersad, A. (1986). *The life of Langston Hughes: Vol. 1. 1902–1941.* New York: Oxford University Press.

Smith, T. M. (1994). *Conjuring culture.* New York: Oxford University Press.

Somé, M. P. (1994). *Of water and the spirit.* New York: G. P. Putnam's Sons.

Stuckey, S. (1987). *Slave culture.* New York: Oxford University Press.

Thurman, H. (1975). *Deep rivers and the Negro speaks of rivers.* Richmond, IN: Friends United Press.

Van Debury, W. L. (1979). *The slave drivers.* Westport, CT: Greenwood Press.

Webber, T. L. (1978). *Deep like the rivers.* New York: W. W. Norton.

Woodson, C. G. (Ed.). (1942). *The work of Francis J. Grimké (Vol. 1).* Washington, DC: Associated Publishers.

Work, M. N. (1909, August). The African family as an institution. *Southern Workman, 38,* 433–442.

CHAPTER 6

Black Clients, Social Work, and the Inability to Mourn

*R*ural black people used their own mourning institutions and techniques to help them overcome the crippling psychologies of cultural sickness, cultural paranoia, and cultural claustrophobia and thus become daring, motivated, confident, and determined to seek a better life and put their destiny in their own hands. However, the ways of the city were antithetical to their rural traditions, and the rural cultural tools black people had developed to combat or cope with negative psychologies became weakened. They sorely needed the help of the social work professional not just to find jobs but to help keep the old psychology of cultural paranoia, deep mistrust of white people, from turning into a deep distrust in themselves and thus creating social antagonism and divisiveness at variance with their development. Without societal intervention and a synthesis of professional social work and the black helping tradition, the secularistic, individualistic, and materialistic thrust of urban culture caused deep erosion in black mourning work, creating a disturbing and widespread pattern of an inability to mourn among urban black people.

THE DESTRUCTION OF THE OLD–TIME RELIGION

Even before black people moved to the city, bourgeois black people and liberal white people had manifested a belief that the religious practices of the rural black masses were excessively emotional, primitive, savage, and even un-Christian. Litwack (1979) wrote that shortly after emancipation, hordes of black and white missionaries and ministers went to the South to impose their "civilizing"

124

influences on these "backward" people. He wrote that white ministers conceded a certain admiration for the "simple and childlike"
faith of the freedmen, their evident "sincerity and earnestness,"
their "implicit belief in Providence," their demonstrated love of
prayer, and the powerful emotional impact of their music and
hymns, but he said the ministers were appalled by "the emotional
wildness and extravagance, the unlettered preaching, the incoher-
ent speeches and prayers, the 'narrowness' of the religious knowledge, and the evidently strong survivals of superstition and pagan-
ism" (p. 459).

The organized black churches, such as the African Methodist
Episcopal (AME) church, and the educated black ministers felt
embarrassed by such excessive emotionalism, frenzy, and religious
"heathenism" and declared war on the old-time religion of the rural
people. The *Christian Recorder,* the official news organ of the AME
church, declared:

> *There was a time when ministers thought any kind of preaching*
> *would do for colored people. . . . There was a time when colored*
> *ministers could glory in their own ignorance before a congregation,*
> *and succeed in making the people believe they were divinely inspired,*
> *and secure their respect and homage. There was a time when*
> *clownishness and incorrect speech were admired, and a swollen*
> *pomposity and conceit were mistaken for ability.* (quoted in
> Litwack, 1979, p. 459)

AME church ministers made it clear that those times were over.
Even the militant, nationalist, pro-black minister Bishop Henry M.
Turner thought the religious worship of the black masses was crude
and operated "under a lower class of ideas" (quoted in Litwack,
1979, p. 458). Turner viewed as ludicrous the way black people carried on in black religious revivals. He said, "Let a person get a little
animation, fall down and roll over awhile, kick a few shins, crawl
under a dozen benches, spring upon his feet, . . . then squeal and
kiss (or cuss) for awhile, and the work is all done" (p. 458). Another
prominent black minister, Thomas W. Cardozo, remarked "I won't
go to the colored churches, for I'm only disgusted with bad grammar and worse pronunciation, and their horrible absurdities"

(p. 458). The AME Bishop Daniel A. Payne even went so far as to apply physical force to any group of black people he saw engaging in barbaric religious practices such as the ring shouts. Payne (1969) recorded in his autobiography an incident where he personally took a hand in breaking up a ring shout among black people on the Sea Islands:

> *After the sermon they formed a ring, and with coats off sang, clapped their hands and stamped their feet in a most ridiculous and heathenish way. I requested the pastor to go and stop their dancing. At his request they stopped their dancing and clapping of hands, but remained singing and rocking their bodies to and fro. This they did for about fifteen minutes. I then went, and taking their leader by the arm requested him to desist and to sit down and sing in a rational manner. I told him also that it was a heathenish way to worship and disgraceful to themselves, the race, and the Christian name. In that instance they broke up their ring, but would not sit down and walked sullenly away.* (p. 253)

Although both white missionaries and educated black ministers waged war against the old-time religion, the "unlettered" rural people remained steadfast. In defending their time-worn religious practices, one black woman stated,

> *I goes ter some churches, an' I sees all de folks settin' quiet an' still, like dey dunno what de Holy Sperit am. I fin's in my Bible, that when a man or a woman gets full ob de Holy Sperit, ef dey shoud hol' dere peace, de stones would cry out's an' ef de power ob God can make de stones cry out, how can it help makin' us pour creeturs cry out, who feels ter praise him for his mercy. Not make a noise! Why we makes a noise bout ebery ting else but dey tells us we mustn't make no noise ter praise de Lord. I don't want no sich 'ligion as dat an I wants ter go ter heaben in de good ole way.* (quoted in Litwack, 1979, pp. 461–462)

Even the leader of the ring shout whom Bishop Payne chastised held his ground. The bishop wrote that after having another chance to speak alone to "this young leader of the singing and clapping ring" (Payne, 1969, p. 254), the young leader said,

Sinners won't get converted unless there is a ring. Said I: "you might sing till you fall down dead, and you would fail to convert a single sinner, because nothing but the Spirit of God and the Word of God can convert sinners." He replied: The Spirit of God works upon people in different ways. At camp meeting there must be a ring here, a ring there, a ring over yonder . . . : This was his idea, and it is also that of many others. These "bands" I have had to encounter in many places . . . to the most thoughtful. . . . I usually succeeded in making the "band" disgusting; but by the ignorant masses . . . it was regarded as the essence of religion. (p. 254)

When the black migrants took their old-time religion with them to the big city, they found themselves met with stiff resistance by the educated class of black people. In 1934, Carter G. Woodson (1921), the renowned black historian, stated, "The educated Negroes could not accept the crude notions of Biblical interpretation nor the grotesque vision of the hereafter as portrayed by the illiterate ministers of the Church" (p. 250). Educated ministers of large institutional black churches often led the battle to get rid of, dethrone, and exile the old-time religious preachers. Rev. Francis J. Grimké, pastor of the powerful Fifteenth Street Presbyterian Church in Washington, DC, chastised the old-type black preachers for thinking that to be an effective minister "all that is necessary is lung power, fluency of speech, and the ability to strike attitudes and make gestures" (quoted in Woodson, 1942, p. 229). However, the old-time religion did have its defenders among powerful educated ministers. For example, Adam Clayton Powell, Sr. (1980) stated that he built his new Abyssinian Baptist Church in Harlem especially for black people who "still cling with a childlike faith to the religion expressed in the spirituals" (p. 273). To Powell, "these spirituals are the finest revelation of the will and heart of God outside of the Bible" (p. 273). Powell was one of the few to recognize the therapeutic value of the old-time religion:

We have learned from Freud and other modern psychologists the evil effect of suppressed emotions. I have often wondered what would have happened to the Negro if the church had not given him the opportunity to sing off, pray off, and shout off his suppressed emotion. During my ministry, I have heard thousands of testimonies like the following: "I intended to commit suicide, I intended to kill a man who had wronged me, I intended to sell myself, I intended to give up God and the church, but after hearing the sermon, the prayer, the singing, I changed my mind." (p. 276)

Powell was a firm believer that the "extravagant emotionalism" of black people in their religious worship was "not to be either crushed or civilized" and that those who defied it were not "serious students of psychology, philosophy, or religion" (p. 280).

The defenders of old-time religion were few in number. Many rural black people wanted modification of the old ways. Even when they sought not to leave all of the rural past behind them, they were beginning to demand more of traditional rural mourning institutions such as the black church. Johnston (1954) held that even before black people migrated in large numbers to the city, many of them had begun to grow coldly unresponsive to preachers who sought "to arouse feeling by referring to trials and tribulations, heavenly expectations, and other traditional responses" (p. 93). She wrote that black people were growing increasingly more responsive to the thought-producing "biblico-religious type of sermon in which stories and events of the Bible are related to life-situations" and wanted their religion to be more practical in respect to helping "to remove some of the crushing, frustrating conditions under which they live" (p. 93). Johnston wrote that the preachers who asked and admonished "Wanna see your Mama? Wanna see your Papa in the great gitting-up morning? They're up there waiting for you. Then hold on and be in that number. I'll be there with my robe on, some sweet day" were beginning to be viewed as "ridiculous and illogical" (p. 93). Rural black people were calling for a more practical method of mourning and problem solving that showed more concern for their situation in this life. Although many black migrants too were seeking a religion more amenable to addressing their hardships in the urban environment, Fisher (1953) held that the bulk of these people continued to prefer what he called the "moaning'" preachers over the educated or intellectual ones.

The war waged against old-time religion did not stamp it out by any means but curtailed its influence considerably. In the big cities, old-time religion was driven underground, finding refuge in small storefront, fundamentalist black churches. In an offensive mode and outside the context of extreme overt racial persecution, these churches tended to not be as flexible as the spiritual tradition allowed. They continued the mourning work to some extent, but this work now was not only excessively emotional but also strictly otherworldly and escapist, a retarding factor as far as challenging the status quo and even as far as racial uplift or inspiring hope for a better life. The black migrants who attended the myriad storefronts sang more loudly than ever:

> *Gimme that ol' time religion*
> *Gimme that ol' time religion*
> *It was good enuff for my mother*
> *It was good enuff for my father*
> *and it's good enuff for me.*

However, the mourning work among them was not as effective, profound, or influential in helping them cope emotionally, psychologically, and spiritually with the vicissitudes of the new times.

THE CO–OPTATION OF THE SPIRITUALS AND THE BLUES

Although the old-time religion of the slaves and the rural black people was being driven underground, the spirituals and the blues traditions, which were also crucial to mourning work, were being co-opted for commercial purposes. Ever since the days of slavery, white people had loved listening to the spirituals, although they often viewed them with amused contempt and saw them as the barbaric, albeit melodious, utterances of a group of savages. After slavery the spirituals, like the old-time religion, were practically "driven out of the church worship by the conventions of respectability and the repressions of puritanism as the Negro church became more sophisticated. A second-generation of emancipated blacks disdainfully looked upon the spirituals as producers of a slavery time they thought was best forgotten" (Locke, 1969, p. 18).

According to Locke, it was not until a group of singers from Fisk University toured the country, and eventually the world, singing the spirituals, that they were revived as an art form in America. After their first unsuccessful concert, singing contemporary songs to white audiences, the Fisk Singers made an instant impression and became a raving success after they started singing the spirituals. Even then they did not present these songs as slave songs but as "jubilees," calling themselves the Fisk Jubilee Singers. To make these jubilees more palatable to white audiences, the Fisk Singers felt compelled to "whitenize" them by polishing off the crude edges, toning down the emotionalism, and even correcting some of the "bad" grammar. Thus, the spirituals that the Fisk Jubilee Singers and others sang in concert hall and glee club renditions were a far cry from the spirituals of the slaves and the rural black people after emancipation. As Locke wrote, "A genuine spiritual is always folk composition or a group product, spontaneously composed as a choral expression of religious feelings" (p. 21). He wrote that

Negro spirituals thus are not originally solo or quartette material. They are congregational outburst under the pressure of great religious emotion,—choral improvisations on theses familiar to all the participants, each singing of the piece is a new creation, and the changes, interpolations, variations defy the most expert musician's recording. (p. 21)

Hurston (1970) coined the phrase "neospirituals" to describe the artificial derivatives that were so familiar as a form of symphonic entertainment. She held that these "renovated spirituals are a valuable contribution to the musical literature, but they are not the genuine thing. Let no one imagine they are the true songs of the people, as sung by them" (p. 360).

Although these songs were being co-opted for black bourgeois pecuniary purposes, the positive result is that the new popularity and recognition of the spiritual saved it as an art form. Before middle-class black people and white entrepreneurs found they could make money from products of the slave, the spirituals were being driven to extinction. Black migrants continued to sing them quietly and alone as if they were subversive songs, and they stopped composing and improvising them. The social context in which these songs were sung existed only in the rural storefront churches where these songs were no longer being used so much as the "peasant's instinctive distillation of sorrow and his spiritual triumph over it in a religious ecstasy and hope" (Locke, 1969, p. 20) but as songs of resignation and escape. The spirituals sung in the big institutional churches were these neospirituals designed more to entertain than to carry out the work of mourning.

However, although these songs were losing their social therapeutic value, the new popularity and commercial success gained them international recognition and acclaim. After the Fisk Jubilee Singers made repeated tours all over America and Europe, these old songs of the slaves and the rural people gained fame for the singers, fortune for the college, and most important, recognition for black folk music. Other black colleges that had heretofore viewed these slave songs with an arrogant disdain followed the Fisk Jubilee Singers' lead and began their own tours, using the songs of the people they looked down on to bring in considerable sums of money to their struggling schools. Furthermore, these unwritten songs of the black soul were being collected and critics were lauding them as "the purest and most valuable musical ore in America; the raw material of a native American music" (Locke, 1969, p. 21). "The spirituals are the most characteristic product of Negro genius to date. They are its great folk gift, and rank among the classic folk expressions in the whole world because of their moving simplicity, their characteristic originality, and their universal appeal" (Locke, 1969, p. 18). Because the spirituals were lauded as being ingenious, many white critics claimed that black people learned them from white people.

Like the spirituals, the blues also were co-opted—in this latter case largely by minstrel entertainers who stole, borrowed, and imitated black musical, dance, and comedic art forms of all sorts as they blackened their faces to become "mock darkies." With the commercialization of the blues, the white music companies that published and distributed blues songs and that controlled the life and livelihood of many blues artists pushed blues composers to stress the sexual themes in the blues and downplay the tales of woe and protest. However, even with that interference, the worldliness and the secularity of the blues allowed the "down home" blues to be carried over into urban life without being as racially white-washed and virtually amputated as the spirituals. The social context of the blues remained the honky-tonk and the juke joint, where the blues were particularly effective at the Saturday night dances. In an environment of drinking, gambling, fighting, and sexual pursuit, the blues could still create an atmosphere of communal bonding, a mood in which men and women who led hard lives could come and hear lyrics that reflected their experiences. As Titon (1977) wrote, "the lyrics [still] most frequently took for their subject relations between the sexes with mistreatment and the difficulty of maintaining a stable relationship the most common theme" (p. 32). In this sense, the blues in the context of the social bonding of the group still had great appeal to tribeless black men and to the black women who had trouble maintaining stable relationships. Titon wrote that "the large number of singers and listeners who have testified to feeling better after blues performances indicates that the ceremonies were effective, that people were renewed" (p. 33).

Although the blues remained in purer form than the spirituals, they never did become as popular. The blues also were being challenged as they made the transition from rural life to the city. They were being upstaged somewhat by the new black musical sounds called "jazz." This new urban black art form was considered more sophisticated and refined than the blues. Jazz became the musical form in rivalry with blues and contemptuously associated the blues as being "country." The black jazz artists and composers would soon find that their music was not safe either. As fast as they produced it, it was being taken over by white people. White music companies gained considerable control over jazz artists and their music, and white jazz musicians put black jazz musicians on the run as if they were fugitives. One black jazz musician confided,

You see, we need music; we've always needed a music—our own. We have nothing else. You see, as soon as we have a music, the white man comes and imitates it. We've now had jazz for fifty years, and in all those fifty years, there has been not a single white man, perhaps leaving aside Bix [Beiderbecke], who has had an idea. Only the colored man has ideas. But if you see who's got the famous names, they're all white. What can we do. We must go on inventing something new all the time. When we have it, the whites will take it

from us, and we have to start all over again. It is as though we were
being hunted. (quoted in Kofsky, 1970, p. 57)

THE INABILITY TO MOURN

Like the jazz, blues, and spiritual artists, rural black people on the
whole were finding that their culture no longer belonged to them.
Their culture was under attack, under siege. While they were being
called stupid, savage, barbaric, childlike, uncivilized, and dependent, their heart and soul were being torn out of them and being
used to culturally and financially enrich others. Others were stealing their ideas, their techniques of emotional expression, their
philosophies on life, and their experiences and claiming these cultural artifacts as their own while viewing the creators of these with
utter contempt and declaring them to be inferior.

What is even more problematic is that rural black people found
that without their own cultural tools or with a weakening of them,
they were more vulnerable to the oppressive influences of big-city
life. They were losing their way of life and, through the psychology
of cultural amnesia, giving up their culture. They were taking on
the individualistic and materialistic culture of urban life, a culture
that was hostile and antithetical to the communalistic, people-ori-
ented thrust of their own culture. Moreover, they were losing the
social context in which mourning work could take place. Clothed
with the newfound individualism, they were beginning to show an
inability to mourn.

When their music and other cultural art forms necessary for
mourning work were torn from their original cultural moorings, the
old mourning tools of black people began to lose their functional
utility. Without a social context and social institutions in which
mourning work could be carried out, the ability of black migrants
to come together for collective empathy, support, and motivation
was seriously diminished. Tribeless black men, disillusioned black
children, black women carrying the burden of raising children
without the support of fathers, and the black bourgeoisie who were
distancing themselves from the black masses even as they fed off of
them were all beginning to show a marked inability to mourn. Also,
the jazz age had ushered in the era of the "cool" black person who

was too cold, indifferent, and emotionally detached to mourn. Hence, the urban black community was becoming increasingly atomized as the psychology of cultural paranoia was being turned back on black people and steadily evolving into the psychology of cultural terminal illness.

SOCIAL WORK AND MOURNING

Urban black people still went to church, but the church in urban life had so many other lifestyles and influences competing for the attention of black people. The black extended family still served a mutual aid function, but under the economic bombardment of the Great Depression even it could not guarantee all of its members the basic emotional and material support they needed. Black caregiving institutions such as orphanages and homes for older people tried desperately to continue serving black people, but during the Great Depression many of them lacked the funds for keeping their doors open. The Great Depression took away the nickel-and-dime donations that came from the black masses for the support of these institutions. Black music continued to play a large role in the lives of urban black people but mainly now as a source of public entertainment and only privately as a method to soothe troubled souls. Urban black people still had black leaders who felt compelled to honor the traditional obligation imposed on them to be a credit to their race by working for the uplift of the black masses. However, what was significantly problematic in early black 20th-century urban life was that many well-off, educated, and talented urban black people were no longer encouraging the black masses to the highest levels of achievement and no longer hurling themselves against racist barricades so that the black masses might see a brighter day. These black people had trouble organizing among other middle-class black people because of petty bickering as to who would be the boss, who would make the key decisions, and who would bask in the glory of success. Although the rapid enlargement of the black middle class was a result of urban society's making available a black clientele undreamed of in the rural areas and small towns—a clientele largely free from the competition of white people—these middle-class black people came to lose identification with the black masses, and they showed no more of an ability to mourn with them than did the tribeless black people who roamed big-city streets and the criminal black predators who used other black people as prey.

With the breakdown of black folk culture and the lack of a strong institutional context for mourning work, professional black social workers were in a unique position to help the black masses retain some parts of their own helping tradition as well as some semblance of themselves and their cultural identity. Armed with superior analytical tools, these sociologist–social workers could have helped the black masses sort out what aspects of their culture they should give up and what aspects of it would best serve them as they made the transition from rural to urban life. By synthesizing black folk culture and professional social work, black social workers would have been able to establish a closer, more genuine rapport with the black masses and gain their respect. After all, all of their clients were black (at that time, black social workers were not allowed to work with white clients). In fact, most of their clients were poor black people with rural southern backgrounds.

Poor, southern tribeless black men came before black and white social workers mainly through the courts for criminal activities and for the nonsupport and desertion of their families. Disillusioned black children came before social workers mainly through the juvenile court system. The main clients of social workers were black women who, because they were suffering a "caring overload," generally came looking for financial aid to support their children.

With tribeless black men roaming from place to place and not taking responsibility for the care of their children, black women were left to care for them with extremely meager resources. Because many of these women had left rural extended family networks behind, they were without much of the familial support that got them through hard times in the rural South. Many had to go through the daily madness of trying to handle difficult family problems alone. They suffered a caring overload that intensified old psychologies that were products of their rural experiences. The psychology of cultural sickness came back in full force as these women developed symptoms of feeling too sick, too nervous, and too emotionally drained to muster up enough energy to move forward.

Feeling abandoned, rejected, and unloved, these women found that the psychology of paranoia was engulfing them. They often projected their fears and rage back on their children and out of desperation and depression became neglectful and abusive. Feeling hemmed in, overburdened, overwhelmed, and choked by the psychology of cultural claustrophobia, these women often turned to alcohol and drugs for escape or retreated into the fantasy world of the psychotic. Sheer desperation drove them to seek financial support for their children and help to overcome their depression, nervousness, and feelings of being driven insane.

In short, black people generally were brought to social workers through the criminal, juvenile, and domestic court systems, or they came seeking help from social workers out of sheer economic, social, and psychological desperation. Regardless of the reason, they soon discovered that coming before social workers in urban society was a far cry from coming before their own people in the ring shouts, churches, extended families, and honky-tonks. In the context of their own mourning institutions, these black migrants could give help without paternalism and receive help without pity. In their own mourning work they were not helped by professionals, experts, and bureaucrats who viewed them as "clients" and "cases" but by fellow mourners helping fellow sufferers. In traditional mourning institutions, tribeless black men might have been considered deviant because they did not follow the black norm, which stressed social connectedness and collective support, but even they would have been considered human beings worthy of nurturing, support, and respect. It would have been inconceivable to rural black people to tag these men "bums," "low lifes," "thugs," or "criminals," as they were tagged by professional social workers. Rural children might be declared "bad," requiring a balanced mixture of corporal punishment and love to correct or make them "good," but they were not labeled "wayward," "delinquent," or "antisocial," as they were by the courts and social workers. Black women often had problems taking care of their children and needed the assistance of the extended family, but they were never stigmatized as "welfare chiselers," "loafers," or "promiscuous," and their children were never seen as "illegitimate," as they were being viewed by social workers. If these women neglected or abused their children, it was generally because they suffered a caring overload, not because they did not care.

Black professional social workers were in a unique position to gain an understanding of the black masses and to help them by bringing their culture together with the powerful tools of social work. However, they too came to view all aspects of rural culture as inferior, barbaric, backward, and savage—something to be attacked and stamped out in the name of assimilation and adjustment. Therefore, black social workers, like their white counterparts, found themselves working in cold, bureaucratic, impersonal social welfare agencies that were designed not for mourning with black people but for the sole purpose of containing them, controlling them, and forcing them to assimilate Anglo-Saxon culture and give up their own. The goal of social work was to help them, even require them, to "adjust" to their oppression.

SOCIAL WORK AS AN ARM OF REPRESSION

For the tribeless men, disillusioned black children, and overburdened black women, social workers seemed to have one major solution to their problems: Lock these social miscreants up. More and more black migrants found that instead of being helped to help themselves they were beginning to fill the prisons and mental institutions as social work became not an instrument of social change but an arm of repression.

According to Mowrer (1928), the social work profession started out as a reform movement challenging the status quo but began to gain acceptance and legitimacy and to be granted power and authority by the status quo as it became an "extension" of the police, the courts, and prisons. For example, in cases of desertion, which engulfed so many tribeless black men,

> *the case work agency functions as an extension of the policy force, initiating the legal process by which members of society are made to conform to the standards of domestic relations demanded by the group. In this role the caseworker may proceed directly or indirectly. She may cause the issuance of summons to court or by threat of*

> *doing so she may accomplish the same results as would the court,*
> *i.e., get regular support for the family from the husband.* (p. 88)

In this respect, Mowrer held, one can see that the courts and the social work profession were interested primarily in the family as an economic entity, concerned with whether the deserting man supports his family, "leaving untouched the inner conflicts and tensions" (p. 89). Social work not only becomes "an extension of the legal arm" (p. 87) but also an integral part of the process of the courts "to bring to bear the force of the political organization to coerce" (p. 87). The caseworker makes use of the threat, either stated or implied, that if the man does not turn over to his family a specified sum of money each week, his case will be taken before the courts and he may end up in jail. Mowrer stated, "In general practice the defendant is bullied by the case worker, and sometimes by the judge, in an attempt to get as much [financial] support as possible" (p. 87) while "little attention is given to other factors" (p. 87). Black women strained by a caring overload could also easily end up in jail; if their depression and desperation led to the neglect and abuse of their children, they could end up in a mental institution while their children would be taken away from them.

SOCIAL WORK AS A PERPETRATOR OF LOSS

As more and more black migrants found themselves being put in prisons and mental institutions and having their children taken from them and placed in prisons, foster homes, and adoption centers, they came to view social work as the perpetrator of their worst historical and primal fear: the dread of loss and separation. They targeted social work because many times it was the report of the social worker working with the courts that would be the final determinant of whether they would be contained or remain free. Cox (1948) wrote that, as early as the 1940s, when it came to the welfare of black people, reactionary white people preferred to build more jails to contain them than social services agencies genuinely designed to uplift them. McIntyre (1993) stated that declaring black people deviant and incarcerating them has been a major tool used by a racist power elite since the colonial era. She held that *two results occurred from the overall maltreatment of African Americans. The designating of the entire group as outsider deviants ensured that a disproportionate African American population would always be present in American prisons; and this reality has remained since the inception of that institution in 1790. More important, the accusing and punishing of African Americans of more criminality (for whatever reasons) than European Americans for 200 years has reinforced the perception in most Whites' minds that any and all Blacks represent criminals or potential ones. Equally destructive is the development in most African American minds that the criminal justice system has been and is geared to victimize any member of this group. What has occurred in fact is the criminalizing of an entire race.* (p. 186)

The perception that social workers play a major role in maintaining the view of black people as deviant outsiders and in perpetuating loss and separation on them has caused black people to direct their cultural paranoia toward social workers. Social workers must be categorically clear on the point that few problems in black history and black life have created greater fear, anxiety, and dread in black people than the problem of loss and separation. Traditional African people did everything they could to safeguard themselves against this problem occurring in any form except through means such as accident, natural calamities, or natural death. As Clarke stated in a lecture,

The concept of divorce was alien to our [African] culture because no one had ever had one. The idea of jail wasn't part of our language because no one had ever been to one. The idea of old people's homes wasn't part of our language either because no one ever threw away grandma and grandpa. The idea of an orphanage was also alien to our language because we weren't giving away our children. If a child has no mother or father, someone in the community would take him in and give him shelter. It was not a matter of adoption, or a matter of looking for a home, it was an automatic culture container, alien to the one they brought us into. . . . [We] developed certain basic traits in the Western World that we did not have before we got here. (Adams, 1992, p. 92)

From slavery until contemporary times, the problem of separation and loss not only has exacted untold misery on black people
but has become one of their major fears. When social workers
became an extension of the police, the courts, the prisons, and
other institutions of repression, they became perceived as people
who were not seeking to prevent this core problem but ones who
were the instigators and perpetrators of loss and separation among
black people. As black people saw their loved ones carted off to
juvenile centers, prisons, insane asylums, adoption centers, and foster homes, they could see that it was social workers who were given
the authority and power by an oppressive, racist status quo to rec-
ommend and place them in these institutions of coercion, punishment, social control, and containment. Wilbert Walker (1987), who
rose from caseworker to deputy director of the Social Service
Administration for the state of Maryland, held that black people did
not understand social workers when they professed to be promot-
ers of family togetherness and community stability while they
engaged in the practice of denying elderly black people assistance
unless they provided proof of their children's inability to support
them. To many black people, this was an attempt to divide children
from their aging parents. The agency also denied black women
assistance so long as they had men in the home, even their own
husbands. Black clients saw this as an attempt to destroy black family life. The agency also often looked right past extended family kin
and instead chose to turn troubled black children over to foster parents, reform school officials, and others who black people perceived
as "strangers" and "enemies."

Even today when social workers, as in the past, are not the primary decision makers or policymakers in terms of taking loved ones
away and placing them in a social welfare institution, they often are
attributed most of the blame. For example, when Malcolm X was
only eight years old, his mother was placed in a state mental hospital by "the State Welfare People" (Malcolm X, 1964, p. 16), and he
and his brothers and sisters were placed in separate foster homes
(even when, according to him, they had relatives willing to take
them in). Malcolm X wrote that social workers "were as vicious as
vultures. They had no feelings, understanding, compassion, or
respect for my mother" (p. 18). He wrote, "I truly believe that if ever

a state social agency destroyed a family, it destroyed ours. We wanted and tried to stay together. Our home didn't have to be destroyed. But the welfare, the courts, and their doctors gave us the one-two-three punch. And ours was not the only case of this kind" (p. 21). Malcolm X's bitterness toward social workers lasted for the rest of his life.

Black people were well aware that social workers were not very successful in preventing loss and separation. They were equally aware that under some circumstances it was necessary to remove black people from the family and the community. However, they were accustomed to having problem black people moved from one subextended family that was not functional to another subextended family that was. For example, it was standard practice for parents to "put out" their own rebellious adolescents but only with the assurance that they were going to be absorbed into the home of another family member (usually on a temporary basis until the youths could get "their act together" and return home). They had supported black orphanages, homes for older people, reformatories, and the like that were run on the order of the black extended family, but the Great Depression all but wiped out these black mourning institutions. They were not accustomed to placing their loved ones in public institutions where they were under the care of hostile strangers; black people had little faith that their relatives would be rehabilitated, reformed, or uplifted. As the following modern-day case of E. P. Jones (1990) demonstrated, black people could expect that being placed in institutions such as prisons, mental institutions, and even foster care would be like being placed in hell.

Jones's experiences with the foster care system left her voicing a sentiment toward social workers that was similar to Malcolm X's diatribe. At age four, she was separated from her alcoholic mother and younger sister and placed in one abusive foster home after another. She was then declared a "suicidal psychotic" and placed in an institution for troubled girls. She had other relatives, including two aunts, who would have taken her in if they had known about her plight. When Jones was 18, she was released. During her incarceration, she gave credit to traditional black helping techniques for her survival. Black gospel music became her balm in Gilead. She wrote, "I took up listening to gospel on a New Jersey sta-

tion, collecting my thoughts, always feeling soothed by the music"
(p. 85). Because she developed a "love of singing" (p. 97), she joined
a choir. Jones gave little credit to social workers. She wrote that during the entire time that she was being subjected to cruel and abusive treatment by foster parents and their biological children and
treated in an institution as if she were mentally ill, "caseworkers
who believed in me were far outnumbered by those who didn't"
(Jones, 1990, p. 165). She said that overall social workers had been
too "quick to label a child entering the welfare system as emotionally disturbed or maladjusted, and quick to rename that child a
ward of the state" (p. 165). Her questions for social workers were

> How would you react to being removed from your maternal
> environment and placed in a foster home or institution where you
> have no real worth and where negative perceptions of the people you
> were born to are encouraged? How well would you survive the scorn
> of foster siblings and guardians, or worse, the abuse of alcoholic or
> psychotic foster parents in whose care you have been entrusted?
> What effect would it have on you to spend your childhood being
> shifted from home to home, institution to institution? (pp. 164–165)

Jones's case and the cases of thousands of other black people
indicate that as long as black people dread loss and separation and
as long as social workers are the extensions of the police, the courts,
the prisons, and the mental institutions, there is likely to always be
great tension between the social work profession and the black
helping tradition modeled on extended family values.

As Jones's case also indicates, social workers today encounter
black people in many tragic situations of loss and separation and
are just as puzzled as pioneering black social workers were decades
ago about how to prevent black people from filling up the welfare
rolls, prisons, juvenile systems, foster care programs, adoption
agencies, mental institutions, and graveyards. Modern-day social
workers have concentrated on a meticulous and rigorous statistical
counting and recording of black pathologies instead of hearing the
desires and aspirations of black people. They have concentrated on
adjusting black people, one person at a time, to society and have
concentrated only half-heartedly on adjusting society to black peo-

ple; however, they, like the social workers in the past, seldom think of drawing from the black experience to see how black people wished to determine their own destiny as a people. Many still see social work as an extension of the police, the courts, the prisons, and other institutions of social control, punishment, and social containment when it comes to dealing with black people.

In light of black history, one can see how black people easily came to view the police, the courts, and the prisons as instruments of black loss and separation; however, it was not easy for them to see how people who were supposed to help could perpetrate this tragedy. Black migrants' unfortunate encounters with relief workers in New Deal relief programs made them view caregivers differently. These encounters, as Solomon (1976) held, left them with tremendous ill feelings toward social workers in general. However, it was when social work was gaining legitimacy as an extension of systems of repression that black people began to look on it with even deeper disdain and distrust. When social workers' decisions or reports could land black people in prison or mental institutions or have their children taken away from them or relegate them to further poverty, it was difficult for black people to view social workers as friends, particularly when they were well entrenched in the camp of the enemy. This view of social workers as a repressive legal and political arm and the general social workers' view of black people as social deviants and dependents made a synthesis of professional social work and the black helping tradition seem more impossible than ever before. To a people who had known the lash, the chain gang, and the lynch rope, any profession that became an arm of repression was not likely to be viewed as one that understood their problems, that was sensitive to their needs, or that was open to their views.

Rural black people who migrated to urban centers in large numbers during the first few decades of the 20th century were accustomed to a helping context that was modeled on extended family values and that involved them in the process of working collectively to help themselves. They were not accustomed to a helping milieu that enhanced their deep dread of loss and separation and that had helpers who themselves showed an inability to mourn. The helping tradition of the black migrants was guided by the sacred ways of their ancestors who constantly invoked in them a spirit of hope in the sense of the old biblical scripture that reads: "For I will turn their mourning into joy and will comfort them and make them rejoice from their sorrow!" (Jeremiah 31:13, King James Version).

REFERENCES

Adams, B. E. (1992). *John Henrik Clarke: The growth years.* Hampton, VA: United Brothers & Sisters Communications.

Cox, O. C. (1948). *Caste, class and race.* New York: Monthly Review Press.

Fisher, M. M. (1953). *Negro songs in the United States.* New York: Russell & Russell.

Hurston, Z. N. (1970). Spirituals and neo-spirituals. In N. Cunard (Ed.), *Negro* (pp. 359–361). New York: Frederick Ungar.

Johnston, R. F. (1954). *The development of Negro religion.* New York: Philosophical Library.

Jones, E. P. (1990). *Where is home?* New York: Four Walls Eight Windows.

Kofsky, F. (1970). *Black nationalism and the revolution in music.* New York: Pathfinder Press.

Litwack, L. F. (1979) *Been in the storm so long.* New York: Alfred A. Knopf.

Locke, A. (1969). *The Negro and his music.* New York: Arno Press and The New York Times.

Malcolm X. (1964). *The autobiography of Malcolm X.* New York: Ballantine Books.

McIntyre, C.C.L. (1993). *Criminalizing a race.* New York: Kayode Publications.

Mowrer, E. R. (1928). *Domestic discord.* Chicago: University of Chicago Press.

Payne, D. A. (1969). *Recollections of seventy years.* New York: Arno Press and New York Times. (Original work published 1886)

Powell, A. C., Sr. (1980). *Against the tide.* New York: Arno Press.

Solomon, B. B. (1976). *Black empowerment: Social work in oppressed communities.* New York: Columbia University Press.

Titon, J. T. (1977). *Early downhome blues.* Urbana: University of Illinois Press.

Walker, W. L. (1987). *The deputy's dilemma.* Baltimore: Heritage Press.

Woodson, C. G. (1921). *The history of the Negro church.* Washington, DC: Associated Publishers.

Woodson, C. G. (Ed.). (1942). *The work of Francis J. Grimké (Vol. 1).* Washington, DC: Associated Publishers.

Mourning and the
Matter of Color

*A*lthough black social workers failed to get close enough emotionally to the black masses to understand their plight and needs, the black masses were won over by charismatic black leaders such as Marcus Moziah Garvey and Father Divine, both of whom rose to prominence during the era of the Great Migration. Leaders such as these attracted black people from the lower ranks by the scores because they had a basic understanding of the psychology of the black masses. They understood above all else that the black masses were in tortuous search of racial integrity and identity and that finding an authentic sense of racial self was as crucial to them as bettering their lot economically. In fact, mass leaders such as these saw racial unity, pride, awareness, and identity as necessary prerequisites for economic self-help and uplift. Garvey emphasized racial consciousness, indeed overemphasized it, whereas black social workers tended to downplay racial matters in the name of assimilating Anglo-Saxon bourgeois culture and appeasing their white funding sources.

THE BLACK MIGRANT AND THE ISSUE OF RACE

What was it about mass psychology that the black mass leaders were able to grasp given that black migrants in particular tended to swell their ranks? The black mass leaders understood that the black migrants came out of a hostile situation where matters were clearly dictated in terms of black and white. They understood how bruised were the egos of rural black people who had been emotionally referred to as "niggers," "darkies," "spooks," and "coons"; defined as "genetically stupid," "immoral," and "uncivilized"; stereotyped as "niggerish," "clownish," and "buffoonish"; and claimed to have been ordained by God to be the docile servants of the allegedly superior white race. These leaders knew that rural black people longed to combat the perennial onslaughts of racial insults and humiliation and had come to the city in part out of a desire to restore their racial integrity and dignity. Both Marcus Moziah Garvey and Father Divine, for example, were well aware that despite the growing rebelliousness and fear of detachment among the urban black migrants such as the tribeless men, the migrants still longed for a strong sense of community (Hosner, 1971; Martin, 1976). They understood that despite the desire of many black migrants to forget their actual past, black people still longed for a glorious, romantic past that would allow them to hold their heads up with pride and dignity. They understood that despite some movement on the part of black migrants away from heavenly pursuits, urban black migrants still were in quest of the millennium on earth and deeply desirous of an earthly savior. In a nutshell, mass leaders such as Father Divine and Garvey were able to exploit four basic needs in the black masses:

1. the need for a sense of community
2. the need for race pride and self-esteem
3. the need for religious expression
4. the need for economic development.

They understood that the black migrants were torn from strong familial and communal roots and that, despite desires to be coldly detached from others as a protective device, they really wanted a beloved community. Both Garvey's Universal Negro Improvement Association and Father Divine's Peace Mission movement gave urban black people a sense of belonging and made them feel as though they were brothers and sisters, one big racial extended family united around a sacred, noble cause and led by powerful, kind, loving protective fathers.

Both Garvey and Father Divine also realized that black people had come out of slavery and the peonage of the rural South starving for recognition and status. Garvey in particular was adept at instilling in them a great sense of importance and race pride by giving them high-sounding prestigious titles and rank in an all-black organization with a black president; a black vice president; a black congress; a black cabinet; a black army with black generals; a black nurse corps; a black newspaper; black ships seeking to do commerce with the black world; and a black religion with a black Jesus, a black Madonna, and black angels. He satisfied black people's yearning for social status, recognition, and power within their immediate environment; they did not have to wait until they got to heaven to be treated as if they were somebody.

Father Divine's Peace Mission movement appeared to deemphasize instilling racial pride because his organization was interracial, with numerous white followers. However, although Garvey talked repeatedly about the black Messiah and the black Madonna and the need to make saints out of black historical figures such as Sojourner Truth and Booker T. Washington, Father Divine implied that he himself was God, with the supernatural power to heal the faithful and exact revenge on any person seeking to discredit him. His suggestion that he was God appealed both to the need of black people for racial dignity and identity and to their religious yearnings. That this black God held power over thousands of white followers added to the feelings of racial pride and superiority in his black followers. Moveover, Father Divine had a secret weapon: He knew that during slavery and after emancipation when it appeared that black people had been stripped of their African heritage and identity, they took on the heritage and identity of the Hebrew people who were the center of focus in the Holy Bible. The many references the spirituals make to the Hebrew people of the Holy Bible suggest that taking on the identity of the Hebrew people was a purposeful act. Locke (1936) was correct in holding that the spirituals displayed "an epic intensity and tragic profundity of emotional experience, for which the only historical analogy is the spiritual experience of the Jews" (p. 20). Father Divine understood that black people were an oppressed people yearning for a Moses to declare to the American pharaohs, "Let my people go"; that they were the people who had followed Daniel into the lion's den and Jonah into the belly of the whale; that they were the people who were in the fiery furnace with Shadrach, Meshack, and Abendigo; that they were the people who had fought with Joshua in the battle of Jericho until "the walls came tumbling down"; and that they were there with Jesus "when they nailed him to the cross."

Being a religious leader, Father Divine fed off of and enhanced the identification of the black masses with the Hebrew people of the Holy Bible. Although Garvey had little use for spirituals, viewing them as ignorant slave songs of appeasement and docility, he declared that the Hebrew people of the Holy Bible were themselves black and thus, like Father Divine, he used religion to strengthen the identity and unity of black people.

Both leaders also knew that the black masses had come out of slavery starving for material things, to have decent clothing, shelter, enough food, and some of the material trappings they had seen white people enjoy. Garvey and Father Divine promised a black economic kingdom on earth. Garvey did not go out seeking jobs from white corporations and pleading with them to allow black people to get a foot inside the industrial door. He gave black people a vision of conducting commerce with a redeemed Africa and black countries throughout the African diaspora.

Father Divine's Peace Mission movement, in contrast, managed to feed, clothe, and shelter literally thousands of black and white people during the Great Depression. His ability to do this when many government welfare agencies had failed to do so added to the mythical notion among the black masses that Divine must be God to work such miracles. He also had numerous small businesses in which he put his members to work at times when work was virtually nonexistent for white people, let alone for black people, the last ones hired and the first ones fired.

What is most significant is that both Garvey and Father Divine used social work–type community organizations and group work and social action techniques to recruit huge followings of black people to their respective causes. Garvey, in fact, had paid community organizers who received more money than professional social workers for similar work. Later, the Honorable Elijah Muhammad, following in Garvey's footsteps, would use group work techniques to have a far greater success rate than social workers in reforming and rehabilitating criminals, prostitutes, drug addicts, delinquents, and other street denizens thought to be virtually untouchable by social work practitioners. Muhammad and his Nation of Islam also understood the psychological need of the black masses for a sense of community (making their members feel that they were part of a mighty black nation), the need for race pride (the Nation of Islam started an entire religious mythology of black people as God's chosen ones and white people as devils), the need for religious development (the black Muslims sought to propagate Elijah Muhammad's brand of Islam), and the need for economic development (the Nation of Islam also created a number of small businesses so that its members could "do for self") (Lincoln, 1973).

THE DILEMMA OF SOCIAL WORKERS

Unlike the mass race leaders, black professional social workers did not draw from black history the tortuous need of the black masses for racial solidarity, identity, and pride. Because they saw black folk culture as a retarding factor, they never knew that because the black masses were stripped of much of their African identity, they felt that it was crucial to their psychological and spiritual survival to take on the identity of the Hebrew people in the Holy Bible. These social workers did not understand, as the ethnomusicologist Harold Courtlander (1963) pointed out, that if the spirituals "are arranged in a somewhat chronological order, they are equivalent to an oral version of the Bible," that "each song presents in a capsulized or dramatic form a significant Biblical moment," and that if one puts spirituals together in a certain sequence, they could not only "produce an oral counterpart of the Bible" but, if printed, produce "a volume fully as thick as the Bible itself" (p. 36). By identifying with the Hebrew people, the black masses indicated to social workers that they wanted to play a role in history, to be actors in history instead of continuing to be acted on. However, even when the black masses were beginning to become disillusioned with the false hopes and grandiose schemes of mass black leaders, black social workers were not able to rally black people to their side because they themselves were being viewed as the arm of repression and the perpetrators of loss and separation. Moreover, they were caught up in glaring contradictions. They pretended color blindness while simultaneously seeking to impose white values and ways on black people. They were confronted with combating racist stereotypes of black people while at the same time adopting pejorative epithets that white racists frequently hurled at black people, viewing them as lazy, ignorant, immoral, loud, boisterous, and rude. They were devoted to advancing black peasants to the industrial working class while receiving funding from the same white ruling industrial elite that exploited, oppressed, and discriminated against black workers. Most significantly, they sought to play down racial differences when the history of the entire social work profession was steeped in racism from the Poor Laws to the friendly visitors. They seemed to be unaware that the almshouses, asylums, outdoor relief programs, and other private and public charities that were developed in 19th-century America did not consider black people to be among "the deserving poor"; that the white missionaries who flocked to the South to educate, enlighten, and uplift the newly freed black people, while making tremendous gains in wiping out black illiteracy, looked on black folk culture with contempt and did all they could to destroy it at its roots; and that the Progressive-era white social settlement workers, while zealously reform-minded, concentrated their attention on helping uplift white immigrants and viewed black people as virtually hopeless.

WHITE PEOPLE AND THE BLACK HELPING TRADITION

Although it is true that black people in the past were generally treated with contempt in all social welfare endeavors, there were always white people who worked together with black people "as if they were conscious of the fact that developments in the racial situation involved the welfare of the entire nation" (Cox, 1962, p. 256). In other words, there were always white people who could mourn with black people. For example, white abolitionists and Underground Railroad leaders such as Sarah and Angelina Grimké, Thomas Garrett, Levi Coffin, John Brown, and Harriet Beecher Stowe worked well with black people because they were sensitive to black loss and separation, treated black people as equals, and took risks on their behalf.

Sensitivity to Black Loss and Separation

Black abolitionists, black Underground Railroad leaders, and black fugitives got along well with white abolitionists who were sensitive to black suffering, especially to black separation and loss. In this respect, Angelina Grimké said that ever since the death of a slave girl she had befriended, "the cruelty and unkindness which I had from infancy seen directed toward them came back to my mind" night and day (Lerner, 1971, p. 79). Her sister, Sarah, also said that since infancy "slavery was a millstone about my neck" (p. 20). Thomas Garrett, the great Underground Railroad stationmaster, dedicated his life to black freedom after a free black woman in his employ was kidnapped by slave catchers (McGowan, 1975). After that incident, Garrett said that a voice within him told him that "his work in life must be to help and defend this persecuted race" (quoted in McGowan, 1975, p. 26). Levi Coffin (1898/1968), a businessman, recalled that when he was a boy he encountered a coffle of slaves tied and chained up. After one of the slave men denoted "the deepest sadness" when he expressed his longing to reunite with his wife and children, Coffin wrote that "the thought arose in my mind—How terrible we should feel if father were taken away from us?" (p. 13). He wrote that "this was the first awakening of the sympathy with the oppressed, which, together with a strong hatred of oppression and injustice in every form, were the motives that influenced my whole . . . life" (p. 13).

Other white abolitionists had similar motivations for advancing the cause of black people. Harriet Beecher Stowe said that after her own son died in infancy, the pain of that experience made her realize how black people must have felt when for them loss and separation had become a way of life. One of her biographers wrote that "she thought that she herself had been punished for failing to do something about the evil of slavery in her own time" (McLard, 1991, p. 96). Stowe felt that she must write a story that would force its readers to see for themselves how wrong slavery was. *Uncle Tom's Cabin* was that story.

The sensitivity of Elijah P. Lovejoy, an abolitionist, to the plight of black loss and separation caused him to lose his own life (Dillon, 1961). At first, Lovejoy was a gradualist in respect to the slavery issue until he witnessed the lynching of a black man. Then he turned into a radical abolitionist, using his newspaper to wage war against slavery. His mighty use of the pen led a white mob to murder him.

Personal Contact

Another characteristic that endeared genuinely sensitive white abolitionists and Underground Railroad workers to black people was that many of those white people sought not just to learn about black people from books such as *Uncle Tom's Cabin* but to know them through personal contact. For example, Theodore Weld, the husband of Angelina Grimké, said that his contact with black people was so close and extensive that "if I ate in the city it was in their homes. If I slept in the city it was in their homes. If I attended parties, it was theirs—weddings—theirs—funerals—theirs—religious meetings—theirs—Sabbath School—Bible Classes—theirs. . . . I was with black people in their meetings by day and by night" (Lerner, 1971, pp. 157–158).

Treating Black People as Equals

Black people also held in great esteem white abolitionists and Underground Railroad leaders who treated them as equals. The Grimké sisters were constantly chastising white abolitionists for seeing black people "as unfortunate inferiors" rather than as "suffering equals" (Lerner, 1971, p. 158).

Taking Risks

Black people also had tremendous admiration for white abolitionists and Underground Railroad leaders who took risks on their behalf. One did not have to give his or her life in the manner of a John Brown. Black people realized that any white person speaking out on their behalf was likely to be held in contempt by other white people. Thomas Garrett, for example, was constantly brought to court by slaveholders who accused him of hiding "stolen property." Once when a judge ruled in favor of the slaveholders, Garrett rose and said, "Now Judge, Thou hast not left me a dollar, but I wish to say to thee and to all in this court room, that if anyone knows a fugitive who wants shelter and a friend, send him to Thomas Garrett" (McGowan, 1975, p. 27). Levi Coffin (1898/1968) wrote that "if by doing my duty and endeavoring to fulfill the injunctions of the Bible, I injured my business, then let my business go" (p. 109).

Earning Trust

Although black people respected and appreciated white people who were sensitive to their suffering, made personal contact, viewed them as equals, and took risks on their behalf, it was still difficult for them to overcome their deep cultural paranoia. Levi Coffin (1898/1968) wrote that when fugitives first came to his home they were "so fearful of being betrayed, that it was some time before their confidence could be gained and the state of their case learned" (p. 120). The Coffin family strictly adhered to the practice of not pushing the runaways for information, not even to know their names, but to go about tending to their need for clothing, shelter, food, and medicine and treating them as equals. They also treated them not as fugitives, but as guests. This allowed the runaways themselves to make up their own minds, on the basis of concrete assistance, whether the Coffins were trustworthy and sincere.

A runaway slave named William said that when he was directed to the home of the white Underground Railroad stationmaster Wells Brown, every instinct in his body suggested to him that the meticulous attention the Brown family paid to his needs was merely a ploy to hold him there long enough for the authorities to arrive (Osofsky, 1969). He was certain that this was the case when Brown and his wife went so far as to serve him at the same table at which they ate and allowed him to sleep in the guest bedroom. Because he was too sick to leave, William felt that he could only await the terrible fate he envisioned—the coming of the slave catchers. It was not until a few weeks had passed that his doubts began to fade. It became clear to him that Brown and his family were not helping him out of pity or paternalism but out of genuine sensitivity to the travails of a fellow human being. He came to feel so much a part of the family that before moving on he added to his name Wells Brown, becoming William Wells Brown, a prominent figure in African American history.

Reciprocity

Although black people learned to trust white people who demonstrated genuine acts of caring and kindness, they also preferred white people who would allow them to satisfy the need to reciprocate in some way, however small. Levi Coffin learned firsthand how important this principle was to the hundreds of runaways he assisted. Thus, he usually asked fugitives to perform various chores around his home and to promise that they would help other runaways. He spoke of one incident in which a runaway who had successfully made it to Canada returned, "saying that he felt so much indebted to us he had to come back . . . to try to repay us, in some measure, for what we had done for him" (Coffin, 1898/1968, pp. 119–120). Coffin said that the man was not satisfied that he had repaid the Coffins for their kindness until he had worked for them through the winter months before returning to Canada in the spring. White helpers such as the Grimké sisters and Thomas Garrett tried vainly to impress on black people that they (the abolitionists) were getting far more satisfaction and reward from working to advance race relations than they were giving to black people. Sarah Grimké said, "I would not give up my abolitionist feelings for anything I know. They have given a new spring to my existence" (Lerner, 1971, p. 155). Thomas Garrett's biographer said that Garrett left "the impression that he wanted the slave to brave those dangers and run away . . . just so he could help him" and that "had there been no slavery in this country, he probably would have died an unfulfilled man" (McGowan, 1975, p. 79). However, it was not enough for some runaways to have Garrett tell them time and again how intrinsically rewarding his work on their behalf was. They still felt a need to reciprocate. Therefore, some of the black people who Garrett assisted took turns guarding his house throughout the entire Civil War, realizing that because of his efforts on their behalf, he was a marked man for Confederate assassins (McGowan, 1975). This was their way of paying him back.

Emotional Commitment

By showing sensitivity to black suffering, making personal contact, treating black people as equals, taking risks on their behalf, developing trust through concrete assistance, and allowing black people to reciprocate, the white abolitionists and Underground Railroad leaders who were the most successful in working with black people had made not just a professional commitment but an emotional commitment and investment.

THE SOCIAL GOSPEL MOVEMENT

Some of the leading white people of the Social Gospel movement, which became prominent in the second half of the 19th century, also showed an ability to mourn the plight of black people and had no problem discussing the contribution of black people to America and advocating for freedom, equality, and justice. The Social Gospel movement sought to apply the teachings of Jesus Christ to the changing problems of an increasingly industrialized and urbanized nation. It launched a crusade for social justice and social reform in many areas of American life, including race relations. Such white Social Gospel leaders as George Washington Cable, Atticus Haygood, Albion W. Tourgee, Charles M. Sheldon, Wilbur Patterson Thirkield, Edgar Gardner Murphy, Harlan Paul Douglass, Lyman Abbott, and Lily Hammond tried to reconcile American race relations with America's professed belief in Judeo-Christian ethics (Luker, 1991). They felt that a more consistent policy would be to put into practice the concept of the fatherhood of God and the brotherhood of man rather than to promote pernicious notions that black people were forever cursed by the mark of Ham while advancing an equally pernicious notion that white people were God's chosen people. The Social Gospel movement had significant influence on black higher education, black civic organizations such as the National Association for the Advancement of Colored People and the National Urban League, and black churches. Many prominent black social reformists and political activist ministers, such as Reverdy C. Ransom, Francis J. Grimké, and Adam Clayton Powell, Sr., were influenced by Social Gospel ministries.

So enthusiastic was Adam Clayton Powell, Sr. (1938), in his belief that the black church should be a source of social therapy and social service that he wrote an article urging black ministers to "take the lead in relief work" and said that if they do not meet the challenge posed to them by the Great Depression "they ought to close up" (p. 227). He even went so far as to suggest that ministers ought to give a portion of their salary for relief work. However, he quickly learned that many black ministers were not of the same opinion. Groups of them from around the country came together and responded to his article with invectives and threats that shocked him. Powell held that "my most learned antagonists seemingly thought that it was their duty and my duty to feed hungry people on ideals in order that they might physically starve to death and go to heaven quickly for milk and honey, long white robes and golden slippers" (pp. 241–242). Powell took comfort in his belief that the tribe of progressive black Social Gospel preachers was increasing. Although the Social Gospel movement was awakened to the ugly realities of racism and prodded churches to institute broad self-help programs in the black community, sought to remove a stumbling block to fellowship by eliminating divisive formulations of race and faith, and, in the name of hating sin but loving the sinner, sought to address concrete social problems and real human needs, radical black social workers such as Chandler Owens (1920) saw it as a reactionary movement set up to thwart the menacing and fearsome revolutionary potential of the black masses by preaching personal not social regeneration and advocating self-help initiatives rather than revolutionary social action.

THE PROGRESSIVE–ERA WHITE WORKERS

The Social Gospel movement paralleled the reform movement known as Progressivism. Many Progressive-era white social workers worked out of the humanitarian impulse of the abolitionist tradition. For example, it was the Progressive-era white social worker Frances A. Kellor who was among the first to draw attention to the conditions of the black migrants. As early as 1904 she wrote a "muckraking" exposé of the vicious exploitation of southern black girls by white employment agencies in the North (Kellor, 1905a, 1905b). Kellor worked closely with George Haynes and other black social workers in forming the National Urban League. Another Progressive-era white social worker, Mary White Ovington, a descendant of a prominent abolitionist family, became one of the founders of the National Association for the Advancement of Colored People.

Early in her career as a social worker interested in the advancement of black people, Mary White Ovington learned that she was living in a time when a white woman socializing with black people could invite the wrath of the entire white nation. To learn about black people, Ovington had taken a page from the lessons of her abolitionist forebears and found an apartment in a city slum to establish firsthand, personal contact with black people. On one occasion, she invited both black and white people over to her apartment for dinner, and even she was not prepared for the anathema heaped on her by white newspapers across the South:

> *This news, our sitting down and visiting together, while treated without much personal comment in the North, became exciting reading as it moved South. We were reproved even on the floor of Congress and, as we fell below Mason and Dixon's line, our sober dinner became an orgy. Those who made it up did not comment on the white man who sat next [to] the Negro woman who sat next [to] a colored man. We were described as drinking and making love. . . . "We have bitter contempt," the Richmond Leader cried, "for the whites that participated in it and illustrated that degeneracy will seek its levels"; and the St. Louis Dispatch declared, "This miscegenation dinner was loathsome enough to consign the whole fraternity of persons who participated in it to undying infamy."* (Ovington, 1947, pp. 45–46)

Ovington wrote that it was the furor over her living among black people "that clinched my determination to devote such ability as I had to the cause of the Negro" (p. 47). Although trying to get to know black people on a personal level presented its own difficulties, an even greater problem facing Progressive-era white social workers was trying to provide equal treatment within the social work profession itself. Although most white social workers saw black people as inherently inferior to white people, many others took courageous action trying to help black people gain entry into the social work profession. For example, when Marian Pulliam tried to integrate the Missouri University School of Social Work at Columbia, Missouri, she met with resistance too great to overcome (Bowles, 1936). She decided that the only way to get black people trained as social workers, given the racist reaction, was to set up a program that was affiliated with the university but taught and located in a separate facility. The university allowed her to establish such a program in St. Louis, Missouri, more than 100 miles away. However, even with the problem of commuting, Pulliam duplicated the social work curriculum taught at the Columbia, Missouri, campus as much as possible, seeking to give black students the same quality of knowledge that white students were receiving. Pulliam found field placements for her students, made sure they received certificates in social work, and went on to find them jobs in the social work field. Against great odds she was a pioneer in the training of black social workers in Missouri.

Miriam Van Waters (1929), the president of the most renowned social work organization of the time, the National Conference of Social Work, launched a scathing attack against white members of the organization for having conferences in cities and in hotels that erected "a pale so high as to exclude" black social workers "from meeting with us, breaking bread with us" (p. 273). Waters held that social workers had absolutely no business holding to beliefs that black people are members of an inferior race. She reminded white social workers that "there is, as social workers have ample opportunity to know, no biological, no cultural reasons why Negroes should not share life on equal terms with those colored white, yellow, red or brown" (p. 273). Social work, she said, should be based on science, not "on popular prejudice" (p. 273).

Edward T. Devine, the director of the Charity Organization Society, risked hostile white reaction when he appointed George Haynes as the first black research fellow of the Society's School of Philanthropy (which had a social work program at Columbia University) and when he hired Jessie Sleet as the first black family caseworker in the New York Charity Organization. His work on behalf of black social workers prompted Eugene Kinckle Jones (1928) of the National Urban League to credit Devine with being "the first white social work executive to realize the value of using competent, trained Negro social workers for work among their own people" (p. 293).

LEFTIST WHITE PEOPLE

Leftist white people, some of whom were social workers and all of whom talked about social welfare issues, must also be mentioned in terms of their work with oppressed black people. During the era of the Great Depression, for example, white and black members of the Harlem Communist Party staged numerous protest activities on behalf of Harlem black people. They led "don't buy where you can't work" campaigns, rent strikes, relief bureau sit-ins, unionization drives, and rallies against discrimination in education and cutbacks in the Works Progress Administration. Although leftist black social workers such as Chandler Owens and labor leaders such as A. Phillip Randolph called for black participation in the socialist revolution, one of the critiques waged by such prominent black ex-communists as Richard Wright (1944) and Ralph Ellison (1964) was that the Communist Party members and other predominantly white leftist groups tended to downplay racial matters in their emphases on the class struggle. These writers also charged that the leftist white people ignored and sought as much to destroy black culture as did bourgeois black and white people. Leftist white people viewed black culture, these critics charged, as a bulwark in the way of their attempt to build an interracial, proletarian internationalism. In contrast, the black leftist social worker Chandler Owens (1920) waged a devastating critique on black social workers, charging them with allowing their own social class standing and their alliance with the capitalist class to hamper their work with poor and working-class people.

INTERRACIAL COUNCILS

To counteract leftist views in the black community and to create more amiable race relations between bourgeois black people and middle-class white people, pioneering black social workers and progressive white social workers formed interracial councils. Because the Great Depression caused the National Urban League to shift some of its focus away from employment, it launched a program designed to bring together the "best" white people and the "best" black people. Other "goodwill" agencies designed to promote interracial cooperation crept up around the country (Parris & Brooks, 1971). After George Haynes left his government position in the U.S. Department of Labor, he became the executive director of the Department of Race Relations of the Federal Council of Churches of Christ in America, one of the most prominent interracial councils of the time (Parris & Brooks, 1971). Designed to show white people that black people were intelligent, decent, and ambitious—in other words, like them—the interracial councils did indeed bring white and black people together in a highly genteel way; the problem was that these councils attracted only those white people who were already sensitive to the plight of black people and ready for cooperation. They had absolutely no impact on staunchly racist white people. Furthermore, because black participants were so eager to prove to white people that they were exceptional (that is, exceptions to the ignorant, uncultivated black masses), lower-class black people were excluded from these meetings for fear that they might exhibit the stereotypes these councils were seeking to explode. Overall, although the interracial councils did help some middle-class white and black people to establish lasting friendships, they did little to combat the racist practices that black social workers faced daily in the field of social work.

BLACK WORKERS IN WHITE AGENCIES

Although black social workers could point out many examples of white people working with black people for black advancement and although numerous individual white social workers took firm stands against racism, racism continued to permeate the field of social work. Even as early black social workers sought to downplay racial differences in the quest for greater interracial unity, they could not help feeling themselves the full power of the racist sting in their work in white social welfare agencies.

Black social workers working in white social welfare agencies experienced racism firsthand. For example, Benjamin Mays (1971) reported that in 1926 his wife, Sadie, a social worker for the Family Service Association in Tampa, Florida, almost lost her job when her white supervisor insisted that she stop putting titles of Mr., Mrs., or Miss before the names of her black clients. John Beecher (1945), a descendant of the famed abolitionist family of which Harriet Beecher Stowe was a member, said that he came under heavy fire from the state and from white workers under his supervision when he gave a black social worker, Victoria Appleby, a raise that was "more than a lot of white people in the organization were getting" because he said that Appleby was "the best social worker I ever knew" (p. 56). He wrote that "when I explained that it was because Victoria Appleby had professional training which they didn't have," they wanted to know "what difference did that make . . . wasn't she colored and weren't they white?" (p. 56). Beecher wrote that after Miss Appleby received the raise, she became known thereafter to her white colleagues as that "uppity black bitch" (p. 56).

Wilber Walker (1987) reported that his wife, Grace, a caseworker for the Baltimore Department of Social Welfare, aroused the disapproval of her white supervisor when she interviewed a white client. In those days black workers were to see only black clients and black supervisors could supervise only black workers. Walker reported:

> The secretary ushered Grace into Miss Lazarus' [the assistant director] office as soon as she arrived. She was greeted warmly and offered a seat at the conference table, as the secretary closed the door to give them privacy.
>
> "Mrs. Walker, I understand that you interviewed a white client today," she began.
>
> "Yes, I did. My supervisor asked me to see her because her worker was in the field."
>
> "I guess she didn't know the client was white. Now, I'm not blaming you, but you know agency policy is for colored workers to work with colored clients."
>
> Grace remained calm as she told Miss Lazarus that she thought it was a ridiculous policy. "I didn't learn colored social work in school, I learned to help all people in need whatever their color," she said.
>
> "I know how you feel," Miss Lazarus replied. "We would love to throw out that policy, but the community's not ready to accept colored people giving case work to whites. Now, don't worry. The client wasn't really upset about being interviewed by you, but I thought I should remind you of our policy." (Walker, 1987, pp. 16–17)

At the time Walker's wife wrote him about the incident, he was thousands of miles from home in Korea leading an integrated platoon in combat to save democracy.

After the war ended, Walker resumed his role as a caseworker in the Baltimore Department of Public Welfare. While there, he detected an informal ranking among its services that mirrored the racial customs and practices of the larger society. It ranked adoptions at the top of the hierarchy, followed by foster care and protective services. Public assistance and medical care were ranked at the bottom. Accordingly, adoptions and foster care were "disproportionately staffed by white graduates from prestigious colleges or from prominent city families" (Walker, 1987, p. 8), whereas public assistance, with a clientele consisting largely of poor inner-city black people, was staffed almost exclusively by black social workers.

Some early black social workers who worked in predominantly white social work settings during the first four decades of the 20th century felt that part of their responsibility was to help white social workers regain the abolitionist tradition. For example, Ellen Tarry saw this as part of her role as a black community organizer at Harlem's House of Friendship during the 1930s. The House of Friendship, under the auspices of the Catholic Church, was responsible for bringing white students from nearby colleges and universities in contact with Harlem black people in an interracial "experiment in social action" (Tarry, 1955, p. 146). Tarry reported that many of the white students had "come to Harlem to tell us how to run things," hoping that "St. Peter will throw open the pearly gates as soon as they tell him they've been working for the 'poor dear Negroes'!" (p. 143). She felt strongly that the House of Friendship needed her "and many other Negroes . . . to explain to these well-intentioned white boys and girls that instead of working for the Negro, they would have to work with us" (p. 144).

Tarry (1955) wrote that her biggest problem was not with the students but with the founder of the House of Friendship, Catherine de Hueck, who Tarry referred to as the "B" for "Baroness" (p. 147). Hueck had fled from Russia. Most of her relatives were killed during the Russian revolution. Tarry said that somewhere between leaving Russia and coming to America, Hueck had convinced herself that her mission in life was "to combat the forces of Godless communism in Harlem" (p. 144). Hueck was absolutely convinced that she knew what Harlem black people needed and felt no need "to explain her reason for being among us" (p. 147). After failing to convince Hueck that "the least fortunate of my people needed an opportunity to help themselves instead of an angel of mercy to dole out food and clothing" (p. 203), Tarry wrote that she finally had to quit herself so as not "to lose the respect of my people" (p. 212).

E. Franklin Frazier also lost his job at Atlanta University in his confrontation with white paternalism. Helen Pendleton, a white field supervisor, had problems with Frazier being her boss. Aware that the white-controlled Board of Trustees of Atlanta University was already wary of Frazier's views, believing they were too radical and uncompromising, she constantly complained to the board about Frazier's allegedly belligerent behavior. When Frazier stormed out of a meeting held by the Atlanta Chamber of Commerce saying, "I have told you white people not to invite me to any meetings where you are going to place the Negroes to themselves as if they were roaches or fleas unfit for human association" (Platt, 1991, p. 75), Pendleton reported that. When Frazier published an article declaring that white racism was a form of insanity, Pendleton also reported that. Her accumulated accounts of how Frazier had consistently violated the southern etiquette of racial relations finally caused the board to dismiss him. He left the profession of social work and went full-time into sociology. His biographer wrote that after Frazier's clash with white paternalism and recalcitrant white racism, he no longer had any hope, "as he did in 1924, that social work might be 'the force that will remold southern institutions and customs so that the Negro will occupy a place in society affording his personality maximum development.' After all, social work had effectively blunted the maximum development of his own personality" (Platt, 1991, p. 81).

BLACK CLIENTS IN WHITE AGENCIES

Not only did early black social workers feel the pain of racial prejudice, exclusion, and rejection, but they were also aware of how badly black clients were treated by white social workers who saw black people as inferior beings. It must be understood that the relationship between the black client and the white worker was not just a clash of colors but a clash of cultures. White workers worked under the assumption of white cultural supremacy, and this assumption dictated every phase of their work with black people. From the black client's standpoint, just to seek help from white social welfare agencies was to reinforce old stereotypes of black dependency, and just to receive help from white workers was to advance the notion of white superiority. This view explains why black people were so eager to reciprocate when they were helped by white abolitionists and Underground Railroad workers.

Furthermore, short of seeking food, fuel, clothes, and other direct material relief from white workers, black people never felt so sure that white workers could help them with their emotional and psychological problems. For as much as individualism permeated white social work practice, when the black individual brought his or her emotional problem to them, white social workers tended to diagnose and treat him or her in terms of alleged afflictions of the entire black race. In other words, the diagnoses would generally be made in accordance with prevailing racial stereotypes. Hence, even deep-seated emotional problems would be seen in terms of the individual black person's alleged laziness, promiscuity, immorality, or treachery. Furthermore, many black socioemotional problems in accordance with the prevailing stereotypes could be diagnosed as insoluble because they were programmed into the black individual's genetic make-up. According to many white social workers of that time, black people were born ignoramuses, thieves, criminals, and moral and sexual perverts. They were also born liars, which meant that any emotional problem they were having was probably imaginary or fabricated. What kind of emotional problems could black people have anyway when they possessed no meaningful relationships, no subjective life, no commitment or obligation to anyone, and no desire other than to have sex, get drunk, and avoid work? If they indeed had anything resembling emotional sensitivity, as they lacked the ability to articulate emotional content, what was the use in wasting time trying to diagnose and treat their feeble, minuscule, so-called emotional problems? With this kind of relationship with the white social workers, it is no wonder that many black clients took their emotional and psychological problems to root doctors and ministers; tried to work them through by shouting them out in churches or honky-tonks; or tried to escape from them through alcohol, drugs, and mental illness.

The most significant cultural problem the black client had with the white social worker was that although the white workers viewed even individual problems in terms of stereotypes applied to the black race on the whole, they never viewed the problems in respect to the history of the black race on the whole. Black clients sensed that their problems were not just individual problems but collective problems stemming from their history in racist America. Their poverty, hunger, lack of decent jobs and political power, economic exploitation, and web of dehumanizing psychologies all had to do with their history as black people in white-dominated America. Black individuals suffered psychological and emotional problems because they felt the full, burdensome weight of black history. Hence, black clients were specifically uneasy and naturally anxious when they came before white social workers for anything other than basic material assistance. When white social workers asked, "What's wrong?," how could the black client answer, "My history"? And if the white social worker asked, "What's the problem?," how could the black client say "The problem is you"?

THE PERSISTENCE OF THE PROBLEM

The matter of color is still a salient issue in social work. Although a far cry from what it was, color still affects social workers in their work with black clients. Davis and Proctor (1989) found that the following was true, even in contemporary society:

- Most white workers prefer to work with white clients.
- White workers "generally are not knowledgeable about minority persons, their lifestyles, and communities" (p. 13).
- "White workers are likely to bring preconceived ideas and attitudes about minorities to their practice" (p. 13).
- "Most programs of professional education have not adequately addressed deficits in students' understanding of ethnic groups, nor do they adequately prepare them for effective work with minority group clients" (p. 13).
- Many white workers "avoid direct discussion of race, especially with minority individuals, and minimize the salience of race in interpersonal relationships" (p. 14).

- "Whites prefer not to discuss racial issues . . . [and] feign blind-ness to their client's race maintaining that they strive to treat minority clients like 'any other' client" (p. 14).

A PERSONAL EXPERIENCE

We have found from personal experience that many undergraduate and graduate programs of social work are still not adequately preparing students to deal with the sensitive matter of color. For example, at predominantly white universities where we have lec-tured or taught classes, we have found that white social work majors on all academic levels tend to mistake any kind of passion directed against racism as hostility directed against them personal-ly and any detailed analysis of the impact of racism on black life as a plot to instill guilt in them. In other words, many of these stu-dents could not even bear to hear about black pain let alone to mourn with black people. When, for instance, E. Martin taught a summer school graduate course in social work at a predominantly white midwestern university, he was surprised to learn that some of the white students took his analysis of racism as signs that he him-self was a bitter black man with latent hostilities toward white peo-ple. One white student's evaluation of the course read as follows:

> *I feel this is a very important subject which should be looked at for what it exactly is. I understand the hardships we, as humans, as humans first and different races second, must live with but the constant talk of discrimination and unfairness towards blacks need not be discussed in such a manner as to make white students embarrassed, angry, guilty or numb. The white students in a graduate level social work class are well aware of the inequities in society. They can be reminded of these differences but not so much as to be ashamed of one's own race.*

Another white student wrote:

> *I detected some hostility to whites by him [Dr. Martin] in the beginning of the summer. He made references to "you white people" on more than one occasion. I am concerned that his anger of the way*

whites have treated blacks has made him assume we are all racist. It took all my energy to listen to the wonderful teachings of the black family instead of being offended by some comments he made. He also made jokes on several occasions that only the black students understood. It made me feel awkward and left out.

Still another student then directed remarks directly to Dr. Martin:

Dr. Martin, some of us really care about the black community. I fear your good intentions may be clouded by your anger and white people won't listen to you. Racism breeds racism in whites and blacks and it will only make black prejudice far worse if whites feel blacks hate them. The whites today are not the people who condoned slavery but I felt as if we are blamed for it. I wish you the best of luck in your endeavors and hope you are able to make the same positive changes for whites that you do for blacks. I know there are real cruel white people out there but an ass comes in all colors.

We have encountered these kinds of remarks whenever we have taught or lectured to a group of predominantly white students. It did not matter how much we tried to assure them that we were not "bitter black people" who hated white people. It did not matter how hard we tried to convince them that the black story had to be told and that the facts about racism, as harsh as some of these truths are, were not aimed at beating them over the head. They still acted as if race was a matter that should not be discussed at all (except maybe to reinforce the idealistic notion that we are all human beings who should love one another).

Pinderhughes (1989) sought a clinical explanation of the uneasiness of white social work students and white social work educators and practitioners with the matter of color. She recognized that anger "is a common response by whites when people-of-color confront them with racism" (p. 86). Pinderhughes wrote,

The anger some whites experience may be a general reaction to confronting feelings that have been hidden and protected. . . . [T]hey resent being lumped with all whites as part of a racist system and not seen as individuals who are in pain, in conflict, and confused, or

who have tried to fight racism and help people of color. . . . The pain
expressed by people-of-color is hard for whites to hear. . . .
Understanding and empathy fade when whites turn off or get angry
about the guilt and sadness they experience. (p. 86)

In contrast to the white students, we have found that we were
well received by black social work students, particularly those at
predominantly white colleges and universities. They were glad to
have someone who could mourn with them. These black students
had grown tired of white social work professors who adopted a
color-blind perspective to the matter of color, downplaying or
denying the realities of race and racism in America by promoting a
naive notion about universality and the "brotherhood of man."
They were tired of having to pursue a curriculum that was almost
totally "Eurocentric." They were tired of social work teachers who
expressed racism with total disregard to the feelings of black students, teachers who were so "liberal" and "humanitarian" that they
had no idea how racist they were even when their mouths were
frothing with it. They were tired of the fact that when black people
were discussed at all in social work courses, they were usually
viewed as pathological, deviant, or at best, victims. Martin himself
attended a postgraduate class in social work in which nearly every
time the white professor talked about poverty, illegitimacy, or crime
he would turn to black students in the class for firsthand accounts.
He assumed, without checking first, that black students naturally
had special insights into those areas of pathologies that they could
share with their white colleagues. Most important, black social
work students on predominantly white campuses complained that
departments and schools of social work were so caught up in the
pretense of color blindness that they did not wish to hear what
black students wanted to tell them regarding how black students
felt and what they thought.

Olmstead (1989) showed how listening to and incorporating the
perspective of black social work students could help enhance social
work academic programs in field placement settings. Olmstead said
that she made considerable headway in the area of race relations
and cultural diversity when she coordinated a training project that
placed "minority group" students in a child and family service

agency run by middle-class white people but serving a clientele consisting largely of black and Hispanic people. The objective was "to find out what the students felt could be done to improve service to minority clients" (p. 105). The first problem the students pointed out was how wary, anxious, and vulnerable clients from racial and ethnic groups must feel when, on making initial contact with the agency, "the first people encountered—the security officer, the telephone operator–receptionist, the maintenance staff, and the fee clerks—are likely to be Anglo" (pp. 105–106). Olmstead wrote that the problem was compounded because "the permanency-planning professional staff, both administrators and practitioners, are white" (p. 106). She wrote,

> *The student expressed concern that this lack of minority staff at the professional level was a deterrent to the effectiveness of the program because minority staff are likely to remind their colleagues to be constantly aware of cultural and racial issues. The students, as well as minority employees in other departments of the agency, pointed out that the agency's employment of minority persons only in lower positions appeared to be a reflection of racism.* (p. 106)

Students also felt that the agency's outreach program was weak. They suggested that instead of relying basically on home visits to conduct outreach, (1) the agency place value on "understanding and relating to the minority client's culture" (Olmstead, 1989, p. 107); (2) when directing clients to other community resources, the agency stress talking to clients "in person rather than on the telephone" (p. 107); (3) the agency establish rapport with people in the racial and ethnic community, such as ministers, grocers, and neighborhood leaders; (4) the agency emphasize locating "people who are not asking for or looking for help but who are clearly in need" (p. 108); and (5) the agency advertise in newspapers and journals that serve racial and ethnic groups.

Regarding diagnostic issues, the students pointed out that, in their view, the staff did not emphasize environmental factors enough when diagnosing clients. Many pointed out that it was important for agency workers to "recognize that anger and depression in minority clients often results from privileges denied because of bias, not just as a result of intrapsychic factors" (Olmstead, 1989, p. 109). They recommended that the focus not be on the client's pathology but on the client's competence, "strengths, assets, and striving" (p. 109). They also suggested that in diagnosing clients, "derogatory labels should be reserved for social ills such as poverty, discrimination, unemployment, poor housing, lack of opportunity, and other indicators of oppression" (p. 109) instead of being applied to people. The reward to the students was that their perspective was being considered; they were being used in a positive and productive way that gave them a sense of belonging, self-esteem, and pride; and white people in charge were taking broad steps to confront the matter of color instead of denying its existence.

THE HIDDEN INJURIES OF RACE

White social work faculty and white students tend to think that because they are not personally involved in keeping black people down, somehow the race problem does not exist. As Pinderhughes (1989) observed, many of them feel that because they too are in pain, in conflict, and confused, their "human" problems are no different from those of black people.

McIntosh (1988) held that when white people adopt the color-blind, "we are all only human beings" approach, they are generally utterly unaware of the advantages that white skin color automatically confers on them. McIntosh wrote that white people generally take "white privileges" for granted and "are carefully taught to remain oblivious to them" (p. 4).

McIntosh (1988) began to count the ways in which she enjoyed "unearned skin privileges" (p. 1). She first had believed that being white had not put her ahead in any way and that she had earned all of her status, rank, and power through hard work, drive, and determination. However, after listing 46 ordinary and daily ways in which she experienced white privilege, she was shocked at the extent to which it provided her with "an invisible package of unearned assets which [she said] I can count on cashing in each day" (p. 4). McIntosh wrote that "as far as I can see, my Afro-American co-workers, friends, and acquaintances with whom I come into daily or frequent contact in this particular time, place, and line of work cannot count on most of these conditions" (p. 2).

MICROAGGRESSION

Although white social workers are generally unaware of the hidden, unearned privileges of being white, black social workers are often confused by the routine "microaggressions" (Pierce, 1970) that are waged against them on a daily basis in predominantly white schools and departments of social work and in predominantly white social welfare agencies. Black social workers are so accustomed to raw, overt racism that the usually invisible, habitual microaggressions that are so minor and so much a part of the texture of their daily lives often elude them. These microaggressions are harder to identify. They are a chronic scratching away at the surface; they are minor assaults that keep black people spending valuable energy on the defensive, on guard, and uptight for apparently no reason at all. The microaggressions are so subtle and slight that they can leave black people not knowing what is bothering them and not certain whether minor assaults are racist. Microaggressions are cumulative in their impact. Black social workers can find themselves ducking so many small, practically invisible racist darts in white social settings that they soon find that they are totally frustrated, depressed, angry, and burnt out. Microaggressions make black social workers realize how difficult it is in a racist society such as America for white people, no matter how liberal, humanitarian, or color-blind they think they are, to escape the malignancy of racism and for black people, no matter how high they think they have risen in the dominant society, to be totally free of the experience of oppression and victimization.

REFERENCES

Beecher, J. (1945). *All brave sailors*. New York: L. B. Fischer.

Bowles, C. K. (1936, September). Social work among colored people in St. Louis. *Opportunity,* pp. 280–282.

Coffin, L. (1968). *Reminiscences of Levi Coffin*. New York: Arno Press and New York Times. (Original work published 1898)

Courtlander, H. (1963). *Negro folk music.* New York: Columbia University Press.

Cox, O. C. (1962). *Capitalism and American leadership.* New York: Philosophical Library.

Davis, L. G., & Proctor, E. K. (1989). *Race, gender and class.* Englewood Cliffs, NJ: Prentice Hall.

Dillon, M. L. (1961). *Elijah P. Lovejoy: Abolitionist editor.* Urbana: University of Illinois Press.

Ellison, R. (1964). *Shadow and act.* New York: Random House.

Hosner, J. (1971). *God in a Rolls Royce.* Freeport, NY: Books for Libraries Press.

Jones, E. K. (1928, November). Social work among Negroes. *Annals of the American Academy of Political and Social Science, 140,* 287–293.

Kellor, F. A. (1905a, March 18). *Southern colored girls in the North.* Charities, pp. 19–21.

Kellor, F. A. (1905b, May 31). *To help Negro women.* Boston Traveler, pp. 3–4.

Lerner, G. (1971). *The Grimké sisters from South Carolina.* New York: Schocken Books.

Lincoln, C. E. (1973). *Black Muslims in America.* Boston: Beacon Press.

Locke, A. (1936). *The Negro and his music.* Washington, DC: Associates in Negro Folk Education.

Luker, R. (1991). *The social gospel in black and white.* Chapel Hill: University of North Carolina Press.

Martin, T. (1976). *Race first.* Dover, MA: Maturity Press.

Mays, B. E. (1971). *Born to rebel.* New York: Charles Scribner's Sons.

McGowan, J. A. (1975). *Station master of the Underground Railroad.* Moylan, PA: Whimsie Press.

McIntosh, P. (1988). *White privilege and male privilege: A personal account of coming to see correspondence through women's studies* (Working Paper No. 189). Wellesley, MA: Wellesley College.

McLard, M. (1991). *Harriet Tubman.* Englewood Cliffs, NJ: Silver Burdett Press.

Olmstead, K. A. (1989). The influence of minority social work students on an agency's service methods. In D. R. Burgest (Ed.), *Social work practice with minorities* (pp. 104–116). Metuchen, NJ: Scarecrow Press.

Osofsky, G. (Ed.). (1969). *Puttin' on ole massa: The slave narratives of Henry Bibb, William Wells Brown, and Solomon Northup.* New York: Harper & Row.

Ovington, M. W. (1947). *The walls came tumbling down.* New York: Harcourt, Brace.

Owens, C. (1920, December). The invisible government of Negro social work. *Messenger,* pp. 174–177.

Parris, G., & Brooks, L. (1971). *Blacks in the city: The history of the National Urban League.* Boston: Little, Brown.

Pierce, C. (1970). Offensive mechanisms. In F. Barbour (Ed.), *The black seventies* (pp. 265–282). Boston: Sargent.

Pinderhughes, A. (1989). *Understanding race, ethnicity, and power.* New York: Free Press.

Platt, A. M. (1991). *E. Franklin Frazier reconsidered.* New Brunswick, NJ: Rutgers University Press.

Powell, A. C., Sr. (1938). *Against the tide.* New York: Arno Press.

Tarry, E. (1955). *The third door.* New York: David McKay.

Van Waters, M. (1929, September). New morality and the social worker. *Opportunity,* pp. 273–274.

Walker, W. L. (1987). *The deputy's dilemma.* Baltimore, MD: Heritage Press.

Wright, R. (1944). *American hunger.* New York: Harper & Row.

CHAPTER 8

Mourning and the Matter of Gender and Class

*A*lthough racism in social work was a primary problem confronting both black clients and black social workers, the sensitive matters of gender and class also complicated the ability of social workers to mourn with black people. In respect to gender, black women had always been the primary caregivers in the black community; however, when social work became a legitimate profession, black men found social work to be an attractive career to pursue. Class issues have always interfered with the relationships between black clients and black social workers, despite early warnings by leading pioneering social workers to avoid social class cleavage. For example, the first black professional social worker, George Haynes, warned black social workers in the first decade of the 20th century not to take on the class outlook of the dominant society where people in the higher social classes tended to look askance at people in the lower-class ranks. Haynes (1922) wrote,

> *It seems very practicable, therefore, before any such fixed differences of class arise among Negroes, to save them from many of the shortcomings of other parts of our nation, and so to organize and to stimulate them that the business and professional classes may develop their present sense of responsibility to the wage-earning classes and spread a group solidarity, a feeling of social responsibility, throughout the whole people.* (p. 89)

Also during that time the great sociologist and pioneer of black social work, W.E.B. DuBois (1971), was propagating his "talented tenth" idea: that the 10 percent of educated, talented black people had a racial obligation imposed on them by history to uplift the "submerged" 90 percent of black people wallowing in poverty, oppression, and ignorance. Later DuBois (1976) was to grow appalled by the elite direction his talented tenth idea was taking:

> We must admit that the majority of the American Negro intelligentsia, together with much of the West Indian and West African leadership, shows symptoms of following in the footsteps of western acquisitive society, with its exploitation of labor, monopoly of land and its resources, and with private profit for the smart and unscrupulous in a world of poverty, disease and ignorance, as the natural end of human culture. I have long noted and fought this all too evident tendency, and built my faith in its ultimate change on an inner Negro cultural ideal. I thought this ideal would be built on ancient African communism, supported and developed by memory of slavery and experience of caste, which would drive the Negro group into a spiritual unity precluding the development of economic class and inner class struggle. This was once possible, but it is now improbable. The very loosening of outer racial discriminatory pressures has not, as I had once believed, left Negroes free to become a group cemented into a new cultural unity, capable of absorbing socialism, tolerance and democracy, and helping to lead America into a new heaven and new earth. But rather, partial emancipation is freeing some of them to ape the worst of American and Anglo-Saxon chauvinism, luxury, showing-off and "social climbing." (pp. 154–155)

E. Franklin Frazier (1957) wrote a scathing critique of "the black bourgeoisie," charging them with seeking to lose identification with the black masses while seeking desperately to gain status, recognition, and acceptance by the white elite. Moreover, the radical black social worker, Chandler Owens (1920) launched a vitriolic attack on black social workers for not identifying themselves with the black working class and failing to help them advance a socialist revolution.

THE MATTER OF GENDER

Traditionally black people had no problem with women as helpers because they primarily viewed caregiving as a woman's role. Black women received their training as caregivers in the black extended family where they were given the responsibility for the day-to-day care of extended family members who were indigent, sick, old, disabled, and mentally unstable. The caregiving role that fell largely on the shoulders of black women was sacrificial and burdensome, especially given the limited financial resources black women generally had. Many would have suffered a caring overload along with its attendant frustration and depression if they had not been able to rely on female kin and neighbors in mutually reciprocal support networks. Despite the sacrifice, the burden, and the threat of caring overload, black women carried the caregiving function from the black extended family to churches and other caregiving systems and emerged as the leading caregivers in the wider black community. Even when black men in churches, benevolent societies, and fraternal orders established social services programs, they generally expected women to carry out the day-to-day work of these programs.

For instance, although men were the leaders in the black church and were given the credit for the rise of the black church, it was the organizational ability and fundraising activities of black women that allowed the black church to establish and sustain numerous newspapers, schools, social welfare services, jobs, and recreational facilities and to advance most of its programs. Fannie Barrier Williams, the leading black feminist at the turn of the 20th century, was correct in holding that "the training which first enabled colored women to organize and successfully carry on club work was originally obtained in church work" (quoted in Washington, 1900, p. 383).

As the backbone of caregiving in the black community, black women brought extended family values into a larger context of social obligations. For example, as early as 1793, a black woman named Catherine Ferguson used the extended family concept of "informal adoptions" to pioneer the foster care movement in America (Ross, 1978). Ferguson realized the advantage of placing children in private homes rather than having them institutionalized in the poor houses and insane asylums of her time and placed 48 homeless children (20 of whom were white) in suitable private homes. Ferguson also went on to organize the first Sunday school movement in America. But instead of having a secure place as a pioneer in the area of child welfare, her contributions have been ignored and forgotten in social work literature.

Literally thousands of black women over the generations followed in the giant footsteps of women like Catherine Ferguson. For example, Harriet Tubman is well known in black history for her fearless work as a conductor of the Underground Railroad movement, personally assisting more than 300 fugitives to freedom. However, it is little known that she also drew from extended family values and helped to establish a nursing home for older black people. Sojourner Truth is also well regarded for her frank and eloquent utterances on behalf of the abolition of slavery, women's suffrage, and temperance, yet she is hardly known at all for her work with wounded soldiers and older black people.

THE WOMEN'S CLUB MOVEMENT

It was not individual achievements that put black women at the forefront of social services endeavors. Their collective effort gave them this honor, particularly their work in the women's club movement after the Civil War. The women's clubs represented one of the most widespread cooperative efforts on the part of black people to ameliorate the myriad social problems confronting them. There was hardly any welfare activity that women's clubs did not consider as they used extended family concepts to work with black people of all ages to fulfill numerous health, housing, educational, recreational, vocational, and rehabilitative needs (Martin & Martin, 1985).

BLACK MALE SOCIAL WORKERS

Although there were always individual black men leading the struggle for social reform, they generally showed little interest in caregiving until social work had gained legitimacy in the eyes of the status quo and had become a profession. With the professionalization of social work, black men began to see caregiving as more than an overblown maternal and domestic nurturing activity. Social work showed promise as a vehicle of upward mobility. It had the potential to give them a career that had as much status and influence in the black community as did the ministry, which had heaped enormous power on black ministers for decades. In fact, black male social workers began to consider social work as equipping them with a knowledge base superior to the emotionalistic sentimentalizing of black men of God.

Not only did social work promise a new and influential professional career, but it simultaneously satisfied the obligation history imposed on educated black people to be a credit to the race—meaning to take an active role in the advancement of black people. Black men perceived social work as a powerful tool for transforming society and envisioned using this new weapon to lock horns with powerful industrialists and labor union leaders in a struggle to wrest power and salvation for a people. With the professionalization and legitimization of social work, black men not only found the profession attractive but quickly moved into dominant roles. They took over the leadership helm of social work programs at predominantly black colleges and universities and major social services organizations such as the National Urban League. Inabel Lindsay was one of the few black women whose career as a social work educator paralleled that of men such as George Haynes, E. Franklin Frazier, and Charles S. Johnson. She was among the first fellows of the National Urban League and later became dean of the Howard University School of Social Work.

The problem was not that black men were entering the social work profession. Black women had always wanted black men to engage more directly in caregiving functions in the black family and the black community. Also, the problem was not that black men were lured to the profession with the promise of status, power, and respectability, because they generally worked out of a genuine desire to serve black people. The problem was that black men moved away from the black helping tradition as they pursued an assimilationist course and sought interracial alliances. Essentially, they did not continue the helping tradition established by black women caregivers in using the black extended family as a social services model. In this regard black male social workers tended to work for black people, not with them. For example, the black male–dominated National Urban League seemed more content in pleading with industrialists to give jobs to black people than in organizing black groups to exert political pressure on industries that refused to hire black people or to rally black people around their extended family concepts of mutual obligation, mutual aid, and mutual reciprocity. For example, the league's most prominent executive director, Whitney M. Young, was noted for his ability to divest money and influence from wealthy and powerful white people. Therefore, critics often saw the league as little more than a prestigious job-finding agency.

GENDER AND CLASS

Although gender was a salient issue in its own right, given the subordinate status of women in general in American society, it was often intertwined with the issue of class. Even black women's club members found class a persistent matter, despite serious attempts to downplay class differences. Leading black women in the black churches and the women's clubs were primarily educated, middle-class black women. Their organizations not only consisted of teachers, missionaries, and the wives of ministers but also formed part of "an emergent class of school administrators, journalists, businesswomen, and reformers" (Higginbotham, 1993, p. 14). These women often found that despite their zealous racial consciousness and desire to uplift the black masses, their middle-class outlook often colored their relationships with poor, peasant, and working-class black women. Their Victorian moralizing frequently led them to attack the values and lifestyles of poor black people who transgressed white middle-class propriety and to wage war against "improper" and "disrespectable" individual behavior such as drinking, gambling, loud talking, gum chewing, snuff dipping, and even listening to jazz on Saturdays and attending baseball games on Sundays. These women felt it their duty to disavow certain behavioral patterns and opposed the expressive culture of "unassimilated" black people. They believed fervently that the crude, loud, emotional, and superstitious oral folk culture of the black masses had to be replaced by literacy and intellectual acumen—in other words, if black people were going to succeed as a race, they must "move up out of the age of the voice" (Higginbotham, 1993, p. 44) to the age of the written word. Thus, through the written word in the form of leaflets, newspaper columns, and especially tract literature, these upper-class black women called for hard work, piety, cleanliness, sexual purity, and temperance among the black masses and condemned black people who did not conform to their Victorian, bourgeois, assimilationist vision.

Trying to impose middle-class values on poor black women became so outlandish that prominent black women's club leaders called for an immediate stop to it. As early as 1904, black women's club leaders began to chastise middle-class black women for being contemptuous of poor people and disrespectful of their way of life. For example, Mary Church Terrell, the prominent black feminist spokesperson and civil rights activist, urged black women to overcome their class biases and "to go down among the lonely, the illiterate, and even the vicious to whom we are bound by the ties of race and sex, and put forth every possible effort to uplift and reclaim them" (quoted in Higginbotham, 1993, p. 207). Nannie Helen Burroughs, the renowned black educator and fiery orator, fiercely attacked women who engaged in social service as a fad or for "social prestige." She denounced the social butterfly who "smooths her well-gloved hand while she studies the 'wonderfully interesting slum' problem as diversion" (quoted in Higginbotham, 1993, p. 208). Burroughs proclaimed,

> There is an army of them [black women] that you have never seen, and never will see until you walk the streets of the New Jerusalem and go out of your way to get an ordinary, common-sense, spirit-filled everyday woman. There are thousands of them to be had, and you can do more work in one month with this type of woman than you can do in one year with the "would-be" social leader, who is entering these organizations devoted to uplift, for no other reason than to show her finery and to let her less fortunate sisters see how brilliantly she shines. (quoted in Higginbotham, 1993, p. 209)

The campaign against notions of class superiority, the effort to recruit and work with black women from the lower strata of society, and the practice of going among them where they lived instead of trying to save them from afar helped black women's club members soften significantly their desire to make poor women "ladylike" in their own bourgeois image and led them to work with women of lower classes on common problems with mutual respect.

The members of the women's clubs and national organizations also had the lessons of history to teach them. Among their earlier heroines was Charlotte Forten (1969) (who later became Charlotte Forten Grimké after marrying the famed minister Francis Grimké), a black elite-class woman who went to the Sea Islands of South Carolina to teach ex-slaves near the end of the Civil War. Black women such as Forten often were held up by black women's club leaders as epitomizing the kind of social class cooperation that all the women's club members should deem ideal.

Born into a wealthy free black Philadelphia family, Forten was one of the few black teachers chosen for work among the newly freed black people of St. Helena Islands during the Civil War. Once among these newly freed black people, Forten was immediately surprised to learn that although both she and the Sea Island people were black, there was a wide gulf between them as a result of their social class backgrounds. Wanting badly to be of service to her people, Forten genuinely believed that the best help she could give these poor, unfortunate people was to teach them the standards of her social class. She decided that because the language of the Sea Island people was "quite unintelligible" to her ears, she would teach them standard English and clear diction. Thinking that they were probably lacking in good hygienic habits and that they probably preferred "gaudy colored" clothes, she decided that she would teach them good hygiene and proper dress. Assuming that they were "crude" and "coarse" regarding manners, she decided that she would teach them how to behave properly. After witnessing a ring shout she concluded that this practice was probably "the barbarous expression of religion handed down to them from their African ancestors" (Forten, 1969, p. 73) and committed herself to making these barbarous influences "pass away under the influence of Christian teachings" (p. 74).

However, after she had been around the black Sea Island people for a while, Forten was forced to reexamine her notions. She wrote that "we noticed that the people had much better taste in selecting materials for dresses than we had supposed. They do not generally like gaudy colors, but prefer neat, quiet patterns" (Forten, 1969, p. 72). Forten noticed too that the Sea Island black people were not as crude in manners and morals as she had supposed. She admitted that "These people are exceedingly polite in their manner towards each other. . . . The children, too, are taught to be very polite to their elders, and it is the rarest thing to hear a disrespectful word from a child to his parent, or to any grown person. They have really what the New-Englanders call 'beautiful manners'" (p. 72).

Forten (1969) noticed that the people were not as hostile to or incapable of learning as she had believed. She had to confess that "it is wonderful how a people who have been so long crushed to the earth, so imbruted as these have been, can have so great a desire for knowledge, and such a capability for attaining it" (p. 71). Forten also acknowledged that the religion of the Sea Island people was not as barbaric as she had thought. She wrote, "We have heard some of the old Negro preachers make prayers that were really beautiful and touching" (p. 82). The music of the people, whether in church, in the fields, or in their homes, she found to be sweet, strange, and solemn—unmatched. She wrote, "I can't describe the effect that the singing has on me. I believe I was quite lifted out of myself" (quoted in Stevenson, 1988, p. 415).

Immersing herself in their lives, Forten made daily rounds visiting, observing, listening, and learning. One diary entry stated, "Went round to see the people, of whom I haven't seen so much this week, being unusually busy. Had as usual a very pleasant time talking with them all, big and little" (quoted in Stevenson, 1988, p. 421). From listening to their expressions of loss, grief, and despair as well as their expressions of joy, faith, and hope, Forten learned to mourn with them. Furthermore, once the people could see that she was no longer intolerant and judgmental, they were open to her ideas, knowledge, teachings, and expertise. Forten was then able to accomplish the goals she originally had such as teaching the Sea Island people to read and write and to know something about John Brown, Frederick Douglass, Toussaint L'ouverture, and others who had fought for black liberty; introducing the women to the latest fashions; and even teaching the young people clearer diction. Once she saw herself as a sufferer among fellow mourners, she viewed them no longer as "those people" but in her words, "mine own people" (Forten, 1969, p. 86). She rededicated her life to her own people, writing "Let the work which I have solemnly pledged myself fill up my whole existence to the exclusion of all vain longings" (quoted in Stevenson, 1988, p. 403).

Women's club leaders and members could see in Charlotte Forten's work the synthesis of bourgeois culture with rural black culture, a synthesis that was nonantagonistic, based on a two-way process of learning, and based on mutual respect and reciprocity.

Black women caregivers not only had black history to show them how they should relate to women of lower-class ranks but contemporary experiences demonstrating clearly to them how they should not. For example, the experiences of the women missionaries of Spelman Seminary (later renamed Spelman College and currently viewed as the epitome of black women's collegiate education) provide a clear example of what not to do. In 1891 Spelman Seminary opened a missionary training department that endeavored to train black women to live among their people in the most destitute areas of the South (Higginbotham, 1993). These women were to impart to poor and uneducated black people knowledge of the Bible; personal hygiene; temperance; family and household duties; and habits of punctuality, thrift, and hard work. Going from house to house, reading the Bible, handing out literature, praying with families, and instructing on proper behavior, the missionaries led a rigorous campaign against drinking, gambling, chewing tobacco, chewing gum, playing cards, and playing baseball on Sundays. Although the Spelman women put great fervor and effort into their work, they found themselves deeply disillusioned because of the stiff resistance of the black masses to their brand of racial uplift. Poor black people felt that because their lives were plagued by run-down, dilapidated shacks with no inside running water and the inability to afford more than one or two pieces of clothing, it was impossible for them to maintain the kind of cleanliness and duplicate the kind of taste in home decorating and fashion that the Spelman women required. They felt that because they were living on scanty wages, it was practically impossible for them to be as frugal and thrifty as the Spelman students advocated. They felt that because life for them was so tough and brutal, they had a need for the kind of recreational and leisurely outlet (such as playing base-

ball, playing cards, and drinking) that Spelman students vehe-
mently asked them to avoid. As one frustrated Spelman woman
attested to, swaying poor black people from drinking was no easy
task because, as she reported, "None of them considered themselves
drunkards for they never drink enough to lay them in the gutter, or
at least not very often and a moderate drinker is, in their minds, a
long way from a drunkard" (Higginbotham, 1993, p. 38). Most
important, the masses of black people felt that there was absolutely nothing wrong in the way they praised the Lord. So what if they
got openly emotional, shouted, and danced in the church aisles!
Overall, they felt that the Spelman women were too "big-headed,"
too "uppity," and "too fine" to understand them and their ways
(Higginbotham, 1993, p. 38).

With the lessons of the past and the examples of the times, black
women caregivers began to show a remarkable ability to bring black
women together from different socioeconomic backgrounds and to
downplay class differences for the sake of greater race unity.
Although women's clubs were almost always organized by middle-
class or privileged-class black women, these women followed
through on the extended family's emphasis on class cooperation
and made it clear that they were not "slumming" in their work with
black women of the lower social strata. Cynthia Neverdon-Morton
(1989) wrote that "as it became clearer [to them] that all black
women—rich and poor, urban and rural—would have to work
together to achieve the dual goals of racial and individual better-
ment, class differences among the women diminished in importance" (p. 6).

BLACK MALE CAREGIVERS AND CLASS

When black men took charge of professional caregiving in the black
community, they undid most of the work early black female caregivers had done in terms of black social class unity. Instead of seeking to purge the arrogant bourgeois attitudes and beliefs within
them and gain closer ties with the black masses, black male social
workers tended to exacerbate class differences by siding with and
promoting the interests of the ruling white elite and by seeking to
transform rural peasants into an urban black bourgeoisie.

The Great Depression of the 1930s stripped black male social workers of the illusion of using social work as a tool to gain industrial democracy and caused them to direct their attention to seeking to improve the character of the black masses. The "partnership" that the National Urban League social workers had, for example, with the capitalist class subjected it to scathing attacks from radical black critics. For example, Chandler Owens, the social worker turned socialist, and A. Phillip Randolph, the radical labor organizer, accused the league of providing "scabs for the industrial magnates and capitalists" who financed the league and held that "it is the instrument of Wall Street, an organization of, for and by capital" (Owens, 1920, p. 176). Therefore, many radicals concluded that "the capitalist Urban League cannot represent the working class Negro race" (p. 176). This critique was particularly painful to the league because it had footed Owen's graduate school expenses in social work and made him a fellow of the league.

Not only did black male social workers, who dominated the National Urban League, the black YMCAs, and black higher education in social work, not go as far as black female caregivers in bridging the gap between the social classes, but there is also little evidence that they sought or respected a black female perspective. For example, the black social worker Sarah Willie Layten, one of the first female field secretaries of the National Urban League, urged the Urban League and other black private charities to break their dependency on powerful white philanthropists. She and other executive board members of the Baptist Women's Convention asked, "Do you wonder how Jane Addams built up that great Hull House? She has done it because her people have invested faith, money and lives in it in response to her appeals. It is not large gifts that we need, but a large number of givers. We can do as much with small gifts from a large number of givers as Miss Jane Addams has done with large gifts from a small number of givers" (quoted in Higginbotham, 1993, p. 175).

Layten, a leader in the National Association of Colored Women as well as the Association for the Protection of Colored Women, also called on Urban League members to focus as much attention on the plight of female migrants as on that of male migrants. The theory of male Urban League members seemed to be that if the black men had steady jobs paying decent wages, then the quality of life among black women and black children would automatically improve. Layten herself devoted considerable attention to keeping black women and girls from falling victim to "the wharf sharks" (Higginbotham, 1993, p. 181), her term for exploitative labor agents and other unscrupulous people who waited on the docks of various cities to intercept black female migrants. Layten felt that there were issues confronting black female migrants that were very different from issues facing black men, issues such as the legacy of black women being raped by white men and battered by black men, the growing feminization of poverty, and the political disfranchise- ment of black women.

Layten, as a leader of the Baptist Women's Convention, urged the National Urban League to work with black churches to deal with both the secular and the spiritual social services needs of the people. Furthermore, Layten urged the league to engage in politics and directly challenge the status quo. A staunch exponent of women's suffrage, Layten urged black people to "turn their Great Migration into a political advantage" (quoted in Higginbotham, 1993, p. 221). She challenged the National Urban League, the black churches, and other male-dominated organizations to assist in the political mobilization of the masses; to politicize them to fight for women's suffrage; to educate and encourage black men to exercise their right to vote; to use the ballot to end discrimination, lynch law, and the rape of black women; to obtain better education; and to secure greater legal justice. There is no evidence that the male- dominated National Urban League heeded Layten's call on any of these pertinent issues.

BLACK MEN LEAVE THE PROFESSION

Instead of changing direction or rearranging priorities, black male social workers in general began to drop out of the profession after the Great Depression revealed the limitations of social work. Most of them, already extremely career-minded, simply sought more- promising and -lucrative careers. For example, when black male sociologist–social workers dropped out of social work, they merely moved forward in other professional careers. Charles S. Johnson left the National Urban League, one author speculated, because "he liked to be in complete control, [and] he may have become restless in his subordinate position" (Stanfield, 1985, p. 122). Whatever the reason, Johnson used his foundation contacts to secure the directorship of the Fisk Social Science Department and later used foundation influence to become the president of Fisk University itself. E. Franklin Frazier left the social work profession in controversy but he moved on to become the chairman of the Sociology Department at Howard University. He rose to prominence as a sociologist and was the first black person to become president of the prestigious American Sociological Association. George Haynes, the first black person to receive professional training in social work, the first to issue a call for the training of black people as professional social workers, and the first to establish an undergraduate program of social work at a black college, got caught up in a power struggle within the National Urban League, which he had helped found. Haynes had come into conflict with Eugene Kinckle Jones, who had replaced him as executive director of the league, after Haynes vigorously espoused an old Booker T. Washington philosophy of concentrating attention on rural black people. Haynes proposed to set up centers to train black social workers to go among their people in the rural South. He believed that providing rural black people with needed social services right where they were would discourage them from migrating to the northern cities (Parris & Brooks, 1971). Haynes's opponents, who represented a break from the old Washingtonian school of black caregiving, argued that the migrants were already in the city and that the league should concentrate on finding jobs, housing, health care, and recreational outlets for them. The new philosophy that Jones espoused won out, and Haynes left the league to score another first. He became the first black director of the Division of Negro Economics under the U.S. Department of Labor (Parris & Brooks, 1971).

By the 1940s and 1950s the dropout rate of black men from the profession of social work was so significant that professional caregiving was turned back over practically exclusively to black women. Overall, although black social workers, male and female, wanted to impose middle-class values on the black migrants, most sincerely wanted to advance the race. In fact, they genuinely felt that imparting bourgeois morality was a step toward racial uplift and that the two went hand in hand. Moreover, they believed that they were engaging in radical activity, particularly because white people in the South were so racist that they would just as soon lynch a black person for trying to impose bourgeois values as they would for burning the Confederate flag. White southerners saw trying to instill middle-class values in black people as a subversive attempt to make "niggers" the equal of white people.

It was not so much the resistance on the part of the black masses to this bourgeois encouragement and opposition that blocked black social workers' efforts of uplift as it was the rising tide of commercialism, materialism, and individualism among black people. For example, many of the early black caregiving systems such as black hospitals, orphanages, and homes for older people were funded not by wealthy philanthropists but by the nickel-and-dime donations of the masses of black people (Martin & Martin, 1985). As black people became more organized, they also became more influenced by the rise of department stores, mass advertising, and installment buying. These black people had been dirt-poor and were starving for material goods. Hence, it did not take much to arouse their consuming passion and to quell the old black values calling for even the black poor to make financial sacrifices on behalf of the race. In urban America, the masses of black people were steadily finding that to "be somebody" meant having things, not helping others. The black elite had also come out of the black helping tradition that obligated the more educated and talented black people to make sacrifices on behalf of the poor, uneducated black masses. As these black people began to define their status and worth in terms of conspicuous consumption and material trappings and to value easy living, status, and money over an obligation to the struggling masses, the old black helping tradition that valued social class cooperation began to decline drastically.

The old black helping tradition declined to the point that even in social work it was becoming increasingly difficult to ascertain whether black people were entering social work to help their people or just to pursue a respectable professional career that would land them in the middle class, if not in terms of salaries, certainly in terms of social prestige and status. As black social workers became more concerned with social status, legitimacy, and power, class matters began to drive a deeper wedge between them and the black masses. Even black women's clubs began to become class exclusive. For example, with the formation and popularity of black Greek-letter sororities, middle-class and privileged-class black women were beginning to set up educational and cultural membership requirements that excluded the vast majority of poor and working-class black women. Although national women's organizations such as the National Council of Negro Women continued to do commendable work in the area of black uplift, even these organizations adopted the practice of working on behalf of the masses of black women rather than with them around class-cooperative endeavors.

A CONCEPT OF VULNERABILITY

Overall, early black social workers did not avoid the social class pitfalls that leading sociologist–social work pioneers such as George Haynes, W.E.B. DuBois, and E. Franklin Frazier warned them about. By taking on a bourgeois outlook, they were unable to create a concept or theory of black vulnerability that would have been the key to a closer relationship with the black masses. A concept of vulnerability would have proposed that in a virulently racist society black people from all social class backgrounds are vulnerable. With such a concept, black social workers would have seen that if lower-class black people were subjected to brutal forms of overt oppression and hostility, then middle- and upper-class black people were often victimized by the racist microaggressions hurled at them perceptively, but nevertheless destructively, in their accumulated effect. Such a concept would have been totally in line with both the blues and the spiritual tradition.

The spirituals view all black people as fellow sufferers and fellow mourners, meaning all black people are vulnerable. The blues philosophy also asserts that everybody, regardless of class status, has to "pay dues" and that everybody is subject to "goin' through changes," meaning experiencing mental, emotional, or spiritual turmoil and anguish that will put them outside their natural, normal, or ideal self. Black humor and black folklore often made fun of "dicty" or high brow black people who thought that their status exempted them from paying dues only to discover that trouble dogs them as much as it does anybody else.

Black social gospel ministers and mass race leaders tried to develop a concept of vulnerability based on the shared historical black experiences. For example, the black social gospel minister Francis J. Grimké recognized that whether black people were lower class or upper class, integrationist or black nationalist,

> *as a race we are to sink or swim, live or die, survive or perish together. We can't get away from each other. Never mind what progress I, as an individual may make, never mind how intelligent or wealthy I may become, the social laws and customs that operate against the Negro as a class, will operate against me. His fate will be my fate. We are all classed together, and are treated alike, whatever our condition—rich or poor, high or low, educated or uneducated . . . our fate is one. We rise or fall together. Such being the case, our duty is to recognize that fact, and in the light of it to pull together for the common good.* (quoted in Woodson, 1942, p. 392)

Pioneering black social workers were not likely to be able to develop a social work practice based on the black experience without a concept of vulnerability and of linking the precarious fate of black people of all socioeconomic status backgrounds to their ancestral and historical connections.

REFERENCES

DuBois, W.E.B. (1971). The talented tenth. In A. G. Paschal (Ed.), *A W.E.B. DuBois reader* (pp. 31–51). New York: Collier Books.

DuBois, W.E.B. (1976). *In battle for peace.* Millwood, NY: Kraus–Thomson Organization.

Forten, C. (1969). Life on the sea islands. In L. C. Lockwood (Ed.), *Two black teachers in the Civil War* (pp. 67–86). New York: Arno Press and New York Times.

Frazier, E. F. (1957). *Black bourgeoisie.* New York: Collier Books.

Haynes, G. (1922). *The trend of the races.* New York: Council of Women for Home Missions and Missionary Education Movement in the United States and Canada.

Higginbotham, E. B. (1993). *Righteous discontent.* Cambridge, MA: Harvard University Press.

Martin, E. P., & Martin, J. M. (1985). *The helping tradition in the black family and community.* Silver Spring, MD: National Association of Social Workers.

Neverdon-Morton, C. (1989). *Afro-American women of the South and the advancement of the race, 1895–1925.* Knoxville: University of Tennessee Press.

Owens, C. (1920, December). The invisible government of Negro social work. *Messenger,* pp. 174–177.

Parris, G., & Brooks, L. (1971). *Blacks in the city: The history of the National Urban League.* Boston: Little, Brown.

Ross, E. L. (1978). *Black heritage in social welfare: 1860–1930.* Metuchen, NJ: Scarecrow Press.

Stanfield, J. N. (1985). *Philanthropy and Jim Crow in American social science.* Westport, CT: Greenwood Press.

Stevenson, B. (1988). *The journals of Charlotte Forten Grimké.* New York: Oxford University Press.

Washington, B. T. (1900). *A new Negro for a new century.* Chicago: American Publishing House.

Woodson, C. G. (Ed.). (1942). *The work of Francis J. Grimké (Vol. 1).* Washington, DC: Associated Publishers.

PART 3

Mornin'

CHAPTER 9

The Foundation of Black Experience–Based Social Work: Perspectives

*B*aer and Federico (1978) held that social workers must develop skills in recognizing, respecting, and accepting diverse cultural and lifestyle groups and their relationship to the social institutions of the dominant society. However, the authors acknowledged that in social work the area of human diversity "is generally troublesome" because the human diversity content "is usually only vaguely conceptualized" (p. 25). They maintained that the "lack of a clear conceptualization of the meaning and significance of human diversity makes it difficult to achieve the objective of educating practitioners who are aware and respectful of such diversity" (p. 25).

We hope that our conceptualizations drawn from the black helping experience have been clear to social work practitioners thus far. We have propagated the image of a people whose lives have been plagued by the problem of loss and separation and who have expressed their dread of this adversity through their music, folktales, narratives, sermons, poetry, and other black cultural forms. We see these people adopting various techniques of survival and patterns of reaction to minimize the danger and reality of losing their loved ones to oppressive racist forces. They accommodate, they role play, and they take flight. Nevertheless, their environment is so repressive that they cannot avoid incorporating negative psychologies that stifle their development. The psychology of the sick grew out of their constantly being treated like helpless dependents, social diseases, and economic pariahs. The psychology of cultural paranoia grew out of their deep mistrust of white people. Could they trust that the master would not sell them even when they behaved themselves? Could they trust that they would not be lynched even when they were "good niggers?" The psychology of cultural claustrophobia grew out of their limited, restricted environment that left little room for realizing their true self-aspirations.

We show that in order to quell their fears and to hold fast to their dreams, this people heavily engaged themselves in the work of mourning. Being a people of loss and separation, they lent one another support in times of trouble, and through empathy and catharsis they sought to maintain some semblance of sanity and humanity. This mourning work also included the instillation of hope and the constant testing of reality. The goal was to make them culturally versatile enough to break through the feelings of sickness, to gain enough confidence and trust in themselves to prepare for the realization of their true self-aspirations—to take these aspirations out of the realm of fantasy and imagination to the realm of possibility and fact. The aim was also to make them versatile enough to take advantage of what little room their stifling environment made for them to avoid societal pitfalls and to grow—to constantly push against the boundaries of reality, "to make a way out of no way."

We trace these people from slavery to emancipation and show that in freedom they developed mourning institutions and modeled their social service programs on the black extended family. We show that the hope, faith, and confidence that these institutions inculcated were largely responsible for these people taking the risk and migrating to urban centers in hopes of fleeing persecution and leading better lives. It is in the urban center that we find that these people began to develop an active sense of cultural amnesia and tried to shed their old ways. Caught up in the commercialism, individualism, and materialism of urban culture, they began to privatize their troubles and camouflage their pain. Without strong social support and strong institutions of mourning, the old psychologies of cultural sickness, cultural paranoia, and cultural claustrophobia began to rise to unprecedented heights and even showed signs of leading to the most destructive psychology of all, the psychology of cultural terminal illness. Caught up in this state of social disorganization, these people began to draw the attention of the professional social workers, particularly as they appeared in the courts and on the relief roles. At first the advocacy, social action, and enthusiasm that social workers displayed gained their admiration. But then it appeared that social workers were part of a repressive legal arm and major players in institutions that perpetuated black loss and separation. In many of these institutions of loss, black people often found themselves handled in ways that intensified their traumatization and deepened their primal fears. Instead of being healed and helped, they were humiliated and brutalized and then dropped back into the black community to turn their bitterness back on their own people.

This is our conceptual perspective of the past black experience in a nutshell. The key issue of this chapter is to see where social workers are in contemporary society. In other words, what relevancy does this theoretical perspective have for social work practitioners in their work with black people today?

MORNING

In this part of the book we concentrate on the concept of morning because, as we indicated earlier, in black culture morning represents being on the verge of achieving or actually realizing the desired goal. For example, in the spirituals, morning was the time when black people would find Jesus:

He's comin' in de mornin'
He's comin' in de mornin'
He's comin' with a rainbow on his shoulder
He's comin' again bye and bye!

That morning was going to be the start of a great day:

Great day! Great day, the righteous marching
Great day! God's goin' to build up Zion's wall.

Individuals would sing,

One o'dese mornin's—it won't be long
You'll look fo' me, an' I'll be gone.

Everybody had better be ready:

> *O mourner, have you got your ticket signed?*
> *O mourner, have you got your ticket signed?*
> *In-a that morning, oh my Lord, . . .*
> *In-a that morning when the Lord says "Hurry."*

Morning suggested that many black people believed staunchly in such biblical scriptures as Psalms 30:5 that reads, "Weeping may endure for a night, but joy cometh in the morning" (King James Version). The pertinent questions of this chapter are: To what extent have the hopes and aspirations of the ancestors been realized in the lives of the current generation? How much unresolved work of the past is left for contemporary social workers to do? What does black experience–based social work have to offer?

PHILOSOPHY

We hope that we have made it clear by now that by focusing on the spirituals and the blues traditions, we are not making a case for music therapy or for turning social workers into musicologists or musicians. We analyze the spirituals and the blues for the insights these cultural forms can provide because they are more than just classical black music art forms. Both represent the voices of ancestors expressing their needs and their hopes for the race, and both contain a philosophy by which countless numbers of black people over the generations were expected to conduct their lives.

The spirituals and the blues imparted a philosophy of survival, endurance, and transcendence. Johnston (1954) wrote that "by singing and shouting, the slaves received strength to endure physical and mental cruelty" and that "without music, it is doubtful that blacks would have survived" (p. 41). Neal (1989) stated that black music advocated a philosophy of spiritual resiliency, that the freeing of the spirit is an essential aspect of the philosophy of the spirituals, and that "toughness of the spirit is an essential aspect of the ethos of the blues" (p. 110).

By imparting a philosophy of spiritual endurance, resiliency, and toughness, the blues and the spirituals represented a problem-solving philosophy. The singer of the blues and spirituals did more than sing to ease his or her troubled mind, to get things out of his or her system, or to feel better. As Keil (1966) stated, the singer "sensed broader and deeper obligation to the community" (p. 76). The singer "must not only state common problems clearly and concisely but must in some sense take steps toward their analysis and solution" (p. 76).

In this regard, the philosophical worldview of the spirituals and the blues placed value on collective problem solving, viewing the world as too hard and brutal for the individual to go it alone. In the blues and the spirituals, individuals can go solo so long as they stay within the group structure. They can, through improvisation and creativity, stray beyond the group with their own individual mark of distinction as long as they get back in rhythm with the shared experience of the group. The important point is that after soloing and listening to one another, they find common ground. The key question facing the modern social work practitioner is: To what extent have black people in contemporary society taken on a philosophy of spiritual toughness, transcendence, and collective problem solving? And to what extent have contemporary social workers been any more successful than social workers of the past in helping to move black people in this direction? Currently, the problem with mainstream social work, as Lum (1986) pointed out, is that it tends to take an individualistic stance without recognizing that many people of color operate on the basis of a communal or group approach. Black experience–based social work learned from the philosophical worldview of the spirituals and the blues that the line between individual problems and structural defects is thin. There are just as many blues songs about structural or societal oppressions, such as being in prison or on the chain gang or owing one's soul to one's boss (Oliver, 1970), as there are about individual loneliness, alienation, and mistreatment. When slaves sang about all God's children having shoes once they got to heaven, this was a subtle protest about not having shoes on earth; when they sang about wearing starry crowns and long white robes and walking through pearly gates on streets paved with gold and drinking milk and honey when they got to heaven, they were addressing the cruelty and coarseness of their wretchedness and their desire to live a better life on earth. When black people sang blues songs such as the following, they were protesting current social conditions:

> *I'd rather drink muddy water sleep in a hollow log.*
> *Rather drink muddy water sleep in a hollow log*
> *Than to be in Atlanta [or wherever they are]*
> *And be treated like a dog.*

In black culture, there is a fluidity of individual problems and structural defects and a connection between private concerns and the collective problems of history.

Black experience–based social workers learned from the philosophical worldview of the spirituals and the blues that there is an overlap between the sacred and the secular. Titon (1977) wrote that the same troubles of the soul that black people brought to church services they brought to the Saturday night dances, and they expected the same kind of emotional release and the same kind of healing. The synthesis of the sacred and the secular in the black experience makes the blues the reality principle of the spirituals. When the spirituals overemphasize longing for that hope-filled, freedom-filled, great gittin'-up morning, the blues bring it back to reality with their own hard version of "morning." Morning in the blues is a time when one can fully see the light but not in terms of finding Jesus or heavenly joy, but seeing clearly the nature and the tenacity of life's pains. Titon wrote that "such formulas as 'I woke up this morning,' 'got up this morning,' 'soon one morning,' and 'early this morning' certainly are related" (p. 181) in the blues and imply that black people had better be mentally tough and spiritually prepared in case more hell than heaven comes knocking at their door. Hence, blues songs follow refrains like this one:

> *I woke up this mornin' blues all 'round my bed*
> *Mm woke up this mornin' blues all 'round my bed*
> *Couldn't eat my breakfast and there's blues*
> *all in my head.*

or

Early one morning the blues came falling down
Mm mm soon one mornin' blues come fallin' down.

Sometimes even in the blues, morning was a time for sacred rituals:

I woke up this mornin' said my mornin' prayer
I woke up this mornin' I said my mornin' prayer
I woke up this mornin' babe I said my mornin' prayer.

Although contemporary social work practice tends to be primarily a secular profession, this can be said categorically: There can be no social work based on the black experience that does not consider both the secular and the sacred world of black people. Thus, black experience–based social work is primarily a secular practice with a deep spiritual emphasis. It does not operate from a theological framework, but it recognizes that black people historically are a spiritual people not only in the religious sense but also in terms of the role of historical empathy, ancestral connectedness, and faith and hope. Black experience–based social work advances the idea that it is imperative for any social worker working with black people to recognize the primary role and important function of the sacred as well as the profane in black life.

PROBLEMS

As we examine the relevancy of the problems of the black past to the problems of black people in contemporary society, we can only say this: The problems of the past are still with us. For example, few problems in the black experience have been lyricized in black music, preached about, worried over, prayed over, and shouted out more than the problem of separation and loss, the problem of troubled intimate relations, and the problem of racial oppression. These problems are still with us, posing a serious challenge to professional social workers.

The Problem of Loss and Separation

Marian Wright Edelman (1992), the prominent child welfare advocate, held that we are still losing our children to the city streets and to societal neglect. She bemoaned, "we are on the verge of losing two generations of black children and youths to drugs, violence, too-early parenthood, poor health and education, unemployment, family disintegration—and to the spiritual and physical poverty that both breeds and is bred by them" (p. 15). Edelman's observations are supported by the prominent black psychiatrist Margaret Morgan Lawrence (1975), who wrote that urban black children are often brought up in families with "three generations of loss, and destructiveness" (p. 73). She wrote,

> *A severe blight among young Harlem children, as perceived by those who care for them, is the trauma of separation and loss. Not infrequently, in three successive generations, we see separation from would-be "ideal images" during the first three years of life. A young black child may suffer loss of one or both parents for economic reasons, through self-destruction or "accident," through violence inflicted by others, or through drug addiction, illness and death. These parents may range in age from 12 to 13 to 48. . . . Separation from significant adult figures is damaging to the image of the self. It interferes with identification with ideal images, those of missing parents. It makes it unlikely that the ego so damaged will find its way to social group acceptance. Above all, there is a deep anger whose original target is the lost person; but the target easily fades and the anger becomes all pervasive. It remains as years pass.*
> (pp. 69–70)

Experts in modern society show that the problem of loss and separation is intertwined with many other serious social and psychological problems. Bowlby (1973), in his pioneering work on attachment and separation, held that people who have experienced object loss go through "a sequence of responses" of "protest, despair, and detachment" (p. 26). Marris (1974) maintained that object loss brings about physical distress, an inability to surrender the past, expressed, for instance, by brooding over memories, sensing the presence of the dead, clinging to possessions, being unable to comprehend the loss, experiencing feelings of unreality, withdrawal into apathy, and hostility against others, against fate, or turned in upon oneself. Parkes (1972) explained that object loss leads to responses of intense grief, yearning, anger, guilt, searching, and attempts to mitigate the pain by maintaining that the bereaved person is nearby, although he or she may not be seen or heard; Simos (1979) stated that not only can object loss result in numerous emotional and psychological disorders, such as grief, rage, guilt, stress, depression, phobias, schizophrenia, and senile psychosis, but that "loss, separation, and fear of loss have also been recognized as underlying dynamics in a variety of physical disorders, such as asthma, ulcerative colitis, heart attacks, cancer [and] rheumatoid arthritis" (pp. 2, 3).

In contemporary society numerous blacks have unresolved conflicts of loss and separation that can have devastating, lifetime consequences. As Rochlin (1965) held, when a people fail to resolve the problem of loss and separation, they are in danger of going "on to adulthood with an inability to form lasting ties of intimacy, with problems regarding task completion, phobias about success, difficulties with normal separations, lives of achievement below one's full potential, psychiatric disorders, and most serious of all, the propensity for self-or-other-destructive behaviors" (p. 121).

In our experience, drawn from many hours of counseling, advising, and motivating, we have found that when black students and other black people seeking our help have not resolved the problem of loss and separation, they have had problems completing other crucial life tasks such as finishing their education, finding work or completing work assignments, and maintaining steady intimate relationships. It is as if they cannot fully complete any other serious life task until they bring this mourning work to completion. These black people with unresolved, hidden tension tend to be unfocused and to always be living on the level of intention. They never quite get around to fulfilling true self goals as they waste considerable time daydreaming, fantasizing, and marking time. And what is specifically problematic is that black people still tend to be disproportionately represented in institutions of loss—mental health facilities, prisons, juvenile centers, public welfare departments, adoption agencies, and foster homes. These loss institutions have carried on the traditional practice of culturally and psychologically amputating black clients, monitoring and punishing them, rejecting and excluding them, confirming society's racist attitudes toward them, and isolating them from intimate relations and close contact with their families and communities. Practically every social welfare institution in America that purports to help rehabilitate, reform, and "make productive citizens" out of black people is of an incarcerative nature and has the coercive aspect of internment.

The Problem of "Mistreatment" in Intimate Relations

The blues and the spirituals have different worldviews of intimate relations, but as Titon (1977) held, "they nevertheless preach the same advice: Treat people right" (p. 33). The spirituals stress that people have to treat other folks right to get close to God or to become godly. To not treat people right is to suffer a spiritual poverty every bit as troublesome as material poverty and a spiritual death every bit as tragic as a physical death.

The blues mainly emphasize the need of the black man and the black woman to treat one another right. Hence, there is hardly any problem that men and women have had or can have that is not explored in the blues. For instance, in the blues social workers can learn a great deal about ambivalence in intimate relations:

> *Sometime I think that you too sweet to die*
> *Sometime I think that you too sweet to die*
> *But at other times I think you ought to be buried alive.*

They can learn about revenge in intimate relations:

> *Lord I walked all night long*
> *with my forty-four in my hand*
> *I was lookin' for my woman*
> *found her with another man.*

They can learn about threats:

> *I love you pretty mama believe me it ain't no lie*
> *The day you quit me baby that's the day you die.*

They can learn about violence:

Took my gun and broke the barrel down
Took my gun and broke the barrel down
Put my baby six feet under the ground.

They can learn about the powerful hold that love and sex can have on an individual "in-a-that-morning":

Got's a long tall woman tall like a cherry tree baby
Got a long tall woman tall like a cherry tree baby
She gets up 'fore day and puts that thing on me.

or

Bumble bee bumble bee please come back to me
Bumble bee bumble bee please come back to me
He's got the best old sting any bumble bee that I ever seen.

Overall, the blues sees intimate relations free of mistreatment as the ideal goal and often subjects "a mistreating man" or a "mistreating woman" to severe scolding and scorn:

Babe if your heart ain't iron it must be made of stone
if your heart ain't iron it must be made of stone
for you're a mistreatin' mama babe sure as you born.

In contemporary society, black male–female relationships are filled with ambivalence, revenge, threats, violence, and sexual control.

The Problem of Oppression

In many cases, the problem of mistreatment in intimate relationships easily signifies blacks people's veiled, unconscious, or subliminal hatred and protest of mistreatment in general. Oliver (1970) wrote that on a surface level, "sexual blues"

tell of broken love affairs, of unfaithfulness, of family disintegration. On the deeper plane they are indicative of the unrest and uncertainty, the fear and humiliation of the group. In them the blues singer has found, consciously or subconsciously, a vehicle of protest. . . . Neither

the blues singer nor his listener is likely to be aware of the function
of the songs as a sublimation of frustrated desires; They are ready to
take the themes at their face value. But they provide the same
catalyst; They sublimate hostility and canalize aggressive instincts
against a mythical common enemy, the "cheater." (p. 258)

So pervasive is the problem of racial oppression in black life that it
is difficult to tell whether black social problems are a result of black
people's own shortcomings or of the racism that relentlessly pur-
sues black people every second of every day. The negative psychologies instilled in black people by a rejecting, racist, oppressive
culture are still prominent and they still hinder the ability of black
people to stand together as a unified front.

NEGATIVE CULTURAL PSYCHOLOGIES

Black experience–based social work recognizes that there are just as
many black people currently as there were in the past who suffer
from the psychologies of cultural sickness, cultural claustrophobia,
cultural paranoia, cultural amnesia, and cultural terminal illness.
Black people migrated to big cities to escape feelings of being sick,
circumscribed, and constantly looking over their shoulders. They
wanted to be free to express their true inner desires; currently, many
black people still have their ambitions thwarted and feel the agonizing need for creativity, self-expression, and self-realization. They
are beginning to feel that the urban ghettos, as the black revolutionary sociologist Oliver C. Cox (1976) put it, are planned extensions of the slave plantation. They are beginning to feel a terrible
sense of entrapment and of having no exit as they face innumerable
economic and cultural dead ends. Urban society still offers some
educational, cultural, economic, and political room for escape,
although the walls are becoming narrower by a fundamentalist,
racist, and reactionary conservative tide, but already many contemporary black people have given up hope and are seeking escape
into the anesthetized world of alcohol and drugs, entertainment,
sports, and strictly otherworldly religiosity.

The most serious malady in the contemporary black experience
is that many black people have severed all ties with their history.

Wilson (1993) held that black people today are in a state of historical denial. Therefore, their lives "are determined by fear, anxiety, terror and trauma" (p. 35). This historical amnesia deprives black people of the problem-solving methods of the past, forcing them "to lose the priceless wisdom and invaluable coping skills so painstakingly accumulated over eons of trial and error by their ancestors" (p. 123). When black people are not in a state of historical denial, they tend to be in a state where they want to glorify or romanticize black history, emphasizing times when blacks were great kings and queens of ancient African empires. To keep from falling into the abyss of despair and cynicism, they seek a simple, sentimental, optimistic, and romantic history that is blind to the perennial pitfalls and risks of the human enterprise.

Black experience–based social work seeks to have black people listen to the ancestral voices. It realizes that without knowledge and understanding of their history, black people have no sense of continuity and are prone to follow the whimsical fads and fashions of the day as they seek to live for the moment. Wilson (1993) wrote that "many of the murders, deaths, and much of the destruction that we see in our communities today are the result of people trying to escape history" (p. 35). Without a sense of continuity, black people lack a sense of identity and a sense of obligation to one another's well-being.

As a result of historical amnesia and lack of group empathy and identity, black communities across America have their guards up. They are communities on the defensive, many so tension-filled that the slightest provocation, real or imaginary, can ignite individual rage (Grier & Cobbs, 1969). The cycle of mistreatment and mistrust makes black people inflict even more dreaded losses and separations on one another. It causes them to see other black people as the enemy or primary threat to black survival. One modern author (McCall, 1994) wrote that he had to come to grip with the "troubling reality" that as "much as I ranted about white folks messing with us, I felt more threatened—physically—by my own people and the powerful self-hatred driving them" (p. 397).

The psychology of cultural paranoia has grown to be so pervasive and vicious in the black community that many black people have started pursuing a course of living hard, fast, and reckless as if they were going to die tomorrow. In fact, it has become fashionable for young black denizens to pick out their coffins and plan their funerals in advance. The gang wars, the drive-by shoot-outs, the gang banging, and the other negative features of black street life speak brazenly to the low premium many contemporary black people put on black life. Coleman-Miller (1992) wrote,

> *I have been to the prisons and have asked the kids there about death. Most of them said they were already dead. I have a friend who is terminally ill. She went out and bought a big car and full-length mink coat. And I am happy for her because she is doing what she wants to do, busily living her life. I saw on the street recently a young man with a pair of pump-it-up shoes with all kinds of things on them, a running suit that would probably have cost me a month's salary, gold necklaces, and a very fancy car. I decided that this young man bought all these things for the same reason my friend did. He had no concept of the possibility of a future. If that is true, it means that a large percentage of our young African-American males are terminally ill. The choices people make when they think they are already dead are different from the choices they make when they believe they have a future. (p. 57)*

We ourselves wrote elsewhere of this phenomenon of young black men developing a sense of impending doom:

> *By the time these young males [ones brought up in ghetto streets] are teenagers, many are living as if they are doomed men; that is, they live for the moment, for today, as if they have no future. They have a deep sense of futility, of inner rage, like men who feel that life has dealt them a raw deal. And even though most manage to contain their inner rage behind a facade of toughness, smartness, cuteness, and coolness, sometimes the masks crack and they explode. The result too often is violence, bloody and deadly. Instead of seeking to give young black males a feeling that they are not outsiders and that the society cares about them and wants them to lead productive lives, American society too often acts as if it is at war with young black males. Young black males seeing the onslaught of negativism against them feel that they are justified in feeling the threat of impending*

disaster, especially when powerful forces such as the police, courts, and media seem arrayed in war against them. (Martin & Martin, 1992, p. 16)

In the past, tribeless black men tended to show this indifference to black life because many had been so brutalized, traumatized, and hurt that they harbored a deep death wish. Some became "bad niggers" who were so reckless and unpredictable in their insane bravado that they frightened both black and white people. Currently, the cool black people are the children of the tribeless black men. Cool black people who roam big-city streets throughout America have a philosophy of being indifferent to suffering and of flirting with and inflicting death. Coolness today allows black people to hide their fears, vulnerabilities, pain, and weaknesses behind a mask of indifference, even callousness, to suffering and to camouflage their poverty and ignorance behind clothes, jewelry, and other material trappings. Majors and Billson (1992) wrote that

presenting to the world an emotionless, fearless, and aloof front counters the low sense of inner control, lack of inner strength, absence of stability, damaged pride, shattered confidence, and fragile social competence that come from living on the edge of society . . . the cool mask belies the rage held in check beneath the surface. (p. 8)

Although Majors and Billson (1992) saw cool as a unique coping mechanism among oppressed black men, they were also aware of its destructive nature, its inherent psychology of cultural terminal illness, and its ideology of a sense of impending doom:

Some black males have difficulty disclosing their deepest feelings even to those with whom they are expected to be closest: good friends, wives, mothers, fathers, girlfriends, and children. Keeping their guard up with white people makes it next to impossible to let their guard down for people they care about and interferes with establishing strong bonds with families and friends. (p. 41)

Majors and Billson (1992) also pointed out that these bottled-up emotions, in other words, the inability to mourn, often explode in aggressive acts by these men against those who are closest to their daily life—other black people.

In the cool world of big-city streets, the drug epidemic has enhanced the psychology of terminal illness to the level of a catastrophic crisis situation. It has led to a kind of cold and shocking destructiveness that has literally led thousands of black people to an insidious bondage, a modern-day type slavery. More than 40 years ago, Brown (1956), remembering when heroin was a "new thing" in New York and considered the "hippest thing to do," recalled that only five years after its introduction it had just about taken over Harlem:

> It seemed to be a kind of plague. Every time I went uptown, somebody else was hooked, somebody else was strung out. People talked about them as if they were dead. You'd ask about an old friend, and they'd say, Oh, well, he's strung out! It wasn't just a comment or an answer to a question. It was a eulogy for someone. He was just dead, through. (p. 179)

Forty years later McCall (1994) still wrote of the walking dead victims of illegal drug use and abuse:

> There weren't many in my bunch you could point to and say, "He's doing fine." . . . It seemed I could associate every other house I passed with a tragedy. The list of those dead was far too long for guys our age. Worse still was the list of those brothers who were drug zombies. They were breathing, but were more dead than alive. Teeth missing from their mouths. Skin palled and ashen. Eyes vacant, and hearts cold as ice in winter. It was depressing, and reminded me why I couldn't bear to go home too often or stay too long. (pp. 361–362)

Black experience–based social work recognizes the psychology of cultural terminal illness as an indication of a people who have given up hope and who are like the walking dead with no one to mourn over them or to mourn with them. The black revolutionary Huey P. Newton (1973) held that the psychology of cultural terminal illness amounts to what he called "reactionary suicide," a physical self-murder in the form of alcoholism, drug addiction, homicidal tendencies, and other self-destructive acts, acts that are responses to social conditions that overwhelm black people and condemn them to helplessness. He wrote that reactionary suicide is a form of spiritual death:

> Its victims have ceased to fight the forms of oppression that drink their blood. The common attitude has long been: What's the use? If a man rises up against a power as great as the United States, he will not survive. Believing this, many blacks have been driven to a death of the spirit rather than of the flesh, lapsing into lives of quiet desperation. Yet all the while, in the heart of every Black, there is the hope that life will somehow change in the future. (pp. 4–5)

Unfortunately, Newton himself became the victim of reactionary suicide as he became a drug addict and a gangster who was brutally murdered on one of America's cool, mean streets.

CULTURAL VERSATILITY

The challenge for contemporary social work practitioners is to help black people become culturally versatile enough to face up to and collectively solve their core problems and to overcome the negative psychologies stifling their emotional, social, cultural, economic, and political development. In the past, social workers failed to meet this challenge and black people who migrated to the big city gave up many of the traditional techniques of keeping these immobilizing, debilitating psychologies under control. As the following spiritual poignantly shows, rural black people wondered what was the matter with black people in the new urban Zion:

> I wonder what de matter with Zion, O my Lord,
> I wonder what de matter with Zion, good Lord, . . .
> My preacher don't preach a like a used to, O my Lord
> My sister don't shout like she used to, O my Lord,
> My mou'ner don't mou'n like a used to, O my Lord,
> My leader don't lead like a used to, O my Lord
> My deacon don't pray like a used to, O my Lord
> Oh, the people don't sing like they used to sing,

The mourners don't moan like they used to moan,
The preachers don't pray like they used to pray
That's what's the matter with the church today.

Without the old, dynamic, resilient culture that was highly adaptable to practically any situation, regardless of how extreme, it appeared that black people no longer had the weapons to combat negative psychologies. In slavery black people had a strong faith and belief in their powers to endure and overcome, had a deep trust in themselves, and used their religion, their crafts, their music, and their humor to expand their horizons and develop their own means of self-expression and creativity. They were plagued by the negative psychologies, but they had a flexible culture that allowed them to function with some degree of integrity and emotional fulfillment despite oppression. Their primary goal was for each black person to become more versatile and maneuverable as he or she sought both individual and racial uplift. Versatility, not adjustment, was the chief morning goal.

As the great civil rights leader, Martin Luther King, Jr., said,

I say to you, there are certain things within our social order to which I am proud to be maladjusted and to which I call upon all men of good will to be maladjusted. . . . I never did intend to adjust to the evils of segregation and discrimination. I never did intend to adjust myself to religious bigotry. I never did intend to adjust myself to economic conditions that will take necessities from the many to give luxuries to the few. (quoted in J. M. Washington, 1986, p. 216)

Cultural versatility alone would allow black people to avoid the entrapments set up by an oppressive society and to move on to take control over their own destiny. In seeking to become culturally versatile, black people have to become great students of examining objective conditions and social reality and learn from the past.

For example, during the Civil War, Thomas Wentworth Higginson, an abolitionist Union officer commanding a black regiment in the South, often wondered why the black troops who showed such daring and bravery on the battlefield had not kept the South "in a perpetual state of insurrection" (quoted in Litwack,

1979, p. 49) when they were on the plantation. Higginson attributed the absence of any large-scale slave insurrection to the slaves' religious faith and to "the habit of patience that centuries had fortified" (quoted in Litwack, 1979, p. 49). However, when he broached the subject with the black soldiers, "they spoke of lack of ammunition, money, arms, drill, organization, and mutual confidence—'the tradition' that nearly every revolt had been betrayed at the outset" (quoted in Litwack, 1979, p. 50). Also, they were well aware that to rise up and fight for their liberty before the war meant that they would have to face the cannons of trained white soldiers from both the South and the North. As one black journalist of that time explained, it was not that the slaves were too ill informed, too cowardly, or too patient or long-suffering to revolt but that they were "too well informed and too wise to court destruction at the hands of the combined Northern and Southern armies" (quoted in Raboteau, 1978, p. 248). Even during the war, black people wanted to see which way the wind was blowing, to see whether the Union army had a chance to win the war, and more important, to see whether the Union army would betray black people once they joined the fight to save the union. Even under the harsh, circumscribed conditions of slavery, black people developed a repertoire of behavioral choices, ranging from quiet patience to indirect sabotage and open revolt. This meant that they had to be culturally versatile to know when to act or not to act and when to move forward or pretend not to be moving at all.

Being culturally versatile meant more than having a keen eye for objective conditions and social reality; it also meant being prepared. For example, it took more than bravery for slaves to plan to run away, particularly because many were illiterate and had little knowledge of simple geography, had never been any more than a mile or two away from the plantation, and had little idea what life had in store for them in freedom. While pretending utter stupidity before white people, many slaves secretly learned to read and write and to master work skills that would be of service to them once they were free. These slaves often secretly collected information for years concerning how to get North and what it would take in terms of supplies, endurance, and daring. Some struck out when they felt the conditions were ripe; others never struck out but remained stuck on the level of intentions, always intending to be free, and even making preparations to be free, but never gaining enough faith, confidence, hope, or risk-taking ability to actually make an attempt to run away. Many black people who never saw the opportunity to escape while they were slaves found it during the war and left in droves. Their years of planning and preparing to seize the time finally paid off.

Black people used their entire culture to promote cultural versatility as a chief morning goal. For example, the spirituals themselves were flexible, versatile songs. They could appear to be calling for adjustment and appeasement while having secret coded messages calling for slaves to run away or even take up arms. In times when objective conditions were ripe for striking for freedom, the lyrics of the spirituals would become bolder, more explicit and less ambiguous in the call for liberation. Raboteau (1978) recorded that before the Civil War black people sang:

> *Go down Moses,*
> *Way down into Egypt Land*
> *Tell ol Pharaoh*
> *To let my people go.*

During the war, they sang:

> *Oh! Fader Abraham [a reference to Abraham Lincoln]*
> *Go down into Dixie's land*
> *Tell old Jeff Davis*
> *To let my people go.*

Their desire for freedom and a better life became more explicit as they longed for a time on this earth when

> *Dere's no rain to wet you,*
> *   O, yes, I want to go home,*
> *Dere's no sun to burn you,*
> *   O, yes, I want to go home,*
> *O, push along, believers,*
> *   O, yes, I want to go home,*

Dere's no whips a crackin',
  O, yes, I want to go home,
Where dere's no stormy weather
  O, yes, I want to go home
Dere's no tribulation
  O, yes, I want to go home.

Booker T. Washington (1901), recalling his last days in slavery, pointed out the flexibility of the spirituals:

As the great day [of emancipation] grew nearer, there was more singing in the slave quarters than usual, it was bolder, had more ring, and lasted later into the night. Most of the verses of the plantation songs had some references to freedom. True, they had sung those same verses before, but they had been careful to explain that the "freedom" in these songs referred to the next world, and had no connection with life in this world. Now they gradually threw off the mask; and were not afraid to let it be known that the "freedom" in their songs meant freedom of the body in this world. (p. 39)

The blues also showed this cultural versatility. For example, as Oliver (1970) pointed out, a blues song such as the one that follows can have numerous meanings depending on the subtleties of interpretation:

The sun's gonna shine in my back-door some day
My back-door some day . . . mmm,
The sun's gonna shine in my back-door some day,
And the wind's gonna change, gonn' blow my blues away.

Oliver asked,

What is the meaning of the verse? Why should the sun shine one day in the back-door—is it because the sun usually shines in the front door? Is it because the sun normally shines on a closed door and the song implies that the door is open and the occupant gone? Or does it imply that the dark recesses of the interior are at last illumined in some complex metaphor of good fortune? Is the emphasis on the back-door an allusion to the illicit lover, the "back-door man" of so many blues, or is the singer himself the back-door man who has left for good? Does the front-door at last face north, when the sun shines in the back, suggesting that the singer has migrated to a more liberal, if less warm, Northern climate? And what is the wind of change that is going to blow away the blues— merely changing circumstances? good luck? Or is the line a subtler one with overtones of eventual racial equality and the dispersal of the conditions that cause the blues. (p. 19)

Nowhere was the cultural versatility in the black experience more pronounced than in the black folktales. Black people required that their folk heroes be able to outmaneuver the oppressor and be able to use wit and agility to get themselves out of situations that seemed to offer no way out. Levine (1977) wrote that "the enduring plight of black Americans produced a continuing need for a folklore which would permit them to express their hostilities and aspirations and for folk heroes whose exploits would allow them to transcend their situation" (p. 370). In seeking to transcend their situation, black people called for the folk hero to be so versatile that he or she had to be a "hero with a thousand faces" (p. 370). Like music, black folktales had to express the common need that called them into being during a specific time in history. "The appearance of new heroes, the alteration of old ones, and the blending of the new and the old that went on continually have a great deal to say about the changes in black situations and consciousness that were occurring" (p. 370). Black folk heroes such as Brer Rabbit, High John the Conqueror, John Henry, the Signifying Monkey, Shine, and Stackolee were so flexible that they could be on the defensive or the offensive, be cautious or reckless, use guile or sheer physical strength, and use malice and mayhem or maudlin tactics and mischief. No matter what situation these black folk heroes found themselves in, they had to show versatility to maneuver their way out. As in the spirituals, they had to be able to express a wide range of emotions and hit high notes and low notes, and as in jazz they had to be able to improvise.

The fact that contemporary black people are not as in tune with their history and ancestry, that their music is more a form of entertainment than social therapy, and that their folktales no longer serve the social function they once did makes the effort of creating culturally versatile black people even more challenging.

VULNERABILITY

In order for social workers to advance the goal of cultural versatility, they must develop a theory of black vulnerability that holds that all black people, regardless of social class standing, are highly susceptible to victimization in a society that places little value on black life. A theory of black vulnerability must imply a concept of entrapment and a belief that the American society deliberately sets snares, traps, and lures to keep black people subordinated. The black experience suggests that black people must be versatile to avoid the planned pitfalls of an oppressive society. It suggests that such factors as education, racial consciousness, political awareness, knowledge of black history, hope, and being reality-based help black people develop greater versatility in avoiding societal entrapment, breaking through oppressive barriers, and rising above oppression.

SELF–DETERMINATION

To promote the goal of cultural versatility, social workers must also develop a concept of black self-determination that is rooted in black history. The history of black people in America has been the history of a people longing for, praying for, and fighting for control over their own lives. Two of the first massive government programs pertaining to the welfare of black people demonstrated clearly that black people preferred social welfare programs that would help them become more self-sufficient over those programs that amounted to a major government handout. One of the programs was the establishment of the Bureau of Refugees, Freedmen and Abandoned Lands (popularly known as the "Freedmen's Bureau"). Under the auspices of the War Department, the Freedmen's Bureau provided food, clothing, shelter, medical service, and protection to thousands of freed slaves. Although black people, given the desperation of their situation, were deeply appreciative of any help they could get, they wanted self-determination rather than to become dependent wards of the state. Therefore, they preferred the second type of program that was established by the War Department. In 1861 the War Department set up a social experiment with the black people of the Sea Islands of South Carolina and Georgia (Hoffman, 1956). These black people had been freed by the Union army under the command of General Sherman.

The purpose of the experiment, according to General Rufus Saxton, the man in charge, was to test the "capabilities of the Negro for freedom and self-support and self-improvement, to determine whether he is specifically distinct from and inferior to the white race, and normally a slave or dependent, or only inferior by accident of position and circumstances, still a man, and entitled to all rights which our organic law has declared belongs to all men by the endowment of the Creator" (quoted in Hoffman, 1956, pp. 9–10). Most witnesses agreed that if the ignorant and brutalized black people living on islands bearing the names St. Helena, Edisto, Port Royal, and Hilton Head could move from dependence to self-reliance, then black people everywhere could.

The white Northerners and a handful of educated free black people involved in the experiment could immediately see the difference between newly free slaves receiving a handout and those given the opportunity to take full control over their own lives. As one author wrote, the people involved in the experiment were shocked to see how quickly the "island people had already begun to shake off their old servility" (Hoffman, 1956, p. 9). These black people stopped singing their old sad moaning spirituals and began to sing more cheerful, defiant songs:

No more driver call for me
No more peck of corn for me
No more hundred lash for me.

In their demands, they made it clear that their goal was self-determination. Hence, they had only three demands that they wanted to be guaranteed: (1) that no driver, black or white, would supervise their labor; (2) that they would be able to profit from their labor; and (3) most important, that they would be given or allowed to purchase land.

Their dream of owning land was realized with General Sherman's 1865 decree, when his famous Field Order 15 allotted plots of land to Sea Island black people. With their own land and with no master, overseer, or driver telling them what to do, the black residents of the Sea Islands produced record-breaking crops as they raised cotton, corn, tomatoes, okra, melons, and potatoes. General Saxton was so proud of their achievement that he declared the Sea Island experiment an "unqualified success" (quoted in Hoffman, 1956, p. 12). General Saxton stated,

> *Amid all their obstruction and in spite of all, the freemen have made constant progress and proved their right to be received into the full communion of freemen. They have shown that they can appreciate freedom as the highest good; that they will be industrious and provident with the same incitement which stimulates the industry of other men in free societies; that they understand the value of property and are eager for its acquisition, especially of lands; that they can conduct their private affairs with sagacity, prudence, and success; . . . that they are intelligent, eager and apt to acquire knowledge of letters . . . ; that they aspire to and adopt as fast as means and opportunity admit, the social forms and habits of civilization; that in short, they are endowed with all instincts, passions, affections, sensibilities, powers, aspirations and possibilities which are the common attributes of human nature.* (quoted in Hoffman, 1956, p. 12)

The jubilation of General Saxton and the black residents of the Sea Islands did not last long. When the war ended, President Andrew Johnson, eager to appease the white Southerners, took the land from the black residents and gave it back to their former slave owners. The effort to move black people from slavery to first-class citizenship had failed, and once again, Sea Island black residents and black people throughout the South were left largely at the mercy of the bitter and vindictive white people who had once enslaved them. Once again they had reason to moan and they did. General Saxton said that "the disappointment and grief . . . were in proportion to their previous exultation in the certain hope of soon becoming independent proprietors, free men upon their soil" (quoted in Hoffman, 1956, pp. 15–16).

A goal of black experience–based social work is to help black people develop the kind of cultural versatility to avoid oppressive pitfalls and to achieve the kind of self-determination that eluded black people in the past. This goal involves helping black people become careful students of reality or objective conditions so that they can break beyond the stagnancy of negative psychologies and be able to determine when objective conditions are ripe for survival, reform, and even revolution.

A FAITH IN BLACK PEOPLE

Furthermore, in order for social workers to advance the goal of cultural versatility they must have faith in black people—faith in their strengths, their potential, and their promise. Solomon (1976) wrote that this faith rests on social workers seeing black people "as causal forces capable of bringing about some desired effect" (p. 27). Chestang (1972) wrote that this faith lies on social workers believing that black people can shed their "depressive" character and develop a "transcendent" (p. 3) personality. Social work as a profession has not always had this faith. Social workers traditionally have viewed black people as the undeserving poor, social problems to be solved, a permanent "underclass," and dependent wards of the state who needed the paternalistic guidance of helping experts. Even in contemporary society many social workers see black people as social deviants to be controlled or contained, whereas vestiges of racism in the profession still hold black people as culturally unfit for full participation in the dominant American culture and incapable of playing a significant role in solving the problems confronting them. Even today the invisible rewards of white privilege and the hidden injuries of race and class hamper the ability of social workers to mourn with black people.

A faith in black people means that social workers must not view themselves as being above black people or as saviors seeking to rescue black people from themselves. The black experience shows that the helpers who have been the most successful in working with black people have been those who viewed themselves in communion with the people, as fellow sufferers in a two-way process of communication, and as fellow mourners seeking common solutions to common problems. This means that black social workers in particular must see themselves as being just as vulnerable to victimization as black people in lower ranks. Their education, income, and social status might make black social workers more versatile and grant them more room for maneuverability, but given the microaggressions that are often hurled at them daily, they too often find themselves fighting off subtle oppression even as they fight against overt oppression against the black masses. They too can become so alienated from ancestral and historical connections, their racial self, and the black masses that negative psychologies of cultural sickness and cultural paranoia overtake them. For example, just before one prominent black woman who was highly successful according to all standards of the dominant society took her own life, she said, "I . . . have made it, but where?" (Campbell, 1989, p. 28).

The faith that black experience–based social workers have in black people rests ultimately on trying to restore the faith that black people once had in social work. Hence, an objective of black experience–based social work is not only to provide social workers with fresh insights into the problems facing black people and to help social workers gain more faith in the ability of black people to rise and overcome but also to help social workers improve their image in the black community and take a leadership role in the black community as genuine, effective advocates of cultural versatility, empowerment, and social change. In other words, the primary goal is to ultimately help social workers have faith in themselves, to start anew, to experience that great "gitting up" morning longed for and hoped for by the people of the spirituals and the blues.

REFERENCES

Baer, B. L., & Federico, R. (1978). *Educating the baccalaureate social worker.* Cambridge, MA: Ballinger.

Bowlby, J. (1973). *Attachment and loss (Vol. 3).* New York: Basic Books.

Brown, C. (1956). *Manchild in the promised land.* New York: Dutton.

Campbell, B. M. (1989). To be black, gifted, and alone. In N. Hare & J. Hare (Eds.), *Crisis of black sexual politics* (pp. 25–38). San Francisco: Black Think Tank.

Chestang, L. (1972). *Character development in a hostile environment* (Occasional Paper No. 3). Chicago: University of Chicago.

Coleman-Miller, B. (1992). You can make a difference. In L. W. Abramczyk & J. W. Ross (Eds.), *Nurturing the black male adolescent* (pp. 55–57). Columbia: University of South Carolina.

Cox, O. C. (1976). *Race relations.* Detroit: Wayne State University Press.

Edelman, M. W. (1992). *The measure of success.* Boston: Beacon Press.

Grier, W. H., & Cobbs, P. M. (1969). *Black rage.* New York: Bantam Books.

Hoffman, E. D. (1956). From slavery to self-reliance. *The Journal of Negro History, 16*(1), 8–43.

Johnston, R. F. (1954). *The development of Negro religion.* New York: Philosophical Library.

Keil, C. (1966). *Urban blues.* Chicago: University of Chicago Press.

Lawrence, M. M. (1975). *Young inner city families.* New York: Behavioral Publications.

Levine, L. W. (1977). *Black culture and black consciousness.* New York: Oxford University Press.

Litwack, L. F. (1979). *Been in the storm so long.* New York: Alfred A. Knopf.

Lum, D. (1986). *Social work practice with people of color.* Monterey, CA: Brooks/Cole.

Majors, R., & Billson, J. M. (1992). *The cool pose: The dilemmas of black manhood in America.* New York: Lexington Books.

Marris, P. (1974). *Loss and change.* New York: Pantheon Books.

Martin, E. P., & Martin, J. M. (1992). Young black ghetto males and the sense of impending doom. In L. W. Abramczyk & J. W. Ross (Eds.), *Nurturing the black male adolescent* (pp. 10–16). Columbia: University of South Carolina, School of Social Work.

McCall, N. (1994). *Makes me wanna holler.* New York: Random House.

Neal, L. (1989). *Visions of a liberated future.* New York: Thunder Mouth Press.

Newton, H. P. (1973). *Revolutionary suicide.* New York: Harcourt Brace Jovanovich.

Oliver, P. (1970). *Aspects of the blues tradition.* New York: Oak Publications.

Parkes, C. M. (1972). *Bereavement: Studies of grief in adult life.* New York: International Universities Press.

Raboteau, A. J. (1978). *Slave religion.* London: Oxford University Press.

Rochlin, G. (1965). *Griefs and discontents.* Boston: Little, Brown.

Simos, B. G. (1979). *A time to grieve.* New York: Services Association of America.

Solomon, B. B. (1976). *Black empowerment: Social work in oppressed communities.* New York: Columbia University Press.

Titon, J. T. (1977). *Early downhome blues.* Urbana: University of Illinois Press.

Washington, B. T. (1901). *Up from slavery.* New York: Doubleday, Page.

Washington, J. M. (Ed.). (1986). *The essential writings and speeches of Martin Luther King, Jr.* San Francisco: HarperCollins.

Wilson, A. N. (1993). *The falsification of Afrikan consciousness.* New York: Afrikan World InfoSystems.

The Foundation of Black Experience–Based Social Work: Pedagogy

A perspective of black experience–based social work involves the merging of art and science, the complementarity of the secular and the sacred, and the communion of the client and the worker as well as their unity as fellow sufferers with faith in one another's ability to solve social problems. This perspective shows that the ideal morning goal of black experience–based social work is to help black people become a culturally versatile people dedicated to one another's well-being and organized for collective action against their oppression. The morning objective is to eradicate the hurting, hating, and harming elements that impinge on the black community and create conditions that are conducive to healing, health, and hope. In this sense, black experience–based social work takes up where early black lay caregivers and professional helpers left off in seeking to build a community that collectively tries to relieve pain, mend wounds, and fight oppression, in other words, a healing community. Similar to lay and professional black caregivers of the past, black experience–based social workers believe that a healing–developing community is a precondition for much-needed structural change. In other words, before a people can organize for numerous assaults on an oppressive society in quest of their rights and entitlements, they have to be culturally versatile enough to avoid the many societal entrapments designed to keep them subordinate, be so reality-based and focused as to be able to move as far forward as objective conditions will allow, and be able to overcome negative psychologies, immobilizing remnants of the past, that keep them divided and straining toward self-destructiveness. As Wilson (1993) pointed out, for a people to develop economically, they must create a healing–developing community to the point that they can trust, rely on, and cooperate with one another. Early black people believed that helping professionals had a leading role to play in the development of the healing community. It was not until environmental burdens became overwhelming that professional black helpers began to lose faith in the black masses to take responsibility for their own lives and, hence, to lose faith in their own ability to alleviate social problems and effect social change. Black experience–based social work is founded on the premise that social workers still have a vanguard role to play in this regard. It believes that social work as a profession offers black people what no other helping profession offers: the opportunity to attack problems confronting them on numerous fronts. Whether the problem is on the micro, messo, or macro level, social work, with its emphasis on casework, clinical work, group work, community organization, social advocacy, social action, and research allows black people to fight on a broader front and to be more culturally versatile than helping professions such as psychiatry, psychoanalysis, and psychotherapy.

Even as social work brings its varied arsenal of weapons to the crisis confronting the black family and community, black experience–based social work holds that much more is needed. What is needed is for social workers to dig deep down into black history and black culture and take out those salient features of the black experience that are relevant and useful to contemporary social work practice. What we have shown throughout this book is that traditionally black people have had their own ways of viewing the problem, relieving suffering, and fighting for social change. Black experience–based social work maintains that the black perspective of helping must be seriously considered in any effort to improve the quality of life of black people. It maintains that the black helping experience will strengthen social work practice and that social work, with its superior scientific, organizational, administrative, service delivery, research, and problem-solving skills, will in turn gain from more-effective use of the black helping experience.

EDUCATION

Before social workers can effectively use the black helping experience, they must be educated differently from the way they are currently trained. They cannot go on taking a surface look at black history and black culture and paying lip service to incorporating "minority content" into the social work curriculum; they cannot continue to pretend color blindness or act as if certain social work methodologies apply to all people at all times without modification; they cannot continue to look at black social workers who vociferously draw their attention to the pervasive problem of racism and black exclusion as if they are fanatics or "reversed racists"; and they cannot continue to expect social work students with so few realistic insights into black life, history, and culture to be prepared to help black people once they become social work professionals.

TOWARD A BLACK IDENTITY OF SOCIAL WORK

In preparing students for black experience–based social work practice, a black presence or identity must be established in social work curricula and social work literature. This means that the history of social work must be less "Eurocentric" and focus much more on the role black people have played in shaping that history and in constructing a social welfare history of their own. For example, establishing a black identity in social work cannot be based on tracing the origin of social welfare policies and programs back to the barbaric English Poor Laws. These laws were too oppressive to be the foundational source for an oppressed people. Establishing a black presence in social work requires tracing the historical origins of black social welfare back to the massive public work projects, the social welfare programs and the community development efforts of ancient Ethiopia, Egypt, and other African civilizations of antiquity. It requires examining the clinical work or casework of traditional Africa that, according to Davidson (1969), "anticipated Freud and what evolved from Freud" (p. 151). It requires looking at how traditional African secret societies, rites-of-passage groups, councils of elders, and circle ceremony groups used group work skills to promote black social welfare and group cohesiveness. Establishing a black presence requires an in-depth look at how black people during slavery used their entire culture—their music, religion, humor, and folk tales—to identify with and soothe one another's suffering as they carried out the therapeutic work of mourning. It requires examining how early black caregivers used the black extended family as a model for their social services programs and exploring the viability of such an approach in the contemporary black community.

Most important, establishing a black identity in social work demands a look at the day-to-day battles of pioneer black social workers as they struggled to get black migrants on a solid economic footing, combated discrimination in New Deal policies, waged ideological warfare against welfare stereotypes, combated racism in the social welfare workplace, and tried to wrestle with some of the most complex problems ever to confront a people. To establish a black social work identity, black experience–based social work attempts to fill the cultural gap left by pioneering black social workers.

In hindsight, and judging from contemporary standards, it is easy to point out the shortcomings of early black social workers, but their strong points must be highlighted as well. Pioneering black social workers understood that the problems confronting black people were too massive and too overwhelming to be tackled successfully solely by black self-help initiatives or white private charities. They knew that these problems would require government intervention as well as self-help efforts and they knew that the problem of racism and economic oppression had to be addressed if black people were going to move upward in society and not suffer so much pain, misery, and hardship and so many premature deaths. Their use of the scientific method to investigate social problems in a systematic way was an improvement over the use of gut feelings, mother wit, common sense, guesswork, and other traditional ways black people determined reality. Early black sociologists such as E. Franklin Frazier, Charles S. Johnson, Ira de A. Reid, and Oliver C. Cox provided black social workers with sophisticated scholarly and theoretical insight into the nature and dynamics of racism, its impact on black life, and the social psychological reactions of black people to it. The pioneering black social workers also were highly dedicated and sincere in their determined effort to uplift the black masses.

One problem, as we see it, is that they failed to make full use of all that social work had to offer in terms of operating on the individual, group, community, and societal levels. They concentrated on societal change and, failing that, resorted to moralizing about the shortcomings of lower-class black people. Attacking on the micro, messo, and macro level would have allowed social workers to tackle racism, economic deprivation, poor health care, emotional instability, and other problems on innumerable battlegrounds. They also failed to explore what the black experience could teach them in respect to how the black masses themselves viewed the problem, what kind of helpers they preferred, what methods they viewed as helpful, and what goals they viewed as ideal.

Contemporary social workers have paid lip service to drawing from black culture, but other than viewing the black church and the black extended family as main support systems, they have not delved too deeply and have made little attempt to operationalize and systematize the black experience for it to be functional to social workers. Black experience–based social work then seeks to fill in this knowledge gap by drawing from the black experience insights and paradigms that can be helpful to social workers in their work with black people. In drawing from the black experience, this approach seeks a synthesis of the best helping practices of the black experience and the best ones of mainstream social work practice. Its use of the concepts moaning, mourning, and morning has provided a theoretical framework that involves an identification of the problem, a helping process, and a desired goal.

Establishing a black identity in social work also means examining how people who were not social workers in the black experience used social work techniques for effective work with black people. For example, it entails examining how Marcus Moziah Garvey's Universal Negro Improvement Association used community organization techniques to organize more black people worldwide than any other organization before or since; how Elijah Muhammad's Nation of Islam used group work skills to reform and rehabilitate criminals, drug addicts, alcoholics, and other street denizens who are practically untouchable in mainstream social work practice; how Martin Luther King, Jr.'s, Southern Christian Leadership Conference used community organization, social advocacy, and social action techniques to create the most effective movement for civil rights in the nation's history; and how the Black Panther Party used a social work–type "Survival Program" to provide free breakfast, free legal counsel, free clinics, and free clothing to poor, downtrodden inner-city black people in its effort to bridge the gap between reform and revolution. Overall, establishing a black presence or identity in social work requires connecting the past experiences of black people to contemporary black life as we look for patterns, parallels, and fresh perspectives and as we seek to complete unfinished business.

Clearly, the establishment of a black presence in social work means changes in the social work curriculum. To date, most social work academic programs on the undergraduate, graduate, and postgraduate levels have made little progress in incorporating the black experience into the social work curriculum. Generally, most programs offer a single course on the black experience, with claims that this satisfies accreditation standards regarding ethnic or cultural diversity. We have found that the lone course is generally taught by someone who knows little about the life, history, and culture of black people, let alone has any idea of how to incorporate the black helping experience into the curriculum or how to make it functional to social work practice. Many social work programs are still resistant to any notion of incorporating such content. Hence, they are very creative in masking the fact that they have done little or nothing in this respect. Some resist by lumping the black experience with the experiences of other "minority groups" in a way that presents only a watered-down, distorted, fragmented version of black life. It is still rare to find the black helping experience spread throughout the social work curriculum of most academic programs except to continue the pejorative tradition of seeing black people as deviant, pathological problems to be solved. When the black experience is taught across the social work curriculum, the curriculum has to undergo some significant changes.

SOCIAL WELFARE AS AN INSTITUTION

For example, classes on social welfare as an institution will have to be set up so that the black helping experience is included with the American social welfare experience. Students must know that black people were not considered to be among the "deserving poor," even in respect to the barbaric almshouses, asylums, and other 19th-century social welfare programs. They need to see that even in contemporary society the need is great for more-effective grassroots social welfare programs directed by black people, funded by the public, by private foundations, and by black self-help efforts, and administered to the needs of black people. They also need to see that in creating the healing black community, social work needs to be taken out of the social welfare agency and taken to the community, the streets, and the families where black people are.

Social welfare policy courses will have to be designed in ways that cover the policies that gave birth to the Freedmen's Bureau and the social experiments on the Sea Islands; examine "the Black Codes" that relegated black people to semislavery conditions during the Reconstruction period; critically assess "separate-but-equal" policies that gave legal sanction to racial segregation and injustice, vestiges of which still exist in American life today; explore the impact of New Deal policies and programs on black people during the Great Depression; examine the effects of civil rights policies on the black experience; look at President Lyndon B. Johnson's Great Society programs and the conservative and racist opposition to them; critically analyze "Reaganomics" in respect to reversal of much of the progress black people had made in the area of civil rights, affirmative action, and social welfare; and, in general, examine health, education, social security, employment, and other social welfare policies in respect to their impact on improving the quality of life of black people.

Despite the ravings and rantings of conservatives and reactionaries that too much public money has been poured into trying to solve the problem of downtrodden people with such little positive result, social work students should understand this point very clearly: America has never seriously considered the social welfare of black people, and much of the social welfare gains that black people have acquired they have fought for. They should understand that, as in the past, America is still primarily concerned with controlling and containing black people, making them invisible, keeping white people from being contaminated by these social deviants and parasites, and making white people feel safe. America still finds, when it comes to black people, it is more to its liking to build more jails than to provide better education, more jobs, greater entrepreneurial opportunity, and better health care.

HUMAN BEHAVIOR AND THE SOCIAL ENVIRONMENT

Courses on human behavior and the social environment will have to be structured in ways that cover such areas as tracing separation and loss throughout the life cycle; exploring the function of an oppressive social environment in creating psychologies that have an adverse impact on black behavior and social relations; and even examining racism as a psychopathology that should be included in the *Diagnostic and Statistical Manual of Mental Disorders* (American Psychiatric Association, 1994). In the current (fourth) edition, black behavior is excluded from "human behavior," and little discussion is given to a racist, sexist, and class-oppressive "social environment."

We will pay considerable attention to this course because it is here that the students' basic ideas, philosophy, and approaches to social work are formed. From courses on human behavior and the social environment students generally learn pet formulas as if they are playing a game of Trivial Pursuit. These formulas generally stay with them for life. For instance, nearly all of them have some familiarity with Sigmund Freud, Erik Erikson, and Abraham Maslow. With Freud, they can cite formulas of preconscious, conscious, and unconscious mental states; oral, anal, genital, and latency stages; and id, ego, and superego personality dynamics. With Erikson they have set to memory his eight "epigenetic" psychosocial stages:

1. trust vs. mistrust
2. autonomy vs. shame and doubt
3. initiative vs. guilt
4. industry vs. inferiority
5. identity vs. role diffusion
6. intimacy vs. isolation
7. generativity vs. stagnation
8. ego integrity vs. despair.

They have learned Maslow's hierarchy of physiological needs: safety needs, belonginess and love needs, self-esteem and self-respect needs, and self-actualization needs, and can cite these needs like kindergarten children reciting their ABCs. Yet, most students leave these courses without the slightest understanding of what these pet formulas mean. They definitely have no idea of how to apply these concepts borrowed from Freudian, neo-Freudian, and humanistic psychology to the black experience or any idea that they are even applicable to the black experience. In their thinking, these formulas are time-worn, unquestionable words of social work wisdom that are applicable to all people and all problems for all times.

Black social work students particularly have difficulty applying these concepts to the black experience. The problem that they seem to be utterly unaware of is that these concepts were never intended to be applied to black people.

Freud

Although Freud's concepts are said to have universal applicability, his theories grew out of clinical observations made in Victorian, bourgeois, European society. Freud (1959a) derived much of his thinking from his "scientific mythology" about so-called primitive society, meaning the society of African, Asian, and other "non-white" people of the world. He thought that a study of the untamed aggression and sexuality of these "primitives" would throw light on the neurotic and irrational behavior of civilized Europeans, particularly as the psychic problems of European people were seen as lying in their unconscious, barbaric, and primal past. In other words, civilized Europeans did not know that they were still primitive. Although this is certainly a simplified account, it nevertheless underscores the fact that black people and other people of color were viewed as backward, and that there is little or no evidence that Freud ever had a black patient, included any black people in his famous circle, or included any serious discussion of the matter of race in his voluminous writings.

Erikson

Erik Erikson (K. T. Erikson, 1969) publicly admitted that when he first wrote *Childhood and Society* he had no thoughts about black people. He said that he wrote from the perspective of a recent immigrant and that perspective colored his perception of the racial situation in America.

*My first book [*Childhood and Society*] was written during the Roosevelt era, when the whole American enterprise, foreign and domestic, seemed to be going in a very different direction, an antitotalitarian and antiracist direction, especially in the eyes of a recent immigrant. Only much later, and only when some young people put their lives on the line, could we too, fully perceive the fact that we had largely overlooked the fate of the black citizenry. . . . But I must also say that immigrants like myself came to this country without any childhood-conditioned awareness of skin color—a fact which made us believe at first that Americans must be on the way to overcoming this historical childhood disease.* (p. 53)

Erikson (in K. T. Erikson, 1969) stated that "when you are welcomed as an immigrant, it is hard to look around and ask whom from abroad they [Americans] are not letting in—and whom at home they are keeping down to a level below that of any newcomer"; "it certainly would never have occurred to me at the time of my immigration as a refugee from European fascism to suspect any fascist potential in the American system"; and "it was only when, in my clinical work, I found social interpretations inescapable, that I slowly became aware of the depth and cruelty of the social conflicts of this country" (p. 125).

Even after Erikson became aware of the depth and cruelty of the social conflicts in America, his later works showed little understanding of black people or the race problems, so cloistered was he in the ivory towers of white academia. For example, in his later work, *Identity, Youth and Crisis,* where he does take up the issue of "race and the wider identity" (see chapter 8, pp. 295–321, in E. Erikson, 1968) he seemed to believe that black people have either no identity, a negative identity (stemming from being viewed as a "pseudospecies" by the dominant white culture and incorporating the negative identity the oppressive culture has of them), or a "surrendered identity," meaning that they were in search of an identity. Erikson asked the questions: "What historical actuality can the Negro American count on and what wider identity can permit him to be self-certain as a Negro (or a descendant of Negroes) and integrated as an American?" (p. 314). Erikson found that there were no historical actualities that a developing black identity can count on and suggested that black people would have to become part of a wider "more inclusive identity" (p. 314). He postulated that because black people were excluded from the technical skill identity—probably "the most inclusive and most absorbing identity potential in the world today" (pp. 316–317)—"the African identity" (p. 317), "the great middle class" (p. 317) identity, religious identity, and "postcolonial identities" (p. 317) were strong contenders for the American black identity.

Because of his typical pathology–disorganization perspective concerning matriarchal black families consisting of domineering black women, absent fathers, and delinquent children, Erikson had no concept of a positive black identity developing out of the black family, the black community, or the overall black experience. For example, he wrote that "the blues may have been at one time an affirmation of a positive identity and a superior uniqueness, even as it 'dealt with' feelings of depression and hopelessness," but that the blues now represented "old images which now have become a sign of discrimination" and a "thoughtless accommodation to a post-slavery period from which we are all emerging" (p. 300).

Maslow

In his effort to create a "psychology of health" rather than a psychology of sickness and pathology, Maslow felt that he could learn a great deal about people, their potential, and positive aspects of human behavior if he undertook the study of exceptionally healthy, mature people. To Maslow, these "self-actualizing" people were great public and historical figures, personal acquaintances and friends in his social rank, and other gifted, exceptional people. In other words, Maslow's psychology was based on a study of elite people, what he termed "the growing tip" (quoted in Goble, 1970, p. 23). Maslow had no use for average or problem-ridden, oppressed people. He stated that "it becomes more and more clear that the study of crippled, stunted, immature, unhealthy specimens can yield only a cripple psychology and a cripple philosophy" (quoted in Goble, 1970, p. 14). In his study of elite people whom he felt were the last possible specimen of the human species, Maslow did not find any black people to fit that category. He had considered studying such great black historical personalities as George

Washington Carver, Frederick Douglass, and Harriett Tubman, but in dividing his study into three categories of "cases, partial cases, and potential and possible cases" (quoted in Goble, 1970, p. 24), he put all of these black people in his category of "potential and possible cases" (p. 24). There is no evidence, that we could find, that he actually studied these black people to sharpen his definition of mental health and his theory of human motivation.

Social work students hoping to become "self-actualized" themselves would be startled to discover that Maslow believed that only an elite few were capable of self-actualization, that is, of reaching their fullest potential and human capacity. For example, he had once considered studying 2,000 college students but found only one sufficiently mature enough. Students would be shocked to learn that according to Maslow, self-actualized people are usually 60 years of age or older. Most black people definitely would not fit into that category because, given black life-expectancy rates. They have trouble surviving to the age when Maslow says that they can become "fully human" (quoted in Goble, 1970, p. 25).

Freud, Erikson, and Maslow and the Black Experience

We are saying that the work of Freud, Erikson, and Maslow was not meant to consider black people, their problems, or their potential. We are not saying, however, that because these works were "Eurocentric" or elitist, or even racist to some extent, they cannot be applied in part to the experience and problems of black people. We ourselves have gained great insight from the work of Sigmund Freud, particularly in the area of "object loss" and "mourning." Freud believed that object loss begins in early childhood experiences in "a situation of the infant when it is presented with a stranger instead of its mother" (Freud, 1959c, p. 169). He wrote that because the infant cannot "distinguish between temporary absence and permanent loss" (p. 169), it feels that every time it loses sight of the mother it will never see her again. The infant in this state not only experiences mourning over "the feeling of loss object" but also "internal, mental pain . . . as equivalent to physical pain" (p. 169).

If this book has demonstrated anything, it is that the black experience has been one of continual mourning and mental pain. Black people have suffered the loss of millions of black lives over the

generations. We are not speaking primarily of the natural separation anxiety that occurs in early childhood experiences or even the
losses that are the result of the natural process of growing up, aging,
and dying. We are speaking of the countless losses caused by slavery, migration, war, abject poverty, and racial terrorism and the
myriad ways contemporary American society still finds to inflict
loss on black people.

Freud (1959b) wrote that "mourning is regularly the reaction to
the loss of a loved person, or to the loss of some abstraction which
has taken the place of one, such as one's country, liberty, an ideal,
and so on" (p. 243). He wrote that the work of mourning is "piecemeal" and painful and carried out bit by bit, at great expense of
time and cathartic energy, because each single memory and expec-
tation in which the libido is bound to the object is brought up and
hypercathected, and detachment of the libido is accomplished in
respect to it.

The black experience shows that mourning to black people was
also regularly the reaction to the loss of a loved person. Although
black people in slavery and after emancipation knew nothing about
libido and hypercathexis, they did know that the work of mourning was indeed a piecemeal, painful, and protracted process. In
their work of mourning, Freud's concept of catharsis might also
apply, not so much in terms of making the unconscious conscious
as responding to the conscious reality of oppression and the need
to channel the rage and anger and pent-up frustrations into outlets
other than suicidal confrontation. Furthermore, a major part of the
mourning work of black people was to instill hope, an objective
that has little place in Freudian psychology.

Our position is that if pioneering black people had incorporated
Freud's thinking on object loss and mourning, they would have had
a better grasp of the situation of the black migrant. It was not until
after World War II, some 40 years after the first major waves of black
migration to Northern cities, that knowledge of the psychological
impact of loss and separation was accessible to social workers.
Psychoanalysis had gained prominence in social work, and World
War II had prompted Freud's daughter, Anna, to conduct a pioneering study on the impact of loss on British children during the
war (Peters, 1985). British psychiatrists and object relations

theorists analyzed the kind of misery and anxiety the millions of deaths during that war caused the British society. In addition, journals such as *Psychoanalytical Study of the Child* examined the impact of "object loss" on white children from practically every conceivable angle. After the war, the writings of Jewish scholars on the genocidal deaths of 6 million Jews in Nazi concentration camps helped provide the field of social work with a knowledge base in the area of loss and separation. However, by this time black people were considered not to be emotionally, intellectually, or verbally amenable to intrapsychic analysis.

Today black helping professionals generally tend to have what one black psychotherapist called "a profound distrust" (Maultsby, 1982, p. 39) of Freudian or psychodynamic approaches to the problems of black people. For example, one group of black social work scholars summarily dismissed psychodynamic approaches with the curt statement that "there is little empirical evidence that such approaches are useful specifically with black families" (Logan, Freeman, & McRoy, 1990, p. 40).

One reason why black people have developed deep distrust of psychodynamic studies pertains to the manner in which white scholars have applied these approaches to the black experience. Maultsby (1982) revealed that as far back as slavery, a prominent white physician received wide acclaim for his alleged discovery of two mental disorders of slaves: "drapetomania" and "dysesthesia aethioptica" (p. 42). Drapetomania, or "flight-from-home madness" (p. 42), was the insanity that caused slaves to run away from their "good lives" in slavery, whereas dysesthesia aethioptica, "an insensibility of the nerves, or hebetude of mind" (p. 42), was the mental disease that caused slaves to try to avoid work, to destroy their master's property, and generally to irritate their overseers. Naturally, slaves who would do these things had to be insane, as happy as the plantation life was alleged to be for black people.

In modern days such Freudian studies as Kardiner's and Ovesey's (1951) *Mark of Oppression* butchered the black psyche and left a bitter taste in the mouths of black scholars and helping professionals. These authors drew from their observations of the psychic life of 25 black patients with mental illness the conclusion that the entire black race is mentally disturbed and suffers from an indelible "mark of oppression." Black people in general so hate themselves, these authors contended, that they identify their black skin with feces.

We might say here too that behavioral approaches also have "a tainted image" (Turner, 1982, p. 13) in the black community. Turner, a black behaviorist, said that negative views of behavioral approaches are largely a result of behavior modification being associated with such procedures as psychosurgery, lobotomy, psychopharmacology, and mind control. Furthermore, he wrote that black people are naturally suspicious of behavior manipulation of any sort because "it can be strongly argued that black Americans have been conditioned to believe that they are inferior, that black is ugly, and white is beautiful" (p. 13).

Although black people have had trouble with Freudian psychology, our position is that just as the class issue cannot be fully understood without a study of the work of Karl Marx, the issue of race cannot be fully understood without examining the work of Sigmund Freud. This means that even the most "Afrocentric" social work theorists cannot escape the work of Marx and Freud if they want to fully grasp the situation of black people in America. In fact, Freudian psychology may be the most "African" of the three streams—Freudianism, behaviorism, and humanism—for although Freud's study of primitive life stereotyped the African experience to some degree, it also paradoxically advanced an African way of viewing the world. For example, as Freud (1943) himself admitted, so-called primitive people are the ones most likely to interpret and find symbolic meaning in dreams. He might have added that although African helping practices were primarily group oriented, African native "psychoanalysis" worked in one-on-one therapeutic situations intended to deal with unconscious content. For example, the id was spoken of in terms of unseen evil spirits or demons that had to be brought to the patient's conscious awareness before he or she could ever hope to be cured. Also, as we have indicated, we have found no theory that can explain the irrational, beastly behavior that drives a lynching or other savage racist acts against black people better than Freudian psychology. For instance, Frazier's psychodynamic study of white racism at the turn of the 20th century created such hostile reactions in the South that he felt compelled to carry a .44 and to call himself E. Franklin Frazier to throw the mob's scent off of the Edward F. Frazier who wrote the article (Platt, 1991).

As for behavioral approaches, it is the firm opinion of black experience–based social workers that they would fare better if they found ways to help black people acquire the kind of behavior that they have historically desired, specifically, flexible, dynamic, prosocial behavior regarding their relationship to one another and protest behavior regarding their relationships to the dominant society. Contemporary behavioral approaches seem to be geared toward adjusting and adapting black people to the status quo; this appears to be a newer version of the old process of "keeping the niggers in their place."

Overall, only a careful study of the work of Sigmund Freud, Erik Erikson, and Abraham Maslow will show students how their theories apply and do not apply to the black experience. For example, we found that Erikson's epigenetic life cycle can be applied only after a thorough understanding of it and a thorough examination of the black experience. If we take Erikson's first oral–sensory stage of trust vs. mistrust, we learn from a careful reading that he himself stated, "Mothers in different cultures and classes and races must teach this trusting in different ways, so it will fit their cultural version of the universe" (quoted in Evans, 1969, p. 15). His beliefs support what the black experience has demonstrated over the millennium that "to learn distrust is just as important" (p. 15). We have previously discussed the psychology of cultural paranoia. Erikson stated that

> If you don't mind my registering a gripe, when these stages are quoted, people often take away mistrust and doubt and shame and all of these not so nice, "negative" things and try to make an Eriksonian achievement scale out of it all, according to which in the first stage trust is "achieved." Actually, a certain ratio of trust and mistrust in our basic social attitude is the critical factor. When we enter a situation, we must be able to differentiate how much we can trust and how much we must mistrust, and I use mistrust in the sense of a readiness for danger and an anticipation of discomfort. (p. 15)

Most social work students are unaware that Erikson added "the virtue of hope" to the oral–sensory stage, calling the psychosocial crisis on this stage "trust vs. mistrust/hope" (Evans, 1969, pp. 16–18). The black experience would validate Erikson in his statement, "children who give up hope because they do not get enough loving and not enough stimulation may literally die" (p. 17).

Overall, what we find from a careful reading of Erikson is that the young Erikson who failed miserably in applying his identity theory to black people was forced to reexamine the issue in his retirement years as shown in a conversation with the black revolutionary Huey Newton (a conversation that is scarcely known by and hardly ever introduced to social work students). In that conversation, Erikson stated that "psychoanalysis will have to go beyond adapting individuals to the status quo, or, for that matter, consider adulthood a mere matter of leaving one's childhood behind. It will have to provide the conceptual means for an adult to recognize his status (or is it flux) in historical change, and his responsibility toward the next generation" (quoted in K. T. Erikson, 1969, p. 86). In that conversation, E. Erikson also stated,

You see, some students seem to hope that by studying my stuff they will learn what a positive identity is and how to get rid of the negative one. Another group of students is afraid of my stuff because they think what I mean by identity is to be so adjusted to the system that you don't want to be anything else but what the system permits you to be. And neither of these explanations represent what I meant. The trouble starts when you project your own negative identity on other people. (quoted in K. T. Erikson, p. 110)

In his conversation with Newton, E. Erikson made his most-detailed and stringent comments against America's racism. He said to Newton that because he (Erikson) was white, "I thrived on that system that exploited your people, thrived in spite of being an immigrant, a former dropout, and a Freudian" (quoted in K. T. Erikson, 1969, p. 98). E. Erikson said that white society has to project its own negative identity onto black people and that white America cannot find its own "most adult identity" (quoted in K. T. Erikson, 1969, p. 60) by denying it to others. He held that black people, through struggle and protest and fighting back, are gaining new communal images for themselves and "that the identity of our black citizens is so central to the future of America and to that of a wider identity anywhere" (quoted in K. T. Erikson, 1969, p. 60).

A careful reading of Abraham Maslow shows where his thinking and black experimental assessment are convergent and consistent. For example, Maslow believed that one has to meet the physiological needs before one can move to the safety needs and meet the safety needs before the individual can achieve the belonginess and love needs and so on up the hierarchy. However, the black experience suggests that when an oppressed people have difficulty in meeting basic physiological needs and can seldom feel really safe given the hostile circumstances under which they live, their need for belongingness and love is even greater. When the group is threatened from without, it must have solidarity from within. Also, contrary to Maslow's conclusions, slaves had to feel a sense of self-esteem and self-actualization first before they would have the will to carry on despite being constantly subjected to loss and separation, hunger, ragged clothing, crude shacks, the cold of winter, the wetness of rain, and the stifling heat of summer. If they had been overly preoccupied with physical survival and safety they would have committed suicide by the scores. They survived because they had the faith, confidence, esteem, and hope that "soon one morning" the sun was going to rise. In other words, their self-actualization lay not in their being able to realize true self-goals or become "truly human" under slavery but in their creation of a culture of transcendence that allowed them to become self-actualized through the hopes they had for their children and for the black generations to come.

Although Maslow's hierarchy of needs would have to be applied in inverse order to apply to the black experience, Maslow's emphasis on having people realize their true self-potential is quite relevant to the black experience. There are few people in America who have had their potential thwarted and their growth stunted as much and as deeply as black people. There are few people who need more motivation to move beyond the immobilizing levels of the psychologies of cultural sickness, paranoia, claustrophobia, and terminal illness than black people. We have found many black people who constantly live on the level of intentions, who are unfocused, and who lack an ability to complete basic life tasks. Maslow's emphasis on mental health too underscores a pressing need in social work to at least balance the profession's preoccupation with black pathology with a concentration on black strength, black normality, and black health.

Furthermore, and most important, there are features of black experience–based social work that only a humanistic psychology such as that of Maslow's will explain and accept. For example, black people historically place tremendous emphasis on ancestral connectedness, and part of their cultural versatility was to let the intuitive self speak to the rational self through their ancestors. Black people would study objective reality but would look also to the voices of their ancestors to tell them when it was time to make a move. They even tried to strengthen the intuitive self with charms, amulets, prayers, hexes, special numbers, special signs, special words, and other magic. Humanistic psychology allows for knowing through feeling and intuition and hearing the voices of one's ancestors, whereas other "scientific" branches of the helping professions criticize such knowing as being subjective, mystical, unscientific, and even the symptoms of a crazed mind.

SOCIAL WORK RESEARCH

Social work research courses must not only borrow from the humanistic approach and present a more balanced perspective on the strength, potential, and promise of black people to offset preoccupation with black pathologies, but they also need to delve profoundly into every phase of black culture. They need to research black music, black folktales, black humor, black religion, black literature and other areas of black life in terms of the impact they have on healing and helping. Social work research must see to it that the black experience is not cut up or distorted to fit social work theory. It must examine the extent to which racism and other structural defects in society hamper the ability of black people to live up to their fullest potential and promise. It must focus on the impact of loss and separation on black people, particularly because black people often view social work as an extension of the police systems, the courts, and the prisons. It must specifically examine what happens to black people, their communities, and their families when they are placed in prisons, juvenile centers, foster homes, adoption agencies, and mental institutions, an effect that often results in part from social work recommendations. In this respect, social workers have to rethink the emphases placed on confidentiality, because many crimes and abuses against black people are hidden behind the cloak of confidentiality. Social work research must find ways to keep black people within communal or familial settings within the black community and ways to humanize loss institutions that are of a punitive, incarcerative character. It must explore the role of hope and faith and spirituality in the uplift of an oppressed people, point out the pitfalls on every class level to which black people are vulnerable, and examine ways that make for greater cultural versatility. The main mission of black experience–based social work research is to develop from the black experience a solid theory to guide social work practice with black people.

Part of the problem of social work research is that it attempts to understand black people without making personal contact with them. It seeks to learn about black people through government sources and by using computerized technology to interpret copious statistical data on black pathologies. It fails to incorporate the lessons imparted by abolitionists and others who have had success working with black people even though they were outsiders. Even contemporary white researchers have found that they are more successful in gaining insider status when they go to black people where they are in their homes, barbershops, beauty parlors, and churches and when, similar to the successful white Underground Railroad leaders of the past, they make a personal or emotional commitment to black people. For example, contemporary social workers Carol B. Stack and Eliot Liebow learned that the old lessons still apply when it comes to getting close to and knowing black people.

Stack (1975) believed that even after a period of intense observation and questioning, she still had not gained acceptance from the black families she investigated. It was not until Stack relaxed her professional role and began to sit with the people and participate in the mundane things they were doing that she was able to make headway. Stack said that just helping one black woman fold newspapers for her son's newspaper route gained her greater acceptance than all her attempts at interviewing. Ironically, it was not until Stack bought a car and used it to help the black families run errands that she really got close to the people. She wrote, "My car did not substantially increase the flow of goods between people, but it did increase daily visiting and the flow of information between people" (p. 17). Stack added that "for a while all I seemed to be doing was taking half a pot roast from one house to another, picking up the laundry from a home with a washing machine, going to the liquor store for beer, or waiting with mothers in the local medical clinics for doctors to see their sick children" (p. 18).

However, what Stack learned was that her car gave her "an easily explainable role in the lives of the families I knew" (Stack, 1975, p. 18) and an opportunity to talk to black people alone in a quiet informal setting and to observe firsthand "the content and styles of social relationships among the residents in the Flats" (p. 20). She wrote that, most important, driving families around the community allowed her "to observe how residents in the Flats got along with white doctors, dentists, social workers, landlords, shopkeepers, and other residents," giving her a close-up view of the "indifference and racism expressed by the larger white society to Flats residents" (p. 19).

After involving herself so intensely in the daily lives of the people, Stack found that her "role in the community at this point was no longer that of an outsider. To many families I became another link in the systems of exchanges that were part of their existence" (Stack, 1975, p. 20). Stack stepped fully outside her role as detached, objective observer when she began to develop a close friendship with one of the black women of the Flats. They referred to one another as "sisters."

Initially, Liebow (1967) went to exaggerated lengths to make himself an insider with the black "streetcorner" men he was observing. He wrote that "almost from the beginning, I adopted the dress and something of the speech of the people," including "cursing and using ungrammatical constructions at times" (p. 255). He also immersed himself in the social and cultural activities of the black men. However, after several weeks of "hanging out" with them, he found that "there was still plenty of suspicion and mistrust"

(p. 243). It was not until Liebow became involved with the murder trial of one of the participants, a man named Lonny, that the men started to relate to him on a more open and genuine basis. Liebow became so personally involved in Lonny's life that he found himself meeting with policemen, judges, lawyers, bondsmen, and probation officers on Lonny's behalf and going into "council several times with various members of Lonny's extended family" (p. 245).

Liebow's work with Lonny demonstrated to the other men that he could see them not merely as objects to be observed, studied, dissected, explained, or described, but rather as real flesh-and-blood men with real human needs. Liebow wrote that it was only after that demonstration that the men started to genuinely accept him, started to call him by his first name, and as he stated, "taking it for granted that I belonged in the area" (Liebow, 1967, p. 247). He wrote that soon

> *the number of men whom I had come to know fairly well and their acceptance of me reached the point at which I was free to go to the rooms or apartments where they lived or hung out at almost any time, needing neither an excuse nor an explanation for doing so. Like other friends, I was there to pass the time, to hang around, to find out "what's happening."* (p. 246)

Furthermore, it was not until Liebow had made an emotional commitment to one of the men that he learned about a basic feature of black life: No matter how friendly black people may be or appear to be to white people observing them and asking them questions, black people are highly prone to an old defensive reaction of "putting whitey on" until they have formed complete trust. Liebow was shocked to learn that the black man whom he felt to be his closest confidant, friend, and "running buddy," Talley, was actually "running a game" on him and telling him just what Talley thought Liebow wanted to hear. Talley admitted to Liebow that he "didn't think nothing of lying to him" at first; but after seeing that Liebow was willing to become personally involved and to take risks on behalf of one of them, he said that "we started getting real tight" (Liebow, 1967, p. 249).

SOCIAL ADVOCACY AND SOCIAL ACTIVISM

Not only has history shown that making a personal or emotional commitment is a great technique for winning the confidence of black people, but it also has shown that at no time was the image of social work higher in the black community than when social workers advocated for the rights and entitlements of their black clients, exploded the stereotypes of black poor people, and took to the streets on their behalf. Social work students need to be taught social advocacy and social activism. We need to revive community organization. Social work students need to be taught how to stand up for oppressed people by first learning how to stand up for themselves. Our experience of over 20 years of teaching social work has been that many come to the profession with a progressive, even radical bent, but by the time they find employment in repressive social welfare agencies, they become passive and cautious, too conservative to fight aggressively for social change.

The black experience shows that power not only does not concede anything without a demand but also that the morning goal of black self-determination cannot be reached without a struggle for power. In the past black people had to be flexible enough to have dual meaning to their spirituals, using them to suggest compliance when it was necessary and to indicate when it was time to fight the battle of Jericho. In their blues, talk of a mistreating woman or a mistreating man could just as easily translate into their distaste for being mistreated by society. Black people are more culturally versatile when they are racially conscious and politically aware. Most significantly, it shows that social activism has therapeutic value in the black community and that social action has helped black people overcome their fear, break out of their feelings of being bottled up inside, feel a sense of black trust and unity, embrace life over physical and spiritual death, and feel empowered. For example, Martin Luther King, Jr., who was generally optimistic, wrote that he had initial doubts about whether young ghetto black men could overcome the psychologies of terminal illness and cultural paranoia and contribute to the nonviolence struggle:

> *I am thinking now of some teenage boys in Chicago. . . . I was
> shocked at the venom they poured out against the world. At times I*

*shared their despair and felt a hopelessness that these young
Americans could never embrace the concept of nonviolence as the
effective and powerful instrument of social reform. All of their lives,
boys like these have known life as a madhouse of violence and
devastation. . . . To these young victims of the slums, this society has
so limited the alternatives of their lives that the expression of . . .
manhood is reduced to the ability to define themselves physically.*
(quoted in Washington, 1986, p. 62)

King wrote that "those of us who had been in the movement for
years were apprehensive about the behaviors of the boys" (quoted
in Washington, 1986, p. 63). However, King found that the boys
"reacted splendidly!" (p. 63). He stated that

*These marchers endured not only the filthiest kind of verbal abuse,
but also barrages of rocks and sticks and eggs and cherry bombs.
They did not reply in words or violent deeds. Once again, their only
weapon was their own bodies. I saw boys . . . leap in the air to catch
with their bare hands the bricks and bottles that sailed toward us. It
was through the Chicago marches that our promise to them—that
nonviolence achieves results—was redeemed, and their zeal for a
better life was rekindled. . . . They revitalized my own faith in
nonviolence. And these poverty stricken boys enriched us all with a
gift of love.* (quoted in Washington, 1986, p. 63)

Himes (1980) held that overall the civil rights struggle served to
give black people a sense of solidarity, helped them overcome alienation, and helped them gain a sense of identity:

*Isolated and inferior, Negro people searched for keys to identity and
belonging. The social forces that exclude them from significant
participation in the general society also keep them disorganized.
Thus, identity, the feeling of belonging and the sense of social
purpose, could be found neither in membership in the larger society
nor in participation in a cohesive racial group. Generation after
generation of Negroes live out their lives in fruitless detachment and
personal emptiness. . . . Yet the search for identity goes on. . . .
Miraculously almost, realistic racial conflict with its ideological*

apparatus and action system functions to alleviate alienation and facilitate identity. Conflict enhances group solidarity, clarifies group boundaries and strengthens the individual–group linkage through ego-emotion commitment and overt action. . . . It may be said that through realistic racial conflict America gains some new Americans. (pp. 254–255)

The civil rights struggle and the black consciousness movement of the 1960s did indeed create new black Americans, Americans who had found a new sense of respect, dignity, and self-determination. In contemporary society, social workers seem to have lost their enthusiasm for social action. They need to draw heavily from the black experience to rekindle their zeal for social activism. After all, the protest tradition in the black heritage is strong, because few people have fought as persistently and vigorously for true American democracy as black people. In their clinical practice, social workers are challenged to incorporate hope, struggle, and liberation consciousness into their therapies, and group workers and community organizers are challenged to help prepare oppressed groups for empowerment. Overall, social workers, again drawing from the black experience, need to see social action as an effort to stop the losses and the suffering and begin the process of healing, self-determination, empowerment, and social change. Through struggle, social workers will not only help to transform black people and the nation, they will also help transform themselves and free themselves from the shackles of their own history and professional culture. After all, as we stated in an earlier work, in capitalist society where "welfare" is considered a dirty word, social workers too are treated like "niggers" (Martin & Martin, 1985).

REFERENCES

American Psychiatric Association. (1994). *Diagnostic and statistical manual of mental disorders* (4th ed.). Washington, DC: Author.

Davidson, B. (1969). *The African genius.* Boston: Little, Brown.

Erikson, E. (1968). Race and the wider identity. In E. Erikson (Ed.), *Identity, youth and crisis* (pp. 295–321). New York: W. W. Norton.

Erikson, K. T. (Ed.). (1969). *In search of common ground: Conversations with Erik H. Erikson and Huey P. Newton.* New York: Dell.

Evans, R. I. (Ed.). (1969). *Dialogue with Erik Erikson*. New York: E. P. Dutton.

Freud, S. (1943). *A general introduction to psychoanalysis*. Garden City, NY: Garden City Publishing.

Freud, S. (1959a). Totem and taboo. In J. Strachey (Ed.), *The standard edition of the complete psychological works of Sigmund Freud* (Vol. 13: 1913–1914, pp. 1–114). London: Hogarth Press.

Freud, S. (1959b). Mourning and melancholia. In J. Strachey (Ed.), *The standard edition of the complete psychological works of Sigmund Freud* (Vol. 14: 1914–1916, pp. 237–258). London: Hogarth Press.

Freud, S. (1959c). Anxiety and mourning. In J. Strachey (Ed.), *The standard edition of the complete psychological works of Sigmund Freud* (Vol. 20: 1925–1926, pp. 169–172). London: Hogarth Press.

Goble, F. (1970). *The third force: The psychology of Abraham Maslow*. New York: Grossman.

Himes, J. S. (1980). The function of racial conflict. In T. Pettigrew (Ed.), *The sociology of race relations* (pp. 253–255). New York: Free Press.

Kardiner, A., & Ovesey, L. (1951). *The mark of oppression*. New York: W. W. Norton.

Liebow, E. (1967). *Talley's corner*. Boston: Little, Brown.

Logan, S.M.L., Freeman, E. M., & McRoy, R. G. (1990). *Social work practice with black families*. New York: Longman.

Martin, E. P., & Martin, J. M. (1985). *The helping tradition in the black family and community*. Silver Spring, MD: National Association of Social Workers.

Maultsby, M. C., Jr. (1982). A historical view of blacks' distrust of psychiatry. In S. M. Turner & R. T. Jones (Eds.), *Behavior modification in black populations* (pp. 39–57). New York: Plenum Press.

Peters, E. (1985). *Anna Freud: A life dedicated to children*. New York: Schocken Books.

Platt, A. M. (1991). *E. Franklin Frazier reconsidered*. New Brunswick, NJ: Rutgers University Press.

Stack, C. B. (1975). *All our kin*. New York: Harper & Row.

Turner, S. M. (1982) Behavior modification and black populations. In S. M. Turner & R. T. Jones (Eds.), *Behavior modification in black populations* (pp. 1–20). New York: Plenum Press.

Washington, J. M. (Ed.). (1986). *The essential writings and speeches of Martin Luther King, Jr.* San Francisco: HarperCollins.

Wilson, A. N. (1993). *The falsification of Afrikan consciousness*. New York: Afrikan World InfoSystems.

The Foundation of Black Experience–Based Social Work: A Practice Model

*U*ltimately not only does a bright new morning in social work with black people hinge on developing fresh perspectives and pedagogical changes but, even more significantly, it hinges on the nuts and bolts of a social work practice derived from the black experience. If we have shown anything in this book thus far, we hope it has been that the black experience is rife with implications for social work practice. Although it does not always demonstrate a clearly delineated step-by-step process, it forces the social work practitioner to focus on the right questions concerning social work practice with black people and to do experimentation to answer these relevant questions. For example, as the problem of loss and separation is a core problem in both past and contemporary black experiences, how do we social workers assess this problem in the lives of our black clients? What are the effects of placing people who already have a history of traumatization in this regard in institutions that store them up and lock them away from their families and neighborhoods? What impact does the problem of loss and separation have on the emotional, social, educational, cultural, economic, and political development of black people? As the black experience calls for creating an extended family–type work or practice atmosphere, what are the best methods for accomplishing this? As the black experience calls for black people to pour out their guts and souls to the group, how best to accomplish this, particularly in light of cultural amnesia, societal stoicism, the privatization of troubles, and cool? As the black experience calls for the instillation of hope to combat alienation, defeatism, and despair, how best to inculcate hope? The black experience demands answers to questions such as how best to deal with the issues of class and race and gender, how best to incorporate spirituality in a profession that is basically secular, and how best to make an ancestral connection in a profession that is basically ahistorical? As the goal of the black experience is to create culturally versatile black people, the questions arise: What qualities or characteristics are more conducive to cultural versatility in contemporary society? How do you teach cultural versatility skills?

What we are saying, in essence, is that black experience–based social work is not a fixed practice that has a specific formula for curing all the social ills of black people. It is a dynamic, flexible approach that requires explanation and experimentation within set boundaries that consider the full range of the black helping experience.

Black experience–based social work seeks not to become so methodologically rigid that it stifles creativity and openness. As in the blues and the spirituals, a central theme might set the boundaries, but room is left for the theme to be approached with numerous variations, to have many subtleties of interpretation, and to be remodeled repeatedly as individuals are allowed to go solo and to improvise, keeping, of course, with the rhythm of the group and within the structure of the central theme. Like the blues and the spiritual tradition on which it is based, black experience–based social work leaves room for improvisation within parameters. The boundaries or parameters of black experience–based social work are set within the framework of the moaning, mourning, and morning themes of the blues and spiritual tradition.

SOCIAL EXPERIMENTATION

Realizing that the black experience raises more questions regarding practice than it answers, we followed a tradition of early black social work pioneers of using students in a "social laboratory" in an attempt to sharpen and refine techniques and methodologies of helping and healing. Our social experimentation with social work students was conducted in our black family classes. Our future goal is to set up black experience–based social work institutes so that questions, issues, and problems concerning social work practice with black people can be systematically addressed and so that the

"scientific method" so highly valued by pioneer black social workers can be rigorously applied. But for now, within the limited setting of our black family classes, we were confronted with how to
prepare students for black experience–based social work practice.

STEP 1. (MOANING) IMMERSING IN BLACK HISTORY AND CULTURE

If black experience–based social work has a step-by-step helping
process at all, the first step is to have social work students learn as
much as they can about black history and culture and to continue
their education in these areas throughout their lives. Social work
practitioners must be thoroughly aware that black people are both
creatures and creators of history in that history has placed them
where they are right now and has shaped their point of view, their
identity, and their aspirations. As the great writer James Baldwin
(1985) pointed out, history is not just something to be read and it
does not merely refer to the past. History, he wrote, is a great force
that "we carry within us," that controls us in many ways, and that
is "literally present in all that we do" (p. 410). Practitioners must
also immerse themselves in every area of black cultural life—art,
religion, music, and folklore. The immersion of students into black
history and culture will help them develop in three areas that are
crucial for effective work with black people:

1. It will foster historical empathy.
2. It will strengthen ancestral connectedness.
3. It will strengthen their black identity (if they are black) and their
   identification with black people (if they are not black).

As we have pointed out throughout this book, ancestral connectedness has been a key factor in the black helping experience.
Historical empathy involves the ability to moan over the suffering
of black people in the past and to connect their pain to the suffering of contemporary black people. When black people can hear the
cries of black people on the slave ships and on the plantation along
with the cries of the oppressed people of the current generation,
they will develop a deeper sensitivity and a more sacred commitment to relieving one another's suffering. The ancestors will in a

sense be with them, strengthening their resolve to continue fighting until the suffering stops.

In our social experimentation with social work students in a black family social work course at Morgan State University, we had to ponder how to develop the skill of historical empathy or ancestral connectedness, particularly because the social work profession tends to be ahistorical as it concentrates mainly on present circumstances. The way to do it, we found, was to incorporate an in-depth social history that is not just about great black people and achievers but that highlights the day-to-day lives and struggles of the black masses during critical moments of their history. The goal of teaching black social history is to develop in students a sensitivity to the plight of black people in contemporary society by providing them with a sense of historical continuity to help them see the relationship and the parallels between the past and the present situation.

One of the methods we have used in training students for historical empathy and ancestral connectedness is bibliotherapy. In bibliotherapy the students read narratives, biographies, and autobiographies of black people during certain stages of history. For example, slave narratives are particularly useful in helping teach historical empathy. We also have students write their own family histories and make comparisons and draw parallels to historical black people and look for unfinished business.

We have found, for example, that many students have so little knowledge of the ways their own grandparents and great-grandparents lived that they view us with suspicion when we suggest that there were times when black people showed more love, care, and respect for one another. So accustomed have they become to black individualism and social atomization that, without some sense of history, they have no idea how rich the helping tradition was in black culture just several decades ago. Hence, exposing them to black history often means just acquainting them with their own family trees so that they can contrast and compare how each generation in their own genealogy lived, what they thought, what they believed, what they valued, and what action they took to improve the quality of their lives.

In seeking to use black history as a weapon for social cohesiveness and social change, we have found that bibliotherapy is a great supplement to black experience–based social work. Reading about the lives and struggles of black people through historical narratives, biographies, and autobiographies can strengthen ancestral empathy and connectedness. There is also ample evidence in the black experience to show how reading has helped black people strengthen the inner self and develop a firm commitment to black uplift and social change. For example, Frederick Douglass (1883) wrote that reading helped transform him from a brute to a man. He wrote that "with a book in my hand so redolent of the principles of liberty, . . . [I developed] a perception of my own human nature and the facts of my past and present experiences" (p. 77). "Light," he wrote, "had penetrated the moral dungeon where I had lain, and . . . it opened my eyes to the horrible pit, and revealed the teeth of the frightful dragon that was ready to pounce on me" (pp. 77–78). Reading helped Richard Wright (1945) articulate his violent rage in political, sociological, ideological, and literary terms. He wrote that "it had been my accidental reading of fiction and literary criticism that had evoked in me vague glimpses of life's possibilities" (p. 283). Wright further wrote that "it had been only through books—at best, no more than vicarious cultural transfusions—that I had managed to keep myself alive in a negatively vital way. Whenever my environment had failed to support or nourish me, I had clutched at books; . . . And it was out of these novels and stories and articles . . . that I felt touching my face a tinge of warmth from an unseen light" (p. 283). Malcolm X (1964) also learned to articulate his rage in political terms after reading opened up to him this avenue of expression:

> I have often reflected upon the new vistas that reading opened to me. I knew right there in prison that reading had changed forever the course of my life. As I see it today, the ability to read awoke inside me some long dormant craving to be mentally alive. . . . My homemade education gave me, with every additional book that I read, a little bit more sensitivity to the deafness, dumbness, and blindness that was afflicting the black race in America. Not long ago, an English writer telephoned me from London, asking questions. One was, "what's your alma mater?" I told him, "books." You will never catch me with a free fifteen minutes in which I'm not studying something I feel might be able to help the black man. (p. 179)

Besides bibliotherapy, students are allowed to pour libation to the ancestors and to commune with them in other traditional ways.

By immersing students in black history, black culture, and the contemporary black experience, we help black students strengthen their identify and consciousness as black people and help students of other races and nationalities develop greater sensitivity to the plight and the promise of black people.

STEP 2. (MOANING) THE IDENTIFICATION OF THE PROBLEM

We found that an immersion in blackness helped students see more clearly that social problems in black life cannot always be defined on an individual basis but must also be viewed in terms of their historical connection. It helped them to see that many individual problems in contemporary society are collective unsolved problems of history. For example, if we were to focus on black youths, we would see that the social conditions of poverty, despair, alienation, and public indifference plagued our youths in the past and still plague them currently. As in the past, contemporary black parents still worry that their children are going to be taken from them and placed in prison, foster homes, adoption agencies, juvenile institutions, or the city morgue. The cry of the black mother in the past over losing her children to the lynch rope or the chain gang is the same primal scream of black mothers today who lose their children to gang violence, incarceration, black-on-black homicide, and the so-called justifiable homicides frequently inflicted on young black people by the police.

Without being able to analyze problems such as black child welfare from a historical perspective, social work practitioners will not have a firm grasp of the depth of problems or a feeling about how deeply entrenched they generally are in the fabric of American society. Without a conception of black history, social workers will be prone to seek simple solutions to complex problems and develop false hopes and illusions about fairness, justice, and equality in an allegedly Judeo-Christian, democratic America, the land of the brave and the free. By entertaining such false hopes and illusions, they will never fully understand what they are up against.

Moreover, without a keen sense of history, social workers will have no conception of the still unfinished business.

Once practitioners have gained a historical perspective and been taught to analyze problems in terms of black history—paying close attention to parallels between the past and the present—they need to focus on the problems that black people have historically identified as the most urgent ones confronting them. Black people have identified as key the problems of loss and separation, troubled intimate relations, and racial oppression.

STEP 3. (MOANING) CREATING ASSESSMENT INSTRUMENTS

Once historical and core social problems had been identified, we found it necessary to experiment with creating new techniques to assess these problems. For example, our students created a "loss/support chart" to be used to identify the major direct losses and separations in their lives on one side and all the supports on the other, in chronological order.

Figure 1 is a portion of a chart submitted by one of our students. She indicates that her mother has been a support source from her birth to her age at the time of this writing (30 years) and that her boyfriend has been a part of her support system since age 28. On the loss side, the chart shows that her father left the family when she was around 12 years old, that her grandmother died when she was 23, and that she broke up with an old boyfriend at age 25. The chart was very effective in giving us a quick overview of the individual's life history with respect to the problem of object loss and object constancy. In their written narrative and their oral presentations, students were required to go into the details of their lives and experiences.

Practitioners should be aware that black people have numerous problems that may not be among the three core ones, but it is hard to imagine any difficulty that is not in some way related to or connected to these core problems. Whatever the case, black experience–based social work practitioners must always be on the alert for spotting these core problems and for creating or borrowing techniques to assess them.

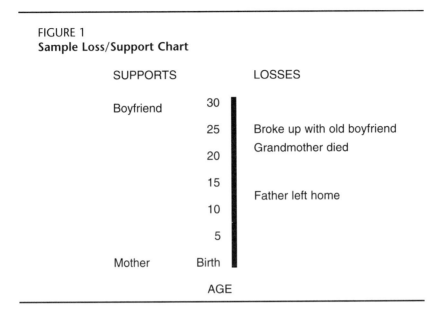

FIGURE 1
Sample Loss/Support Chart

STEP 4. (MOANING) CLARIFYING THE OBJECTIVE

Once practitioners gain thorough knowledge concerning the three core problems—their etiology; black people's reaction to them; and their impact on black individuals, black families, and black communities—they need to be clear about the goal of black experience–based social work. The goal is neither social adjustment nor social adaptation. The goal is to create culturally versatile black people, that is, to help them overcome whatever personal, social, or mental disorders thwart their maximum potential for maneuverability upward in society. This goal stems from the black experience.

As Lovell (1972) stated, "The spirituals demonstrate that even the slave showed considerable flexibility in meeting problems of change" (p. 392). Teaching students cultural versatility techniques involves the following process:

- Identify immediate and long-range plans or life goals.
- Explore the immediate pressing problems serving to keep one from reaching true self goals.

- Recognize the societal barriers against realizing true self goals.
- Anticipate the societal traps and pitfalls that thwart the realization of true self goals.
- Identify the emotional, psychological, intellectual, and cultural restraints within oneself that keep one from realizing true self goals.
- Develop a plan of action for confronting immediate problems, breaking through societal barriers, avoiding societal entrapments, and overcoming one's own internal restraints.
- Follow through on the plan of action.
- Help other black people to become more culturally versatile.

The outcome should be the creation of black people who are able to maneuver around the traps and pitfalls systematically set for them by an oppressive racist society and who are able to overcome their own internal blockages that keep them from confronting difficult problems, keep them living on the level of intentions, and cause them to fear both failure and success. In the black family class, students put together a list of qualities, traits, and characteristics they felt were conducive to cultural versatility in contemporary society. According to their "cultural versatility profile," black people are more culturally versatile when they are educated or skilled, intuitively in tune with the voices of their ancestors, racially conscious, historically knowledgeable, politically aware, communally oriented, and dedicated to the progress of black people in contemporary society and to the well-being of future generations. They are more versatile when they have confidence in themselves, faith in a higher power, and hope tinged with a firm grasp of reality. Creating black people with these qualities, traits, and characteristics presented a huge challenge to our young social work practitioners.

In seeking to create culturally versatile black people, black experience–based social workers have to recognize the barriers to creating cultural versatility. Black experience–based social work practice has identified at least five major negative psychologies that keep many black people from confronting core problems; having the flexibility, mobility, and motivation necessary to avoid societal pitfalls; and gaining the sense of identity and empathy and grasp of objective conditions necessary for collective liberation:

1. cultural sickness
2. cultural paranoia
3. cultural claustrophobia
4. cultural amnesia
5. cultural terminal illness.

Students had the awesome challenge of creating techniques to identify symptoms of each of these negative psychologies.

The most damaging of these negative, immobilizing psychologies from the standpoint of black experience–based social work is the psychology of cultural amnesia. If black people are cut off from history and ancestral connections, they are vulnerable to all kinds of whims, fads, thoughts, and ideologies that are antithetical to their best interests as a people.

STEP 5. (MOANING) CLARIFYING THE GOAL

By creating more-versatile black people, the ultimate goal is to create a healing–developing black community, in other words, a community that must heal many of its emotional, social, and historical wounds as a precondition for economic, political, social, cultural, and intellectual growth. For example, the five negative psychologies identified in this book still thwart development in crucial areas of black life. The psychology of cultural sickness, a vestige of slavery, is still exacting a tremendous toll on the black individual, family, and community. Its symptoms, as identified by our students, are low self-esteem, feelings of inferiority, lack of confidence, and so forth. Just imagine how difficult it is for people to rise educationally and economically if they feel they are of little worth. What is even more problematic is that many black people have developed such a grave feeling of mistrust of other black people and of being hemmed in and thwarted by their environment that they have taken on the destructive cultural psychology of terminal illness. The objective is to create culturally versatile black people to reach the goal of developing the healing–developing community.

STEP 6. (MOURNING) CREATING THE HELPING ATMOSPHERE

The black experience emphasizes taking a collective approach to problem solving. This collective approach entails helping individual black people to pinpoint the social origin of their personal pain to view themselves as fellow sufferers sharing a common history, common problems, and a common racial identity. This collective approach means that the black experience emphasizes group work but allows room for individuals to engage in a one-on-one casework or clinical work situation for more deep-seated mental and emotional problems beyond the scope of group work. The social context of black experience–based social work is of primary importance. In the past, black people used the extended family as a model. Our students also have found the extended family model helpful in creating a nonjudgmental, supportive, cooperative, nurturing atmosphere. Historically, black people have felt more comfortable sharing their pain in a warm, friendly, communal atmosphere. It was in this kind of social context that they could connect not only with other people's pain but also with the suffering of their ancestors. Also, students were sensitive to the historical fact that being black in America has been a traumatizing experience for countless black people over the generations and that their placement in many social welfare institutions has meant further traumatization, given the way many of them have been mishandled and mistreated. Students knew the importance of trying to create an environment where black people would not be traumatized any more than they already are. In the black family class, composed of approximately 35 students per semester, students not only sought to create an extended family–type helping milieu that would allow them to identify with one another's suffering, lend one another support, and instill and reinforce hope, but also relied on the African tradition of the circle. Therefore, students arranged their seats in a circle to allow them to see one another's faces as they disclosed highly personal information about themselves and sought to comfort one another in their suffering as they were mastering the traditional art of mourning. They were encouraged to see one another as fellow sufferers and members of an extended family and not as sick, inferior people, public parasites, or social deviants.

STEP 7. (MOURNING) WRESTLING WITH THE PROBLEM OF DISCLOSURE

We have highlighted throughout this study that black people in the past moaned about their deeply personal problems through their music and other black cultural forms in the context of mourning institutions. Both the blues and the spiritual tradition requires toughening individuals mentally, spiritually, and culturally to the point that they confront problems, not back away from them; disclose problems, not hide them or become silent sufferers. However, we also pointed out that when black people migrated to the big city they began to develop a serious case of cultural amnesia, followed the dictates of the dominant society that extolled the privatization of personal troubles, and were influenced by the street ideology of cool that called for fronting instead of confronting. In contemporary society, taking flight or running away from problems is a primary form of escapism.

Taking flight is no longer physically running away from a totalitarian experience to gain some mastery over one's own life so much as it has become a psychological running away from difficult problems. For example, in contemporary black ghetto life "running" has become a central theme. Black people on the streets are always talking about having to "make a run"; they cannot stay still or settle down in any one place for too long; and they speak of their friends as "running buddies." When they seek to manipulate, con, or exploit other black people, they speak of "running a game on them." When they are living in "the fast lane," they move as if they are "running out of time." Their tendency is to run away from responsibility, relationships, and reality as many continue the "dog-eat-dog" tribeless way of life. The desire is not only to escape current conditions but to escape historical obligations.

Besides recognizing the problem of disclosure in the black experience, students also discovered their own discomfort in articulating their suffering in a collective setting. In seeking solutions to this problem, they explored a number of options. They examined mainstream social work methods of interviewing, asking one another open-ended, nonmoralizing, and nonjudgmental questions, but they also experimented with black traditional techniques. For example, some made use of brief personal narratives on their lives, concentrating on loss and separation; intimate relations; oppressions; and familial, ancestral, or spiritual supports. Other students found stories drawn from black history or from black literature and even examples from contemporary life that paralleled their own lives. Most of our students, however, preferred songs and poems using lyrics that best defined the problems that pained them most and that highlighted their deepest true self-desires or aspirations. In this regard, it was interesting to find that "rap" music served the same function for the students that the spirituals and the blues served for their ancestors: It gave them a means by which their voices could be heard and their deepest hurt and longing could be made public without shame or stigma. For example, one student wrote the following rap poem:

Life in the Day of a Woman

It is not easy being a black woman
every time you think things are going o.k. and you're about to stand
*   tall*
You find yourself faced with another brick wall.
*   Life in the day of a woman.*
*   Life in the day of a woman.*
So you're on your own, living alone.
It's not easy but you manage to survive.
You go through hard times but you keep your head high.
*   Life in the day of a woman.*
*   Life in the day of a woman.*
Life in the day of a woman can bring you rain and pain
but from it all you're not ashamed because you will eventually gain.
*   Life in the day of a woman.*
*   Life in the day of a woman.*
From the time of being molested when you were young;
From the time of being an adult and losing a loved one
This is when you feel that life in the day of a woman is being
*   used,*
*   abused,*
*   and*
*   accused.*

Life in the day of a woman.
Life in the day of a woman.
Then comes love again, at least you think it's love
Until the baby comes, and the love you thought you had is a thing
of the past.
Life in the day of a woman.
Life in the day of a woman.
Each day seems long as you raise your child alone.
But you nurture him, educate him, and teach him to be wise, loving,
and strong.
And once you've done your part
you hope he'll never break your heart.
Life in the day of a woman.
(Edwards, 1995. Reprinted with permission of the author)

This rap poem gave the student an opportunity to express deep, hidden feelings about being sexually molested as a child, losing a husband (to black-on-black homicide), being jilted by the father of her son, and the hardship of a single black woman raising a son on her own. Yet, despite the pain of loss, hurt, and abuse it conjures up (in the tradition of the blues), it also (in the tradition of the spirituals) talks about managing to survive, holding one's head high, gaining from hard experiences, and continuing on with hope for herself and her son. Most social work instruments of disclosure are geared toward the rational self. Songs, narratives, poems, and the like are black traditional instruments for getting in touch with the intuitive self, the soul.

Of course, whether poems, songs, or narratives were chosen, each student eventually had to come before the group and talk about his or her personal narratives, tell how the music lyrics reflected his or her own frustrations and hopes, or discuss the ways that stories mirrored his or her personal life. We were encouraged in our use of traditional black techniques of disclosure and self-expression by the black psychotherapists and educational counselors Alfred B. Pasteur and Ivory L. Toldson (1982), who wrote, "In our therapeutic and educational work with groups and individuals, we use popular forms of black contemporary expression (music, drama, dance, graphic arts, poetry, folklore, fashion, sermons, stories) to help them improve chances of living happily in our modern world" (p. 12). These authors experienced a high success rate in using black culture to lead black people to optimal mental health and social functioning.

Students amazed us and amazed themselves at how creative they were. It was not surprising to us that most of them chose music as the main form of expressing their deepest emotions. Most students were eager to share their thoughts through personal narratives, music, and storytelling and eager to hear the thoughts of others. We found that the best strategy was to let those who were the most eager to disclose talk first. This served to help other more-introverted students break down their wall of silence and be more open to disclosing deeply personal information.

Although the traditional techniques of problem identification helped us considerably, we still detected that each student had his or her secrets, silent spots, and hidden chambers. Students were encouraged to talk about their secrets but they were not pressured to do so.

For example, one of our students, who we will call Ada and follow throughout the helping process, was extremely reluctant to talk about her life. She had not wanted to reveal the problems she was having with her father. She said that when she heard other students revealing even shameful, embarrassing, guilt-ridden episodes of their lives she felt more comfortable. She gained greater confidence after realizing that the students who went first had "horror stories" that were scarier than hers. Also, she realized that the information was not going beyond the group and that it was not a gossipy group relishing in sensationalism.

Because rules were laid down in the beginning informing students that they were to work in the communal spirit of their ancestors and thus avoid at all cost being judgmental, moralistic, condescending, paternalistic, and antagonistic, students such as Ada felt more at ease disclosing personal information to the group.

Ada chose the personal narrative form of disclosure. When she decided that she was ready to talk she stated that her father abandoned the family shortly after her mother began dying from cancer. He left her and her younger sister, both teenagers, to take care of their dying mother alone. Ada had vowed that she would never speak to her father again in life. After her mother died, her hatred increased. She decided to choose a college on the East Coast because she could not bear to live in the same West Coast state in which her father lived. She brought her younger sister with her. They lived on the little insurance money they received after their mother's death.

Probing

After each student made a personal disclosure based on his or her narrative, song, or story, he or she was asked questions by members of the class who used the mainstream social work skills of interviewing. We called this questioning "probing." Thus, each student was "probed" in hopes of reaching the deeper layers of inner feelings and experiences. Many students stated that it was the first time they had revealed areas of their personal lives to anyone, even to close family and friends. They felt relieved.

Ada said that she had convinced herself that her problem with her father was "dead and buried" but learned that although the disclosure conjured up old ghosts and old bitterness, she felt better in confronting the situation instead of continuing to suppress it. She realized that no matter how much she thought she had put the past behind her, her relationship with her father was still a matter that had to be resolved. The probing also made her realize that she and her sister were not actually alone in dealing with their dying mother. Aunts and uncles had been very supportive. Ada even admitted reluctantly that even though her father no longer lived with them, he did make sure that the bills were paid and that she and her sister had money for clothes, school, and other needs.

STEP 8: (MOURNING) MASTERING THE ABILITY TO MOURN

As students became more comfortable disclosing their inner thoughts and purging their personal demons with confidence that they would be listened to with sympathetic ears, it was easier for them to engage in the mourning work of lending one another support and instilling hope.

Lending Group Support

As students conjured up old hurts and unresolved conflicts in their lives, the group sessions were almost akin to being in church. Thus, students who had to pause a moment to choke back tears were told "Take your time, honey!" "It's all right!" "Let it out!" and "We're with you, baby!" Students began to reassure one another with hugs, pats on the back, and words of encouragement as their tears became one when they related tales of hardship, struggle, strangled ambitions, denial, deprivation, and other themes recurrent in all of their lives. The students' joy became one too as they related tales of triumph amidst defeat, hope amidst despair, and courage amidst fear. Although it was easier for the female students than the male students to lend emotional support, many of the male students over the 10-year period in which the social experiment was conducted also learned to give hugs, pats on the back, and words of encouragement and to receive such support with no feelings of threat to their manhood.

In lending group support, students learned to avoid blaming, condemning, judging, and moralizing and to concentrate on recognizing one another's strength and potential. Ada said that the students made her feel good about herself when they pointed out that it took a great deal of courage on her part for her to help care for her dying mother and that it took a great deal of strength to take primary responsibility for caring for her younger sister while holding down two part-time jobs and going to college full-time. For some of the students it was the first time anyone had said anything positive about them or had given them hugs in their suffering. Most had no idea that their fellow classmates had collectively suffered so much and had such strengths. It was the first time they had been able to know one another on more than a superficial level.

Instilling Hope

Lending support went hand in hand with instilling and reinforcing hope, as students articulated their true self-desires and aspirations. As they lent one another support, they were no longer strangers but fellow sufferers conscious of their oneness. It was at this point that they were asked to bring in anything or anybody that inspired them to try to realize their personal objectives. In one class, a student brought in a prayer that she felt would be inspiring to other students because she had received so much encouragement from the prayer herself. This prompted other students to bring in poems, songs, sayings, and even photos of people who had served as major sources of hope and inspiration in their lives. The photos were of the living and the dead, as some students said that they would have given up a long time ago if they had not feared "letting down" deceased loved ones who while living had been an inspiring force. Some believed that the deceased loved ones were still "there for them," watching over them and guiding them in the right direction. Others brought in live people. For example, one student brought in his old high school basketball coach, whereas another brought in her newborn baby as her primary motivator toward success.

Like their traditional African forebearers these students drew strength from both the living and the dead as ancestral memory became a rich source of inspiration, faith, and hope. So successful were students in instilling hope that we sought to sharpen this skill by following the students' lead and having them bring something or someone to class who had inspired them to greater heights of excellence, uplift, and achievement. Ada brought in a prayer that her mother had given from her deathbed.

STEP 9. (MOURNING) EVALUATING GROWTH

As they were undertaking the work of mourning, students were cognizant of the need to develop criteria for which they could evaluate their growth in their quest to become black experience–based social work practitioners. Drawing from the morning theme of the black experience, they evaluated their growth in terms of their ability to (1) identify collective patterns in respect to problems they had in common, (2) explore collective alternatives to problem solving, and (3) make a realistic assessment of objective conditions and develop versatility strategies and skills.

Identifying Collective Patterns

One of the primary morning objectives, as we discussed earlier, is for black people to reach the point where they can resolve the social and psychological problems keeping them from engaging in collective problem solving and seeking social change. After students gave their personal reports and were probed and supported and had their hopes lifted, they came together to look for patterns in respect to problems they had in common so that they could collectively explore alternatives and options. They were assured that they were not expected to solve the problems of the entire black race within a single academic semester. They were to learn not to make quick decisions, give hasty advice, or look for easy, simple answers.

It was important that the students were collectively seeking answers to hard problems, whereas before they were accustomed to handling their problems alone or simply keeping them to themselves, hurting inside but allowing problems to go unresolved. In this respect, they had to learn the skill of partialization, that is, taking in no more of the problem than they could handle and breaking the problem down in ways that made the problem concrete, manageable, and solvable.

What students found startling was that they were still wrestling with core social problems identified by their ancestors, namely the problems of loss and separation, defective intimate relations, and oppression. They could see the historical connection and understood that although the context might have changed, the problems of the past and the present were the same.

In identifying patterns, students could see that they had tended to think that they alone suffered from particular problems only to discover that there were many fellow sufferers with the same problems. For example, students recognized the influence of the five negative psychologies of cultural sickness, cultural paranoia, cultural amnesia, cultural claustrophobia, and cultural terminal illness. They also recognized the debilitating effects that alcoholism and drug addiction had on black family and community life. There were few students over the 10-year period whose families had not suffered in some way from alcoholism and drug addiction. It was easy for students to see that their private concern regarding the problem of alcohol and illegal narcotics was also a problem in the black community beyond the classroom. Students could view the problem of poverty in the same respect.

On the positive side, students found that a common thread that weaved their lives together was that many of them still received support from extended family members, especially from aunts and grandmothers. Granny was still "the guardian of the generation"

(Frazier, 1949, p. 146), although her role was not as extensive as it had been in earlier decades. Students could see the potential of the black extended family as a great source of helping, and they explored ways of strengthening it.

While examining the extended family as a caregiving institution, students recognized an unfortunate family problem that was common to most or all of them, whether they came from middle-class, working-class, or welfare-class backgrounds: Nearly all of them suffered from the absence of fathers or from the peripheral and shadowy roles many fathers tend to play in black family life. This was clearly the problem of intimate relations so often highlighted in the blues, because many of these fathers had problems with the students' mothers; this obviously had adverse consequences for the children. Some of the students were in so much pain in this regard that they had declared their fathers "dead to them," even though they knew that they were still alive. Ada was surprised that she was not alone in the troubles she was having with her father.

When students began to explore options for solving this problem, they came up with a number of suggestions ranging from strengthening the economic base of black men to engaging them in revolutionary change. This recognition of the problem black men have in terms of living up to expected family responsibilities and communal obligations extended from the classroom to the plight of black men in society in general. The students also made ancestral connection by exploring the plight of black men in America over history. Some engaged in the practice of pouring libation as a means of being spiritually connected to the ancestors.

Exploring Collective Alternatives

Besides learning that problems they thought were private ones were core problems suffered by other black people and problems they thought were endemic to contemporary society were also problems black people had suffered historically, they also used their ability to explore collective alternatives as signs of their maturity and growth. This they knew was consistent with black tradition. As Lovell (1972) wrote, "The spiritual's way of putting responsibility on each individual presupposes a unique life for each person, and therefore unique preparation for that life" (p. 392). Students began to judge their own individual growth by how well they could accept and follow up on group suggestions as to how to take responsibility for following up with and tackling their own personal problems once the class was over. As students explored ways in which they might best serve the collective, Ada realized that her unresolved conflict with her father was affecting her studies. She had been an honor student in high school but found that now that she was in college she was too tired, too unfocused, and too content to "just get by" to move her studies beyond average grades. She decided "after much soul searching" to take the group's suggestion and make contact with her father to hear his side of the story.

Examining Objective Conditions

When students explored collective alternatives they found that they had to examine objective conditions to see to what extent their plans were realizable and manageable in whole or in part. We stated earlier that the role of the blues tradition was to bring the high hopes, wild dreams, and utopianism of the spiritual tradition back to earth. In this respect, even as students were mapping out strategies to solve their own personal problems so they could be in a better position to serve the black masses, they were asked to explore social conditions to ascertain how favorable or unfavorable reality was to their best-laid plans.

Ada felt that the strongest opposition to her seeing her father lay within herself because her father had tried on several occasions to talk with her. She understood that just mapping out a strategy for change did not mean that she would carry it out, particularly in light of the fact that like many black people she had a history of not being able to complete crucial and burdensome life tasks.

We must state here that in seeking a collective approach to problem solving, the black experience–based social worker should be keenly cognizant that the problem of loss and separation, poor intimate relations, and oppression has caused many black people to live on the level of intention where they are too unfocused and too lacking in energy and motivation to complete crucial life tasks. Many black people would rather seek escape, accommodation, or adjustment rather than confront social problems and seek social change. We pointed out that black people ever since traditional Africa have been a people in flight.

What students discovered was that when black people sought to escape from the problems, the problems grew larger. Also, they found that escapist tendencies keep black people from seeking collective solutions to their problems. Ada said that she thought she had put her problem with her family behind her but found out in confronting it just how deeply it was still affecting her and keeping her from realizing her fullest true self-desires.

Developing Versatility Strategies and Skills

Once students identified collective patterns, sought collective alternatives, examined objective conditions, and saw the necessity of confronting problems instead of denying, repressing, or trying to escape from them, they also sought (with the help of the group) to develop their own versatility skills. Because the group would break up after the semester ended, the only guarantee that the students had that they would follow up on tackling problems they had identified was to hold students accountable for making sure they took responsibility for addressing their own personal problems, mapping out strategies to avoid the society's oppressive snares, and preparing themselves emotionally, mentally, and spiritually for helping to advance the group. Learning versatility skills became the chief criterion for evaluating their development. Learning versatility skills did not just mean rational analysis or planning, but in keeping with black tradition, it meant listening to and trusting the intuitive self. Both a rational and realistic appraisal and following the lead of ancestral insights are necessary for developing versatility skills. We found that providing students with tasks that they must perform to reach their goals was also quite helpful. In carrying out these tasks, the individuals had to be accountable to the group. Moreover, in carrying out tasks they were taking individual initiative and individual responsibility and not camouflaging inactivity behind waiting for the group to move.

Ada chose to ask a friend to rehearse with her how she would communicate with her father and to practice how she would calm her anger enough to be open to hearing what he had to say. She planned the location where they would talk and met with her role-playing friend to make sure that the area was suitable in terms of allowing for privacy and a quick exit if necessary.

Ada finally felt that she was versatile enough in terms of mental, physical, and emotional preparation to carry to completion this crucial life task. She arranged a meeting, which lasted several hours, with her father. After hearing her father's side of the story, Ada learned that he felt that he simply did not have the emotional strength to watch her mother whom he had loved since they were 17 years old become "skin and bone." She learned that he had kept informed about his wife's health and his children's well-being through Ada's aunts. He also said that Ada's mother understood and had told him repeatedly that she did not want him to see her in such an emaciated state. Ada's mother knew that she was dying and wanted her husband to remember her as she had been in better health.

Although Ada dismissed this as a rationalization or excuse, she learned from the group sessions that her father did what many other black men have done under distressing situations: Instead of seeking group support from family, friends, and church members, they take flight. Ada also learned from the group sessions that she herself had responded to the separation from her father in a way in which many black people respond when they are confronted with a devastating loss or separation. Not only do they tend to have trouble completing crucial life tasks, as Ada was having in her studies, but they also have trouble establishing trust in their relationships with others. Ada felt that she could not trust a man enough to have a romantic relationship. Once she reestablished her relationship with her father and agreed with him to work together to sort out and solve the problems between them, she renewed her interest in her studies and regained her trust in black men enough to start an intimate relationship.

From Ada's experience, we can see that individual problems were not ignored but reframed in the context of the group and dealt with on a collective basis as students learned to translate private concerns into social causes. Holding individuals accountable for making themselves versatile was quite consistent with the responsibility traditional African communities, the slave community, and the rural communities placed on individuals to prepare themselves to overcome personal disaster so they could position themselves to advance the progress of the group. The class held individuals responsible for being flexible, resourceful, and resilient enough to get out of the traps in which they had found themselves and to avoid other pitfalls and to be versatile enough to work collectively for black uplift and social change. In doing so, the individuals were to drop the old individualism and indeed see it as the enemy. In seeking to become versatile, they were to seek help from others and not revert back to the old practice of facing problems alone. For example, a few students had to face the fact that they had drug problems that were not only destroying them personally but destroying black people collectively. They had to realize that even as they were willing to take individual responsibility to handle this problem, they were incapable of solving it alone. In seeking group support, one student found out that even as he was trying to get out of the drug trap, he was about to fall into another societal trap: namely, that there were no drug rehabilitation centers in his community that could take him in immediately. One center had been closed because of a lack of funds, and the other had a backlog so heavy that he was told that he could be seen in nine months or a year. This student found out just how urgent it is for black people to be able to come together collectively and take control of their own lives. Such situations made students generally even more aware of the urgency of their learning to view problems from the perspective of black people in the past and the vantage point of contemporary society and from their own personal stances as well as from the viewpoint of the group. It made them feel a sense of urgency in becoming culturally versatile and strengthening their resolve to turn their concerns as students into commitment to the healing–developing community and change beyond the classroom

STEP 10: (MOURNING) ENGAGING THE BLACK COMMUNITY

Not only did our students see the importance of pursuing their own personal problems beyond the classroom, they also knew that the black experience demands that helping professionals engage themselves in the black community. They understood that early black caregiving systems, such as the black church, the black extended family, orphanages, old folks' homes, and the like, took residence right in the black community where they could not only address hard problems but also seek preventive measures. In contemporary society, as in the past, a disproportionate number of black people are labeled deviants, criminals, mental defectives, incorrigibles, and other pejoratives. They are taken away from their families and out of their communities to be locked up in institutions of loss where they are often beaten, harassed, drugged, and so forth in the name of reforming and rehabilitating them. Social workers play a major role in this repressive system of coercion, control, and containment, although they are skilled at denying their culpability. As Wilson (1993) pointed out, "we have a system that asks the so-called helping professions to 'keep them away from us; make them invisible; convert their behavior; make them adjust to the system in one way or another. Use your diagnostic and treatment powers as a means of giving us peace at night'" (p. 89). Even when black people are placed outside their communities in social welfare institutions that genuinely seek to help them and which have made progress in helping them, once their stint is up and their cases are closed, these institutions tend to drop them right back in the wretched environment that caused their malady in the first place. Even relatively successful outside institutions tend to do very little follow-up with their black clients once they have washed their hands of them and released them back into the urban jungle.

Students see the need to engage themselves, if only on a voluntary basis, in the black community. Many seek field placements in the black community and some even have hopes of building their own social service institutions there. They see their participation as a move toward helping to create the healing–developing community. They have learned that one way to rid themselves of bourgeoisie notions of class superiority and racist notions of white supremacy is to take up the old social work dictum of "starting where the client is," which, in the black experience, also means going where the client is. Moreover, engaging the black community provides fertile ground for social advocacy and political action.

TOWARD THE HEALING–DEVELOPING BLACK COMMUNITY

Overall, for social work students to help black people heal deeply entrenched historical wounds as a prerequisite to realizing their fullest economic, political, cultural, and social development as a people, they must be able to universalize their experiences and recognize what they have in common with black people in the past and black people in the contemporary wider society. Black social workers are expected to play a leadership role in creating the healing–developing community, to follow the lead of black social work pioneers, to learn from their mistakes, and to fulfill and enhance their vision. They must lead the fight in seeing that there are black experience–based social work agencies that are largely funded by local, state, and federal governments in every black community but are also funded by the nickel-and-dime donations of the masses of black people. They must see to it that this approach gets incorporated into social work curricula in colleges and universities across America. Saying that black social workers must play a vanguard role in seeking to heal the wounds that keep black people from coming together to address common needs is not to advance a policy of racial exclusion. Although race is a factor that cannot be ignored, social workers of all racial and ethnic backgrounds can find a place in helping to create the black healing–developing community. What is of crucial importance is how social workers, regardless of their race, ethnicity, or nationality, are educated, trained, and prepared to work with black people, how willing they are to follow the lead and direction of black social workers, and how sincere they are in making America a truly democratic society for all its citizens.

In our classes, social work students are realizing that to create the healing–developing black community, black social workers must take the lead in creating black caregiving agencies and institutions in black communities to tackle the myriad social problems confronting their people. They are aware that black social workers must convince local, state, and federal governments that black people themselves can do a better job, and do it more cheaply, in preventing black crime and delinquency, bringing black ex-convicts and ex-juvenile offenders back in tune with the community, healing people who are mentally ill, caring for the older people, and providing extended family–type support to the thousands of black children in foster homes and adoption centers. Already in our follow-up with our former students, we are finding that some are moving toward creating healing agencies of their own that are based on black experience–based social work concepts. For example, one of our former students has based practically his entire counseling of young black people on combating the five negative psychologies. Another has had success teaching black youths versatility skills so that they can avoid societal traps blocking the realization of individual potential and hampering the advancement of the group. She has her students not only anticipating societal barriers but confronting their own internal restraints to realizing true self-goals. Another student is seeking to build a home for abandoned black children using the extended family as a model. Some plan to conduct research for master's and doctoral dissertations on black experience–based social work principles, concepts, and techniques. Many others are carrying black experience–based social work, sometimes in bits and pieces, into schools, prisons, churches, black families, social welfare agencies, and communities as they work with black people of all ages and all socioeconomic backgrounds. The reports from our students have been encouraging, particularly for a social work approach that is still in its embryo stage. We ourselves are developing black experience–based social work training manuals that will explore how this approach can be used in respect to a variety of cases. This book lays the foundation. The manuals, geared toward helping professionals, lay caregivers, and clients, will go further into the nuts-and-bolts detail of black experience–based social work practice.

Even in its foundation stage, we believe that black experience–based social work offers social workers invaluable insights and new directions. Already, black experience–based social work is distinct from other social work methods in that it emphasizes developing such skills as fostering historical empathy and ancestral connectedness, developing versatility skills and strategies, strengthening the ability to mourn, and mastering the art of collective problem solving, all based on black traditional ways. Black experience–based social work is also unique in that it uses concepts drawn from the black sacred and profane heritage and it uses the moaning, mourning, and morning themes of the spirituals and the blues to guide the social change process. Like all new approaches, it is expected to become sharper as it gains greater acceptance and use and as it undergoes more-critical scrutiny. By synthesizing mainstream social work and the black helping heritage, black experience–based social work may never give social workers the power to lead black people to the promised land, but it will provide social workers with fresh tools and new weapons for liberation and social change as it puts the scientific method, the black tradition, and the ancestors on their side. By focusing on the black experience, it realizes the importance of ancestral and historical connectedness in understanding and solving contemporary problems. At the turn of the 20th century, the great sage and pioneer in black social work W.E.B. DuBois (1903) declared prophetically that "the problem of the twentieth century is the problem of the color line" (p. vi). As we approach a new century, the perspective of black experience–based social work is that the problem of the 21st century is the problem of black people in America, and perhaps throughout the world, regaining their African soul.

REFERENCES

Baldwin, J. (1985). White man's guilt. In J. Baldwin (Ed.), *The price of the ticket* (pp. 409–414). New York: St. Martin's/Marek.

Douglass, F. (1883). *Life and times of Frederick Douglass.* Secaucus, NJ: Citadel Press.

DuBois, W.E.B. (1903). *The souls of black folk.* Chicago: A. C. McClurg.

Edwards, S. (1995). *Life in the day of a woman.* Baltimore, MD: Author.

Frazier, E. F. (1949). *Granny: Guardian of the generation.* In *The Negro family in the United States* (pp. 146–162). Chicago: University of Chicago Press.

Lovell, J., Jr. (1972). *Black song.* New York: Macmillan.

Malcolm X. (1964). *The autobiography of Malcolm X.* New York: Ballantine Books.

Pasteur, A. B., & Toldson, I. L. (1982). *Roots of soul.* New York: Anchor Press/Doubleday.

Wilson, A. N. (1983). *The falsification of Afrikan consciousness.* New York: Afrikan World Infosystems.

Wright, R. (1945). *Black boy.* New York: Harper & Brothers.

Index

About the Authors

Elmer P. Martin, PhD, is professor of social work at Morgan State University, Baltimore. Dr. Martin received his undergraduate degree in sociology from Lincoln University, Jefferson City, Missouri; a master's degree in sociology from Atlanta University; and a PhD in social welfare from Case Western Reserve University, Cleveland.

Joanne Mitchell Martin, PhD, is executive director of the Great Blacks in Wax Museum, Baltimore. She received her bachelor's degree in French from Florida A&M University, Tallahassee; a master's degree in French from Atlanta University; a master's degree in reading from Case Western Reserve University; and her PhD in educational psychology from Howard University, Washington, DC.

The Martins are coauthors of *The Black Extended Family* (University of Chicago Press, 1978) and *The Helping Tradition in the Black Family and Community* (National Association of Social Workers, 1985). They are cofounders of the Great Blacks in Wax Museum, America's first wax museum of African American history. They have conducted numerous lectures, workshops, and seminars and are noted for their work with black youths, black families, and black prisoners. Throughout their professional careers they have been laying the theoretical and practice foundation for black experience–based social work.

Cover and interior designed by Naylor Design, Inc.
Composed by Maben Publications, Inc., in Stone and Caflisch
Printed and bound by BookCrafters, Inc., on 60# Lakewood

Books on Diversity
from the NASW Press

Social Work and the Black Experience, *by Elmer P. Martin and Joanne Mitchell Martin.* The first text to offer a social work technique that incorporates the rich black spiritual and blues traditions specifically into work with black individuals and families.
ISBN: 0-87101-257-X, #257X, **$28.95**

The Helping Tradition in the Black Family and Community, *by Elmer P. Martin and Joanne Mitchell Martin.* The Martins trace the evolution of the helping tradition from traditional Africa to slavery, among free blacks, through Reconstruction, and into rural and urban America.
ISBN: 0-87101-129-8, #1298, **$18.95**

Ethnicity and Race: Critical Concepts in Social Work, *by Carolyn Jacobs and Dorcas D. Bowles, Editors.* Helps the reader understand how social and political realities for people of color have led them to experience life from a dual perspective—that of their own group and that of the predominant cultural group.
ISBN: 0-87101-155-7, #1557, **$23.95**

Color in a White Society, *by Barbara W. White, Editor.* The authors point out the inherent strengths of people of color and reaffirm the profession's commitment to this group of clients and workers.
ISBN: 0-87101-128-X, #128X, **$16.95**

Books on Diversity
from the NASW Press

Social Work and the Black Experience, *by Elmer P. Martin and Joanne Mitchell Martin.* The first text to offer a social work technique that incorporates the rich black spiritual and blues traditions specifically into work with black individuals and families.
ISBN: 0-87101-257-X, #257X, **$28.95**

The Helping Tradition in the Black Family and Community, *by Elmer P. Martin and Joanne Mitchell Martin.* The Martins trace the evolution of the helping tradition from traditional Africa to slavery, among free blacks, through Reconstruction, and into rural and urban America.
ISBN: 0-87101-129-8, #1298, **$18.95**

Ethnicity and Race: Critical Concepts in Social Work, *by Carolyn Jacobs and Dorcas D. Bowles, Editors.* Helps the reader understand how social and political realities for people of color have led them to experience life from a dual perspective—that of their own group and that of the predominant cultural group.
ISBN: 0-87101-155-7, #1557, **$23.95**

Color in a White Society, *by Barbara W. White, Editor.* The authors point out the inherent strengths of people of color and reaffirm the profession's commitment to this group of clients and workers.
ISBN: 0-87101-128-X, #128X, **$16.95**

Order Form

Title	Item #	Price	Total
❏ **Social Work and the Black Experience**	**Item 257X**	**$28.95**	_____
❏ *The Helping Tradition in the Black Family and Community*	Item 1298	$18.95	_____
❏ *Ethnicity & Race*	Item 1557	$23.95	_____
❏ *Color in a White Society*	Item 128X	$16.95	_____
	+ 10% postage and handling		_____
		Total	_____

❏ I've enclosed my check or money order for $ _____

❏ Please charge my ❏ NASW Visa* ❏ Other Visa ❏ Mastercard

Credit Card No. _____ Exp. Date _____

Signature _____

*Use of this card generates funds in support of the social work profession.

Name _____

Address _____

City_____ State/Province _____

Country _____ Zip _____

(Make checks payable to NASW Press. Prices are subject to change.)

NASW Distribution Center
P.O. Box 431
Annapolis JCT, MD 20701 USA

Credit card orders call **1-800-227-3590**
(In metro Wash., DC, call 301-317-8688)
Or fax your order to **301-206-7989**

*SWBEz 8/95

Order Form

Title	Item #	Price	Total
❏ **Social Work and the Black Experience**	**Item 257X**	**$28.95**	_____
❏ *The Helping Tradition in the Black Family and Community*	Item 1298	$18.95	_____
❏ *Ethnicity & Race*	Item 1557	$23.95	_____
❏ *Color in a White Society*	Item 128X	$16.95	_____
	+ 10% postage and handling		_____
		Total	_____

❏ I've enclosed my check or money order for $ _____

❏ Please charge my ❏ NASW Visa* ❏ Other Visa ❏ Mastercard

Credit Card No. _____ Exp. Date _____

Signature _____

*Use of this card generates funds in support of the social work profession.

Name _____

Address _____

City_____ State/Province _____

Country _____ Zip _____

(Make checks payable to NASW Press. Prices are subject to change.)

NASW Distribution Center
P.O. Box 431
Annapolis JCT, MD 20701 USA

Credit card orders call **1-800-227-3590**
(In metro Wash., DC, call 301-317-8688)
Or fax your order to **301-206-7989**

*SWBEz 8/95